Key Text

REFERENCE

Theory, Culture & Society

Theory, Culture & Society caters for the resurgence of interest in culture within contemporary social science and the humanities. Building on the heritage of classical social theory, the book series examines ways in which this tradition has been reshaped by a new generation of theorists. It also publishes theoretically informed analyses of everyday life, popular culture, and new intellectual movements.

EDITOR: Mike Featherstone, *Nottingham Trent University*

SERIES EDITORIAL BOARD
Roy Boyne, *University of Durham*
Mike Hepworth, *University of Aberdeen*
Scott Lash, *Goldsmiths College, University of London*
Roland Robertson, *University of Pittsburgh*
Bryan S. Turner, *University of Cambridge*

THE TCS CENTRE

The Theory, Culture & Society book series, the journals *Theory, Culture & Society* and *Body & Society*, and related conference, seminar and postgraduate programmes operate from the TCS Centre at Nottingham Trent University. For further details of the TCS Centre's activities please contact:

Centre Administrator
The TCS Centre, Room 175
Faculty of Humanities
Nottingham Trent University
Clifton Lane, Nottingham, NG11 ENS, UK
e-mail: tcs@ntu.ac.uk

Recent volumes include:

Simmel on Culture: Selected Writings
edited by David Frisby and Mike Featherstone

Nation Formation
Towards a Theory of Abstract Community
Paul James

Contested Natures
Phil Macnaghten and John Urry

The Consumer Society
Myths and Structures
Jean Baudrillard

Georges Bataille – Essential Writings
edited by Michael Richardson

Digital Aesthetics
Sean Cubitt

FACING MODERNITY

Ambivalence, Reflexivity and Morality

Barry Smart

SAGE Publications
London • Thousand Oaks • New Delhi

First published 1999
Published in association with *Theory, Culture & Society*,
Nottingham Trent University

 SAGE Publications Ltd
6 Bonhill Street
London EC2A 4PU

SAGE Publications Inc
2455 Teller Road
Thousand Oaks, California 91320

SAGE Publications India Pvt Ltd
32, M-Block Market
Greater Kailash – I
New Delhi 110 048

British Library Cataloguing in Publication data

A catalogue record for this book is available
from the British Library

ISBN 0 7619 5519 4
ISBN 0 7619 5520 8 (pbk)

Library of Congress catalog record available

Typeset by Mayhew Typesetting, Rhayader, Powys
Printed in Great Britain by Redwood Books, Trowbridge,
Wiltshire

What is constant is an immense uncertainty . . . The revolution of our time is the uncertainty revolution. We are not ready to accept this. Paradoxically, however, we attempt to escape from uncertainty by relying even more on information and communications systems, so merely aggravating the uncertainty itself.

Jean Baudrillard

The idea of a morality as obedience to a code of rules is now disappearing, has already disappeared. And to this . . . must correspond the search for an aesthetics of existence

Michel Foucault

To listen, to reflect, to criticize, to respond – these are the tasks of social inquiry today, as they always have been

Robert N Bellah

Reason is never so versatile as when it puts itself in question

Emmanuel Levinas

CONTENTS

ACKNOWLEDGEMENTS

The development of this work has benefited from the criticisms, suggestions and support offered by a great many people. In particular I would like to thank Chris Rojek for his encouraging comments on the manuscript and Bryan Turner for his constructive criticisms. I am also grateful to students and colleagues at the University of Auckland for their contribution to the development of earlier versions of some of the chapters in the book, to Ross Abbinnett, Chris Shilling and Keith Tester for 'local' support, and to Robert Rojek for his editorial assistance. Above all I would like to thank my son George for helping me to put everything into perspective.

In writing this book I have drawn on material contained in articles I have published in the following journals and books: *International Sociology*, *Body & Society*, *Philosophy and Social Criticism*, *New Zealand Sociology*, *The Blackwell Companion to Social Theory*, and *The Politics of Jean-François Lyotard*. I would like to thank the various referees, reviewers and editors of these texts for their constructive comments and criticisms.

1
ANALYSIS AFTER AMBIVALENCE

A sense of ambivalence has been a longstanding feature of reflections on modernity. In the respective writings of Marx, Weber, Durkheim, Simmel and Freud traces of uncertainty and conflicting views of the prospects and possibilities inaugurated by the advent of modernity are clearly evident. Marx and Durkheim might have considered the 'beneficent possibilities' to outweigh the 'negative characteristics' (Giddens, 1990: 7), but they nevertheless remained troubled by the development of modernity, and ambivalent about its prospects and consequences. With Weber, Simmel and Freud the costs of the modern world loom larger, and this led them to express concern about the relative balance of benefits and costs following exposure to the brighter and darker sides of modernity, and to raise questions about the 'progress' made. As Simmel was moved to comment on the modern world, 'every problem solved throws up more than one new one' (1990: 475).

Ambivalence about the consequences associated with the modernization of production is a prominent feature of Marx's critical reflections on late nineteenth-century European civilization, the grim reality of perpetual social upheaval being tempered by the prospect of eventual social(ist) progress. For Marx and Engels (1968) the 'uninterrupted disturbance of all social conditions', the agitation and uncertainty unleashed by the perpetual transformation of production, brought with it increases in alienation and exploitation, in short a marked deterioration in the human condition. But at the same time the '[c]onstant revolutionizing of production' was considered to open up the possibility, perhaps even to be preparing the ground, through the creation of appropriate social and economic conditions, for another, better, way of life. However, in so far as history can offer no guarantees, a radical 'reconstitution of society at large' remained no more than a possibility in Marx's view, albeit a preferred alternative to common ruin.

As Marx perceptively anticipated, 'labour in the direct form' still continues to be replaced as the 'great well-spring of wealth' (1973: 705), and social production based upon exchange value continues to encounter contradictions. Reflecting on the growing impact science and technology were beginning to have on production, Marx argued that as labour 'no longer appears so much to be included within the production process . . . the human being comes to relate more as watchman and regulator to the production process itself' (ibid.: 705). As we now know only too well, such a production process, increasingly automated, employing an extended family of complex numerical control technologies, seems to have need of fewer and fewer producers and regulators. In circumstances where there is already a growing 'crisis of work' (Gorz, 1989), where unemployment is recognized to be a chronic problem, it is both unacceptable and inappropriate to continue to treat labour, employment, a job, as the primary measure of worth and principal source of livelihood, while at the same time proceeding to develop and deploy more labour-saving and labour-eradicating technologies. For Marx the solution to the implied uncertainties of capitalist modernity, a resolution of the ambivalence identified with the seemingly inexhaustible disordering capacity of capitalist modernity, lay with what Bauman has described as 'modernity's last stand' (1991: 262), namely the realization of another form of modernity, socialism, and subsequently the development of communism. The idea(l) of socialism, and its status as an achievement (or was 'actually-existing socialism' (Bahro, 1978) merely a distortion or a pathological simulation?) has probably been forever tarnished by the realization that modernity 'pushed to its radical limits: grand designs, unlimited social engineering, huge and bulky technology, total transformation of nature' (Bauman, 1991: 265), has not, moreover, will not, lead to the promised 'free development of individualities' (Marx, 1973: 706), but to more, much more, of the (capitalist) same, namely the persistence of social and economic inequality, increased bureaucratic regulation, continuing exploitation in the workplace, an increase in risks encountered, enforced movement of population, as well as widespread environmental degradation and destruction. To paraphrase Derek Sayer's (1991: 147) remarks, while capitalist modernity remains as invidious as ever, the idea of the moral superiority of an alternative modernity, socialism, has lost virtually all credibility.

More than a degree of ambivalence is also evident in Freud's critical reflections on (modern) civilization and its consequences. If civilization in general requires a combination of externally and internally reinforced 'cultural prohibitions', modern civilization with its seemingly endless pursuit of technical mastery over nature and parallel reconstitution of human conduct through disciplinary and governmental technologies, is taken to task for having placed too heavy a burden on its subjects. While emphasizing that a 'certain degree of coercion' ([1927]1985: 186) is necessary if civilization is to be maintained, Freud simultaneously draws attention to the fact that 'we do not feel comfortable in our present-day civilization' ([1930]1985: 277). Modernity is not a form of life conducive to feeling comfortable, to the contrary the restlessness, uncertainty and agitation which is endemic stimulates and disturbs, precipitates anxiety and produces forms of nervousness (Beard, 1881 cited in Bellah et al., 1996: 117; Simmel, 1950: 409–10; Freud [1908]1985: 34–7). Modernity seduces by holding out the tantalizing prospect of a soon-to-be-achieved 'comfortable' existence, a prospect which frustratingly tends to continually recede from our grasp, but not necessarily from our imagination, with each renewed attempt at realization. Freud doubted that we would ever feel comfortable, that an accommodation would ever be reached between the individual's 'desire', 'urge' or 'claim' for freedom and the 'moral' demands of modern civilization ([1930]1985: 285) – 'The fateful question for the human species seems to me to be whether and to what extent their cultural development will succeed in mastering the disturbance of their communal life by the human instinct of aggression and self-destruction' (ibid.: 339–40). Not only does the fateful question itself remain unanswered, the very terms in which it was posed have themselves become matters of analytical and political disputation. In a context where debate rages over increasing signs of difference and the erosion of cultural values, the loss of hierarchy, and the associated problem of distinguishing worthy 'works' from the merely distracting and entertaining surfeit of 'commodities' produced by global cultural corporations – consider the alleged 'dumbing' of America (Bloom, 1996; Steiner, 1996) and, given the continuing reach of American cultural imperialism, the inference must be of everywhere else too, to a degree at least (Hoggart, 1995) – what are 'we' to make of 'cultural development'? To what now does 'cultural development' refer? And what remains of 'communal life' to disturb? To ask questions such as these is not to imply that no responses can be offered, or that none have been forthcoming, it is rather to draw attention to the fact that what Bauman (1991) has termed modernity's 'cultural crusade' has lost its way, if not run aground. It is also to acknowledge the concern, widely felt and expressed, that under late modern conditions communal life is more than disturbed; it has become increasingly fragile and fragmented, if it has not, in extreme circumstances, been eradicated altogether. It is to suggest that solutions to our problems 'remain opaque because of our profound ambivalence' (Bellah et al., 1996: 285), and that such a condition of ambivalence is, as Bauman (1991) demonstrates, a corollary of modernity itself.

Ambivalence about the fate of humanity under modernity also constitutes the central theme of the work of Max Weber. A prominent concern running through Weber's reflections has been identified as that of the 'possibility of living a life in an ethically interpretable manner under . . . prevailing conditions' (Hennis, 1988: 102). For Weber prevailing conditions meant disenchantment, rationalization and discipline, conditions which rendered social relations impersonal and thereby increasingly inaccessible to ethical interpretation. It is the marginalization or disfiguring of face-to-face ethical relations which Weber identifies as the most significant consequence of modern processes of rationalization: 'Every purely personal relation of man to man . . . is susceptible of ethical regulation; ethical demands can be made of them . . . Commercial rational relations are not like this, and the more rationally differentiated that they are, the less they are susceptible of such regulation' (Weber, 1968: 585; quoted in Hennis, 1988: 97). Accelerating closely articulated processes of economic and bureaucratic rationalization, precipitating a diffusion of forms of organization predicated on objective, calculable rules, were identified by Weber as the source of a growing depersonalization of the life orders that shape human existence and produce an increasing disregard for face-to-face ethical relations. 'Without regard for persons' became, Weber (1970: 215) remarks, the watchword of both modern bureaucratic administration and the economic marketplace. Where official discourse constitutes the 'client' and/or the 'consumer' as sovereign, 'persons' become vulnerable to being treated as objects of disregard.

Located in a modern world, a disenchanted world characterized by increasing 'intellectualization and rationalization', Weber broke with the 'preoccupations implicit in the values of a past world, without at the same time falling under the influence of the contemporary belief in progress' (Hennis, 1988: 64). Indeed Weber was more than ambivalent about the proclaimed 'progress' of modernity, being moved to remark on the way in which the 'rosy blush' of the Enlightenment seemed to be 'irretrievably fading' and to lament, '[s]pecialists without spirit, sensualists without heart; this nullity imagines that it has attained a level of civilization never before achieved' (1976: 182). Concern over depersonalization and the increasing inaccessibility or resistance of the modern world to ethical interpretation, as articulated by Weber, has not diminished over time, to the contrary, as the preoccupations of contemporary philosophers and sociologists such as Emmanuel Levinas, Zygmunt Bauman and Robert Bellah testify, the problems have, if anything, increased in gravity.

From the exposure of modernity's last stand, the illumination of its lost promise, and with that a haemorrhaging of false hopes about the rosy hue of future prospects, has emerged a condition of 'postmodernity', and a need to reconcile ourselves, as Bauman puts it, to 'the non-finality of any order-ing project and . . . the permanence and omnipresence of ambivalence' (1991: 230). In short, there is a requirement to face up to the reality of ambivalence, a need to learn to live with ambivalence, but not in a spirit of resignation, to the contrary: 'The world is ambivalent, though its colonizers and rulers do not like it to be such and by hook or by crook try to pass it off for one that is not . . . Ambivalence is not to be bewailed. It is to be celebrated. Ambivalence is the limit to the power of the powerful' (ibid.: 179). But if ambivalence undermines the ordering and designing objectives of the powerful does it necessarily follow, as Bauman proceeds to suggest, that it simultaneously constitutes the 'freedom of the powerless'? A satisfactory answer to such a complex question lies beyond the scope of the present study; it requires a detailed analysis of the various ways in which ambivalence receives expression in, and impacts upon, the lives of different groups and classes of people, an analysis which needs to include, amongst other things, a consideration of the ways in which the dis-ordering and re-ordering consequences of the surrender of more and more areas of social life to the vagaries of the market, and associated forms of economic reorganization, are lived and experienced positively by some and negatively by others, in, and as, ambivalence.

A sense of ambivalence constitutes a longstanding feature of analytic reflection on modernity, as Levine (1985) demonstrates in his discussion of the 'flight from ambiguity' characteristic of modern societies. The modern response to the ambiguity of language and life has been a pursuit of 'univocal discourse' and communication, a pursuit of precision and clarity. Levine remarks that 'universal discourse serves functions that are indispensable to any high-tech society . . . [it] advances our capabilities for gaining cognitive mastery of the world . . . [and] provides resources essential to life in complex societies by facilitating the precise designation of specific rights and responsibilities' (1985: 39–40). But if the pursuit of 'univocality' is a prominent feature of modernity, Levine argues that ambiguity is no less essential, as a necessary counter to the dominance and, by implication, excesses of 'positive science' and the 'hegemony of rationalized institutions'. It is the ambiguity of language which is identified as serving to facilitate and nurture 'expressivity' and to protect 'privacy in a world of extended central controls'. And it is ambiguous language, Levine continues, which mediates 'the experience of community in a society built of highly specialized units', fulfils the need for 'symbolic forms', and 'enhances adaptiveness to change' (ibid.: 40–3).

Reflecting specifically on the analytic dimension of the 'modern assault on ambiguity', Levine suggests that the pursuit of precision in modern social analysis has tended to under-represent and obscure the ambiguities which are an intrinsic feature of social life. Human realities are held to be 'intrinsically ambiguous', as are the concepts employed by social analysts attempting to make sense of them, but such a diagnosis does not constitute, and should not be read as, a plea for universally applicable univocal definitions, rather Levine's main concern is to counter indifference to, and increase awareness of, conceptual ambiguity, in order to reduce the risk of inconsistent and potentially misleading applications. Indeed, Levine adds that in the case of social analysis 'the very attempt to formulate a universally applicable univocal definition seems ill-advised' (ibid.: 17), for there are important insights to be gained from construing a concept in different ways, in particular, insights into the ambiguities of life, the fact that 'people have mixed feelings and confused opinions, and are subject to contradictory expectations and outcomes, in every sphere of experience' (ibid.: 8–9).

Levine draws attention to forms of conceptual and experiential ambiguity, and recognizes the limitations, and indeed inappropriateness, of attempts to construct 'univocal definitions' and 'univalent methodologies' in the field of social analysis. Although there is some consideration of the ambivalence of modern forms of life, this does not constitute the primary focus of Levine's narrative, rather it represents the briefly drawn context within which the respective writings on modernity of classical figures such as Durkheim, Weber, and Simmel are contrasted and compared. Within the discussion of the modern flight from ambiguity offered by Levine relatively little consideration is given to the respects in which the modern pursuit of precision is itself constitutive of ambiguity and, in turn, ambivalence.

It is really only with Zygmunt Bauman's postmodern 'trilogy' (1991, 1993, 1995a) that a sustained case has been made for regarding ambivalence as an unavoidable corollary of modernity. For Bauman the relationship is clear, '[b]oth order and ambivalence are alike products of modern practice; and neither has anything except modern practice . . . to sustain it' (1991: 15). One consolation with modernity it seems, is that of ambivalence, at least, we can be sure.

The Certainty of Ambivalence

Under conditions of modernity conflicting emotions and attitudes abound: ambiguity and uncertainty proliferate. But of ambivalence we can be reasonably certain, it seems destined not to go away, for it is a product of the modern preoccupation with the pursuit of order, it is the 'waste of modernity', the corollary, or by-product, of seemingly endless processes of 'design, manipulation, management [and] engineering' (Bauman, 1991: 15, 7) of orderliness with which modernity is inextricably associated. Modernity is the making of ambivalence as much as it is the pursuit of order, or constitution of forms of orderliness. And as the institutions of modernity have become global, have become 'stretched', intensifying 'worldwide social relations' (Giddens, 1990: 64), so a condition of 'existential and mental ambivalence' has become 'an ever more universal experience' (Bauman, 1991: 95, 97). The idea of the 'rational "makeability" of the world' (Berger and Kellner, 1982: 14) is no longer simply accepted and embraced without question, both its feasibility and desirability have become matters of dispute.

Ambivalence is a consequence of modernity, a condition of our modern being. Modernity, as Giddens remarks, is 'double-edged' (1990: 7), there is security and danger, trust and risk. Social relations are abstracted from their local setting, lifted out or 'disembedded' and then rearticulated 'across indefinite spans of time-space' (Giddens, 1990: 21). Disembedded, perhaps re-embedded, albeit 'partially or transitorily', and unsettled by the prospect of the recurring removal of social relations 'from the immediacies of context' (ibid.: 79, 28), from the particularity of familiar places, individuals have become more and more reliant on experts and professionals, have been increasingly constituted as clients or consumers of professionally organized and produced systems, services and commodities (Illich, 1978, 1985). The systems of professional expertise on which we rely, to which we are subject, and in which we are inclined to trust, until further notice, until that is increased risk-awareness, itself often triggered by expert systems, occasions doubt and uncertainty, constitute one of the two forms of 'disembedding mechanism' analysed by Giddens, the other being 'symbolic tokens', that is 'media of interchange which can be "passed around" without regard to the specific characteristics of individuals or groups' (1990: 22), without regard for persons. Disembedding mechanisms, the abstract systems constituted by networks of professional expertise and impersonal media of exchange such as money, are predicated on trust, on confidence and faith in what Giddens (ibid.: 26) has described as the 'abstract capacities' of the institutions of modernity. The trust invested realizes security as its dividend. But in so far as expectations raised, promised, perhaps by implication seemingly 'guaranteed', may not always be met, indeed frequently are not met to anything like the degree anticipated, the security built on trust in expert systems and symbolic tokens is liable to dissolve, and following that, trust is likely to be undermined and/or withdrawn. In such circumstances it is questionable whether trust can be restored through campaigns aiming to promote reassurance, and/or references to the prospect of further 'advances' in scientific research finding 'solutions to every problem' (Beck, 1992: 32, 45). The belief 'that we bend the world to our will by means of technology' has been a characteristic feature of modern society, but as Baudrillard adds, in fact 'it is the world that imposes its will upon us with the aid of technology, and the surprise occasioned by this turning of the tables is considerable' (1993: 153).

Consider, for example, the European-wide loss of confidence and withdrawal of trust in the beef industry, particularly the British industry, which gathered momentum in the spring of 1996 following reports of the incidence of Bovine Spongiform Encephalopathy (BSE) in cattle and a possible connection with Creutzfeldt-Jakob disease (CJD) in human beings who had consumed beef products. After almost a decade of denying any possibility that 'mad cow disease' might cross the species barrier into humans the British Government belatedly had to admit that new findings from scientists on the Spongiform Encephalopathy Advisory Committee indicated that '"the most likely explanation" for 10 cases involving a new strain of CJD was exposure to BSE before the offal ban in 1989' (Brown et al., 1996: 1). In 1990 any connection between BSE and a new variant of CJD had been officially denied and British beef had been declared 'safe'. Indeed, John Gummer, the Agriculture Minister at the time demonstrated his confidence by thrusting a beefburger into his daughter Cordelia's mouth as he remarked 'It's delicious. I have no worries about eating beefburgers. There is no cause for concern' (*Guardian* 21/3/96). At the end of 1995 scientists consulted by government continued to offer reassurance that the risk of any connection between BSE and CJD remained 'inconceivable'. However, in the light of accumulating evidence of a new apparently BSE-related strain of CJD which emerged early in 1996 the risk was re-assessed and was deemed to have increased from 'inconceivable' to 'extremely small', a qualification which offered scant consolation to the victims of the industrialization and de-regulation of British agriculture, and which predictably led commentators to ponder 'How big is extremely small?' (Jenkins, 1996: 18). It is a question to which science is unable to provide any firm answer. The loss of confidence and trust accelerated in the summer of the same year following reports of evidence concerning the transmission of BSE from cows to calves – once again contrary to assurances given by

the Ministry of Agriculture in 1994 that the 'theory of maternal transmission is "basically rubbish"' (Bates et al., 1996: 1) – and confirmation of
fears expressed earlier in the year that BSE may be transmitted to sheep.
Later in the same year further research revealed that the experiments on
which the government drew to confirm the safety of British beef were
'seriously flawed' because they were insufficiently sensitive to detect the
presence of small but potentially lethal amounts of the BSE agent (*Sunday
Times* 17/11/96).

A further example, which followed in the wake of the BSE-CJD crisis, is
provided by a British Government Ministry of Agriculture report which
identified traces of toxic chemicals, phthalates, in baby milk formula. The
level of phthalates (undisclosed) found in some brands (unidentified) was
reported to be slightly above the 'Tolerable Daily Intake'. Given the lack of
knowledge concerning the potential long-term effects of many man-made
chemicals, and reports of a possible effect of phthalates on the sexual
development and fertility of infant boys in particular, an increase in
risk-awareness and erosion of trust and confidence in particular expert
systems was to be expected. Moreover, following an intense media debate
about the risks lurking in manufactured foodstuffs, a debate likely to
simultaneously effect a promotion of the virtues of breast-feeding and
'natural' foods, consumers have subsequently been warned that a 'poison
risk . . . lurks in "healthy" eating' and that 'Natural toxins in food pose a
greater potential danger than man-made chemicals' (Connor, 1996: 3).
Awareness of disagreements and changes in scientific opinion, coupled with
an increasing awareness of the range of possible risks associated with the
manufacture and consumption of different forms of foodstuff, makes
the objective of eating healthily both difficult to achieve and hard to feel
confident about.

Such incidents are symptomatic of what Beck (1992) has termed 'risk
multiplication' and they underline the vulnerability of trust: it is always 'on
call', and perpetually liable to recall. There are no guarantees for trust,
merely differing degrees of awareness of and concern over the risks that lie
in wait, which in turn expert systems attempt to address, the strategy
generally being to seek to minimize or reduce, and where possible remove
risks, but also at times to conceal them. If, as Giddens remarks, 'disembedding mechanisms have provided large areas of security in the present-
day world', they have been accompanied by a 'new array of risks which . . .
are truly formidable' (1990: 125). Where once the prospect of advanced
modern society was associated with the promise of greater certainty and
steadily increasing levels of security within everyday life, it is now widely
recognized that the reality is more complicated and uneven, that modern
societies do indeed attempt to increase forms of control and to enhance
security, for example by trying to limit hazards and minimize dangers, but a
reduction in levels of risk has proven difficult to achieve. Indeed it might be
argued that while modern societies continue to market security they also
simultaneously manufacture risk, some manifestations of which are literally

too 'risky' to insure. For example, 'nuclear, chemical, ecological and genetic engineering risks . . . cannot be compensated or insured against', one significant consequence of which is to 'undermine and/or cancel the established safety systems of the provident state's existing risk calculations' (Beck, 1996: 31).

Trust Ambivalence

Reflecting on the substance of relations of trust in modernity Giddens draws a distinction between two categories, *facework commitments*, where 'relations . . . are sustained by or expressed in social connections established in circumstances of copresence' (1990: 80), the other, *faceless commitments*, where abstract systems predominate. The thesis presented is that 'disembedded mechanisms interact with re-embedded contexts of action, which may act either to support or to undermine them; and that faceless commitments are similarly linked in an ambiguous way with those demanding facework' (ibid.: 80). But how are the respective forms of trust and associated commitments articulated? Given the growth of abstract systems and associated forms of trust and commitment, what are the consequences for personal life, for trust in persons and 'facework commitments'?

The position advanced by Giddens is that it is inappropriate to counterpose the pervasiveness and impersonality of abstract systems to the diminishing intimacy of personal life, because the latter has been subject to a 'genuine transformation'. The transformation outlined is one in which the self, personal life, and social ties have had to be reconstituted in the light of the far-reaching dispersion of abstract systems. The modern self has become 'a reflexive project' (ibid.: 114) and relationships of personal trust have also become projects 'to be "worked at" by the parties involved' (ibid.: 121). In short the self has become a constituted identity, open to revision, to being re-thought and re-made – 'We are, not what we are, but what we make of ourselves' (Giddens, 1991: 75) – and personal trust is to be achieved or won, and then continually maintained. But such 'personal' projects are conducted in a context where, as Giddens briefly acknowledges, the routines of everyday life have been reshaped and where 'structured by abstract systems have an empty, unmoralised character' (1990: 120). Within the routines of modern everyday life it tends to be an impression of commitment that is present(ed), the 'engineering of a convincing impression' (Goffman, 1959: 243) that is of most concern, and in consequence it is no suprise to learn that 'trust is always ambivalent' or that 'ambivalence . . . lies at the core of all trust relations, whether it be trust in abstract systems or in individuals' (Giddens, 1990: 143, 89). How could it be otherwise, given our knowledge and experience of the ways in which carefully built forms of trust have been subsequently undermined?

In addition to the 'faceless' commitment of trust in abstract systems and the 'facework' continually required to win and maintain trust for a self

contrived from a 'series of social masks' (Bellah et al., 1996: 80), is there
scope for another type of commitment, one which can serve as a counter or
challenge to the ambivalence of modernity? For Giddens the answer under
present circumstances is clearly no. Modernity is destined to remain beyond
our control, and it is suggested that so long as its institutions prevail
'[f]eelings of ontological security and existential anxiety will coexist in
ambivalence' (Giddens, 1990: 139). Whether in relation to abstract systems
and associated forms of expertise and certified knowledge, or in respect of
more personal, perhaps intimate relationships, ontological security is very
much a matter of emotion rather than cognition. As soon as systems, forms
of knowledge, and interpersonal relations, along with the forms of trust
with which they are closely articulated, are subjected to question, to the
'reflexivity of modernity' (ibid.: 92), feelings of security are liable to
dissolve, to be undermined and inclined to give way to uncertainty and
anxiety. Whether in respect of abstract systems, or personal relationships,
where matters are taken on trust it is, Giddens remarks, because there is a
lack of knowledge, either of technical details, or of the 'thoughts and
intentions of intimates' (ibid.: 89). And where a lack of knowledge exists,
uncertainty, caution and ambivalence are generally not far behind. Under
modern conditions 'trust is always ambivalent' (ibid.: 143).

Sociological Ambivalence

The idea that the social sciences are closely articulated with modernity is
indisputable. It has been widely accepted that '[s]ocial science and modern
society were born together and [that] their fates are deeply intertwined'
(Bellah et al., 1983: 1). The social sciences have been recognized to be
'deeply implicated' in modernity (Giddens, 1990: 40), to be bound up with
it. Likewise, it has been noted that the social and human sciences only
became possible with the emergence of the modern epistemological configuration, in particular with the constitution of that ambiguous figure of
'man', the subject and object of knowledge (Foucault, 1973: 344). Elaborating on the modern experience, Foucault argues that the establishment of
the 'figure of man' within the field of knowledge makes it essential that
thought constitutes both knowledge and, in turn, a modification of what it
is about – what it 'knows'. Thought constitutes reflection and simultaneously transforms that on which it reflects. It is precisely this reflexive
articulation of thought and being which has been identified as a defining
feature of modernity.
    It is the fundamental contribution of social scientific reflection to the
'reflexivity of modernity' as a whole to which Giddens has drawn attention,
with particular emphasis being placed upon the centrality of sociological
reason. Giddens remarks that sociology's pivotal position 'in the reflexivity
of modernity comes from its role as the most generalised type of reflection
upon modern social life' (1990: 41). The social sciences, and sociology in

particular, continually inform and transform those public and private worlds which they address, and to which they belong. The more abstract 'second order' constructs of the social scientist '"circulate in and out" of what it is that they are about' (ibid.: 43), sometimes reinforcing, sometimes transforming, and sometimes undermining the 'first order' constructs in terms of which we routinely operate – understand and act – in and on the world. There is no way of knowing, in advance, what will eventuate from processes of knowledge generation and associated forms of social intervention – the formulation of social programmes, attempts at designing or engineering particular social futures, etc. – because relations of power, value orientations, 'the impact of unintended consequences' and the reflexivity of modernity (ibid.: 44–5) ensure that the relationship between programmes, practices and their effects continually falls short of correspondence. Ambivalence, both analytical and existential, is an understandable consequence of not knowing, and knowing that one cannot know for sure, precisely what will emerge from the various complex processes of restructuring through which modernity is continually (re)constituted. Late modernity, or the postmodern reconditioning of modernity, constitutes a form of social life in which ambivalence is pervasive.

Of all the social and human sciences, sociology represents not only the most generalized type of reflection on modernity, and predominantly *Western* modernity at that, but also possibly the most ambivalent form of analytic discourse, the most ambivalent form of reasoning about the modern social world. Sociological analysis necessarily proceeds from the world as it is, but as social practices, forms of organization and associated structures are revealed to be the momentary manifestations of cultural and historical processes, the reality of the social world is shown to be a continual accomplishment, and thereby it is relativized. It is precisely in this sense that sociology can not help being critical, can not help putting reality in question by alerting us to the possibility that things may (and/or will) be otherwise. Furthermore, insofar as sociological knowledge becomes incorporated into social practices, as it does, it contributes directly, and indirectly, to the transformation of the social world. It is on these grounds that Bauman finds sociology to be 'so internally ambiguous and inherently schizophrenic' (1992a: 209).

From its inception sociology has been preoccupied with modernity as a general focus of analytic inquiry, but how that particular subject matter has been conceptualized and what methods and styles of inquiry have been invoked to bring it into focus have varied considerably, and they continue to do so. It has been argued that evidence of diversity in respect of conceptualization and method signifies that sociology remains in a preparadigmatic stage of development (Friedrichs, 1972), but it would be more appropriate to argue that sociology has always, from the very beginning, been effectively post-paradigmatic, that the prospect of 'progressing' to an agreed shared paradigm has never been a serious option for the discipline because fundamental differences in respect of style of analysis,

conceptualization of subject matter and method of investigation constitute
an intrinsic feature of its field of inquiry, and reflect the increasingly
fragmented and diverse character of modern social life (Levine, 1985).

Sociology not only offers different perspectives on the complex articulation of local and global processes in the contemporary world, but in
addition draws attention to the presence of a multiplicity of different social
worlds, the existence of multiple social realities with their own distinctive
characteristics, structures of relevance and so forth. To paraphrase Berger
and Kellner, sociology has from its beginnings 'discovered its object[s]
along with the methods of studying it[them]' (1982: 10) and the various
objects and methods of inquiry discovered have continued to circulate
within the discipline. In consequence, within sociology it is not so much a
unified body of knowledge as perspectives on the social world, each generating their own forms of knowledge, which have tended to accumulate. The
student of sociology can not avoid encountering a range of objects of
inquiry (i.e. social facts, society, social action, sociation, social systems, etc.
etc.), only some of which may be reconciled, and a comparably wide range
of perspectives, of schools and approaches, not to mention different
attempts to bring more order to disciplinary diversity by introducing
additional classificatory schemas and distinctions (Levine, 1985). The
perpetual reflectiveness of sociology has certainly contributed to the 'high
degree of de-institutionalization' which characterizes modern societies
(Berger and Kellner, 1982: 153). Sociological reasoning has not simply left
us with questions where once we might have thought we had answers, it has
left us with a profound sense of the perspectival character of knowledge and
has, to that extent, made a powerful contribution to 'the deepening sense of
relativity in modern Western history' (ibid.: 61).

Reinterpreting Sociology

Sociology is a discipline which has been continually divided and sub-
divided by theoretical, methodological and, at times, political differences.
Consider the following by no means exhaustive list of schools and
approaches to sociological inquiry – positivism; functionalism; systems
theory; action theory; symbolic interactionism; phenomenology and
ethnomethodology; conversational analysis; structuralism and poststructuralism; rational choice theory and exchange theory; Marxism and critical
theory; and diverse feminist orientations – each of which continues to have
its exponents (Ritzer and Smart, 1999). To the above, far from compre-
hensive list, it is necessary to append the following sets of classificatory
distinctions which have been employed to try to bring a degree of order to a
seemingly increasingly disorganized field of study – Naturwissenschaften
and Geisteswissenschaften; bourgeois and Marxist tendencies; technocratic
or instrumental, and liberatory or emancipatory interests; theoretical and
empirical orientations; quantitative and qualitative methods; and legislative

and interpretive strategies. The controversial modern/postmodern distinction represents one of the more recent attempts to reclassify schools and styles of sociological inquiry. Perhaps it constitutes the end of the classificatory game, its point of exhaustion, the point at which the only remaining option appears to be to continually replay and/or revise existing classifications. The history of sociology is riven with divisions and disagreements about which of the many alternative directions the discipline should take. Perpetually located at one crossroads or another sociology has been continually open to the charge that it really isn't going anywhere. But the charge is unwarranted and the directional metaphor inappropriate.

I am not going to attempt to give a history of the various distinctions and differences which have been a feature of the development of sociology. I have briefly noted above some of the more common distinctions which have been employed to order the field, and they are already well enough known, if not widely accepted features of the discipline. I will merely reflect briefly upon a few responses which the absence of a governing paradigm has attracted, and I will go on to suggest that the preoccupations controversially identified as 'postmodern', preoccupations which have become a prominent feature of contemporary sociology, may ironically be more in tune with the *realities* of social analysis, the social processes such analyses seek to understand, and the complex forms of articulation which exist between the two, than critics have been prepared to allow.

Directional metaphors have been a longstanding feature of sociology, but in practice analysts have found it difficult to leave the concerns of their forebears behind. In consequence, rather than a progressive increase in learning and an associated cumulative ordering of knowledge about social processes, conditions and relations, contemporary sociology has found itself returned, time and time again, to basic questions about subject matter, conceptualization, theoretical standpoint and method of research. This represents a constitutive feature of the practice of sociology as Giddens (1987) has emphasized in his discussion of the 'double hermeneutic'. The practice of sociology – conception(s) of subject matter, theory, and method, and understanding(s) of generated forms of knowledge – is unavoidably an integral part of the social world; it both contributes to the transformation of social processes and, in turn, is itself necessarily transformed, as it attempts to come to terms with the complex mutation of prevailing conditions and experiences. In a context where there is 'wholesale reflexivity' knowledge is continually open to revision and social phenomena to processes of transformation. In such circumstances it is inappropriate, if not self-defeating, to regard sociology as engaged in the pursuit of cumulative knowledge of social phenomena.

There has been no shortage of attempts to set the discipline on a new path, to promote a new direction, or to achieve more coherence through the generation of syntheses which aim to reconcile and build upon different traditions of inquiry – the respective works of Parsons (1977) and Habermas (1984, 1987a) constitute two important examples. But to date such attempts have achieved little more than an increase in the range of variation in theory and method within the discipline.

In 1946, T.H. Marshall gave an inaugural lecture at the London School of Economics on the subject of the state of sociology and its possible futures. Marshall asked: 'Where does sociology stand today?' and 'Along what road should it travel into the future?' (1963: 3). What is striking about Marshall's answer is that most of the general issues and concerns broached at that time remain matters of debate. The reputation and contribution of the discipline; relationships with cognate fields of inquiry; the competing claims of different ways of doing sociology, for example grand narratives claiming to provide a total explanation of social development ('the way to the stars') and empirical studies of social phenomena, involving the collection of a multitude of facts ('the way into the sands'); as well as the connection between sociology and policy, continue to promote detailed discussion and attract controversy. And the very metaphor employed to situate sociology has itself resurfaced once again in Immanuel Wallerstein's (1997) diagnosis that 'sociology as an intellectual and organizational construct is at a crossroads'. It is also worth noting that the new road Marshall proposed sociology should take at the crossroads, namely 'studies in depth of limited areas of selected social systems' (1963: 34), has itself become simply another 'middle-range' option, one route among many along which contemporary sociologists now travel.

The discourse of the 'new' is a modern preoccupation and an effective history of contemporary sociology might well be constructed around the various forms this preoccupation has assumed. The 'new' has continually been presented as that which promises to bring closer a resolution of the problems and paradoxes which have beset sociology since its inception, to finally give it *a* specific direction. During the past 50 years there have been repeated diagnoses of a turning point or crisis in sociology and so many different remedies have been proposed that methodological pluralism has become an almost incontestable feature of the discipline. To illustrate the point I will briefly note a few critical responses to the way in which modern sociology has been developing, responses which have promoted the idea of 'reflexive' and/or 'moral' forms of sociological inquiry.

Sociology has been indicted on several counts during the course of its development, and it is the identification of a neglect of moral questions and concerns which is particularly relevant to my argument. If an interest in morality constituted an important part of the intellectual foundations of the discipline, subsequent developments have been more noteworthy for the way in which questions of ethics and morality have tended to be marginalized, if not excluded almost entirely, until, that is, the advent of an ethical (re)turn taken by social analysts investigating the discontents of modernity (Wolff, 1989; Bauman, 1993, 1995a; Lash, 1996). Concern about the absence of a meaningful ethical and moral dimension in contemporary sociological inquiry has been articulated in a number of ways, and over a considerable period of time. For example, in the early 1960s the discipline was criticized for becoming too preoccupied with the performance of tasks considered necessary to achieve the status of a modern scientific profession and, in consequence, for losing its critical moral sense, that is its ability to reflect critically upon both social processes and sociological practice itself (Stein and Vidich, 1963). In a broadly comparable manner a companion text argued that the increasing amoral scientific packaging of sociology risked putting the discipline 'into a *cul de sac*' (Horowitz, 1965: 3) and made necessary a new direction, if not the construction of a new 'moral' sociology. A similarly critical concern with the way in which modern sociology was developing subsequently led Alvin Gouldner (1972) to argue for a radically 'reflexive sociology', that is to propose, once again, a way of working which would challenge the modern legislative conception of 'sociologist-as-liberal-technologue' and promote instead the idea of sociology as a critically interpretive endeavour and moral activity; a way of working which in effect suggests the possibility of a return to a relatively marginalized and largely devalued conception of sociology as a moral science. Each of the examples I have briefly cited seem to draw inspiration from critical reflections on the problems of modern sociology developed by C. Wright Mills, reflections which anticipate, in some very general respects, preoccupations which have subsequently been identified as 'postmodern'.

Drawing on a tradition of critical inquiry, within which the work of Max Weber occupies a prominent place, Wright Mills argues for the reconstitution of sociology as a form of cultural analysis concerned with 'the present as history and the future as responsibility' ([1959]1970: 183). In a context where the relationship between reason and freedom is identified as problematic, and where the expectations and assumptions of the Enlightenment have proven to be questionable, if they have not collapsed altogether, Wright Mills argues that the practice of social analysis needs to be radically revised and recast. Reflecting on the limitations of modern social thought Wright Mills (ibid.: 184) argues that our basic conceptions are no longer adequate, that our understandings of 'society' and 'self' have been overtaken by 'new realities', realities which have subsequently been explored in greater detail by many others, for example by analysts such as Touraine (1989) and Giddens (1990), both of whom have been concerned with the impact of processes of globalization on forms of social organization and the extension of social relations beyond the geopolitical boundary of the nation-state, an extension which renders the modern sociological preoccupation with a conception of society, itself assumed to coincide with the formation of the modern nation-state, problematic. The new realities overtaking our understanding of 'self' have been explored in a parallel manner in structuralist and poststructuralist forms of analysis. In very broad terms such analyses effectively extend and re-work the criticisms of assumptions about the human subject articulated by Wright Mills, namely that there may be no universals, nothing beyond social and historical specificity, 'nothing but "human culture", a highly mutable [and variable] affair' ([1959]1970: 182).

Wright Mills argued that we are living through the ending of an epoch, perhaps entering what he described as a 'post-modern period'. The sense that we are living in a period of transition, in an interregnum, along with an associated judgement that conventional modern narratives and assumptions about the social world no longer seem appropriate or adequate, have subsequently become prominent elements in the debate over the transformation of modernity and the possible emergence of a condition of postmodernity. In contrast to the designation of the postmodern as a periodizing term, a designation which suggests possible parallels between the respective views of Wright Mills and Toynbee (1954) on the historical development of the West, I take the term 'postmodern' to be synonymous with a radical questioning of modernity, to be literally a corollary of the wholesale reflexivity of modernity, of the process of radical questioning which has been turned increasingly on the project of modernity itself. In short, it constitutes a way of relating to the modern world, as it is, and as it cannot avoid being. In the terms employed by Bauman (1991: 257), postmodern means 'living without guarantee', without security and order, and with contingency and ambivalence. To put it another way, it means living without illusions and with uncertainty. The sociological corollary of the above, or to be more precise the implication of postmodern preoccupations for sociology, is that a number of the assumptions, expectations and objectives conventionally ascribed to the discipline become inappropriate, if not unrealizable (Bauman, 1992a; Seidman and Wagner, 1992; Smart, 1993a).

One response to the idea of a postmodern configuration is to argue that it merely constitutes another version of the 'new', and that with the passage of time it too will be forgotten, or at best may come to constitute simply yet another idiosyncratic position on the sociological continuum. The implication being that in due course we can all either return to business as usual, that is practising our preferred variant(s) of sociological analysis, or embrace yet another new variant. There are two comments to be made here. First scepticism about any 'cult of the new' is warranted insofar as it is analytically constructive. But as I make clear in the following chapter, the concerns associated with the idea of the postmodern have been around, in one form or another, for most of the century, in short for a substantial part of sociology's history, and to that extent it is not appropriate to dismiss the postmodern as simply another new form. Second, issues raised in the context of the debate over the notion of the postmodern call attention to significant and controversial matters that sociology can not simply brush aside. For example, the strategy of 'legislative' reason on which modern sociology has been so dependent has been undermined, not so much by the rise of an alternative 'interpretive' strategy as by its own, increasingly evident, intrinsic limitations, and by a declining demand for its expert services as government of the social through centralized state planning and social engineering has been increasingly handed over to market forces (Bauman, 1992a).

The pursuit of universal epistemic warrants or foundations, on which legislative reason has been predicated, has proven to be a futile task, one increasingly undermined by the recognition of persisting cultural differences which resist the subordination that is a corollary of inclusion within totalizing categories, as well as the silencing which follows exclusion from the same (Readings, 1992). The related question of how modern sociology is to respond to the emergence of different objects of analysis, notably following the impact of transnational or global processes of transformation on social life, and in particular the consequences of complex forms of articulation between local and global processes, is no less important.

On the one hand the increasing internationalization of socio-economic and cultural life appears to be eroding the sovereignty of nation-states and contributing to the emergence of transnational socio-cultural and political forms, 'supranational' communities and Pan nationalisms. But at the same time there appears to be a proliferation of the modern nation-state as regions and *ethnie* pursue modern nationhood (Smith, 1990: 183). Given the conventional sociological equation of the social formation 'society' with the geopolitical formation of the modern nation-state, transformations of the order outlined above raise questions about the appropriate subject matter or focus of the discipline, as do the growth of global or transterritorial forms of communication, the increasing migration of populations (Rouse, 1991), and the greater mobility of an increasing number of people.

As subject matter, theory, and method have increasingly become matters of difference and disagreement, so the remote prospect of a shared paradigm or consensus within the discipline of sociology has receded. Paralleling the social, cultural and political transformations it attempts to interpret and explain sociology itself appears de-centred and pluralistic. Given the existence of a plurality of sociologies, differentiated on epistemological and cultural grounds, nineteenth-century Western European arguments concerning the specificity of sociology appear deficient, if not irrelevant. Whereas the founding figures in the discipline sought to radically differentiate sociology from other social and human sciences, contemporary analysts are inclined to draw attention to the blurring or undermining of disciplinary boundaries and the virtues, if not the necessity, of interdisciplinary work (Giddens, 1987; Touraine, 1984, 1989; Bauman, 1992a). It is in this complex setting that the question 'Whither sociology' continues to be posed.

What are the prospects for sociology? One common response is to attempt to resuscitate the aims and objectives of the longstanding tradition of sociological inquiry which extends back to the work of Saint-Simon and Comte. The idea of an integrated, internally cohesive sociology is a familiar one. It represents the objective towards which the discipline has attempted to move almost from its inception. But to date all attempts have found that the goal continually recedes, like the horizon it is never reached, and for each sociological community, if not for each f(r)action it seems to be a different horizon towards which analysis is drawn. Even what used to be

known as the 'orthodox consensus' (Atkinson, 1971) was in practice a
vigorously contested and internally quite diverse combination of sociological standpoints. The subsequent proliferation of sociologies has only
served to underline and increase the extent of the methodological diversity
that has been a feature of sociological inquiry from the beginning.

Sociology for One World?

A somewhat different argument for a unified sociology has been carefully
outlined in the following terms: 'I want to advocate a single sociology,
whose ultimate unity rests on acknowledging the universality of human
reasoning; to endorse a single World, whose oneness is based on adopting
a realistic ontology; and to predicate any services this Discipline can give
to this World upon accepting the fundamental unicity of Humanity'
(Archer, 1991: 131). It appears to be a laudable objective, but it is one
which requires closer consideration. The idea of an international sociological forum continuing to open up communication between sociologists
across and around the globe and the associated 'call for an internation-
alised sociology to address . . . global phenomena' (ibid.: 132) are pro-
posals to which there can be little, if any, serious objection. What such an
internationalized sociology might look like, is however another matter, a
potentially controversial matter.

   The current condition and recent history of sociology has been diagnosed
in the following terms. As institutional domains have become subject to
'intensified globalisation', sociology in the wake of positivism's demise has
allegedly become 'increasingly localised'. It is suggested that there has been
a massive retreat from 'international endeavour . . . and a re-celebration of
diversity, difference, tradition, locality, context specificity and indigenisa-
tion' (ibid.: 132). The implication is that the universalist assumptions of
positivism have been replaced by no less problematic responses, exemplified
by the 'false universalisms' of (i) modernization theory anticipating forms
of convergence following 'the transfer of capital, technology, and information from the First World' (ibid.: 135); (ii) dependency theory which
effectively mirrors modernization theory; and (iii) postmodernism which it
is argued presents a 'sweeping repudiation of "modernity"'. Ultimately, it is
the awkward, ambiguous, constituted unity of postmodernist discourse that
appears to arouse most concern.

   The idea of a single sociology is not to be equated with the various forms
of unity associated with sociological positivism '(unity of method, universality of laws, uniformity of practice)' (ibid.: 132–3). On the contrary,
the distinction or polarity 'between Unity and Diversity' implicit within
positivism, and shared ironically by its various critics, is itself conceived to
be the source of many sociological problems, in particular of an 'increasing
extremism' which reaches its climacteric in Archer's view with postmodernism. The argument is that postmodernism celebrates difference and restates

the polarity Unity/Diversity as Totality/Locality. In so far as it is the latter terms in the respective dichotomies that are privileged within postmodernism the consequence is said to be 'impotence to engage in international discourse' (ibid.: 133). One of the problems I have with this is that postmodernism, like modernism with which it remains closely articulated, itself seems to be not simply a topic within international discourse, but has been constituted as an international discourse. Whether we like it or not, to a degree, postmodern discourse and associated ideas are shared, discussed and debated around the world. In Europe (England, France, Germany, Italy and Spain), America, Australia, New Zealand, Malaysia and Japan postmodern ideas are employed to make sense of a number of contemporary social, cultural, political and economic developments.

Ironically, the process of globalization highlighted by Archer is frequently associated with the diffusion of postmodern conditions. Indeed it might be argued that what has been termed a 'condition of postmodernity' arises with a series of global transitions beginning in the 1960s, transitions associated with information technology, computerization and the mercantilization of knowledge (Lyotard, 1984a); a prodigious expansion and 'fundamental mutation of the sphere of culture in the world of late capitalism' (Jameson, 1991: 47–8); problems of multiculturality and polyethnicity confronting modern nation-states (Tololyan, 1991); and the growth of institutions, movements and networks of communication addressing, invoking, or attempting to fabricate global constituencies. It is precisely recognition of the increasing significance of trans-societal or global transformations that has opened up the analytic 'frame beyond . . . the usual interpretation of concern with modernity' (Robertson and Lechner, 1985: 105) and has prompted discussion of aspects of contemporary conditions as postmodern.

Globalization has precipitated 'a growing worldwide interconnectedness of structure, culture and agency' (Archer, 1991: 133). But if it has lead to a 'parallel de-differentiation of traditional boundaries' (ibid.), there are signs that a de-differentiation of some modern practices and a simultaneous regeneration or reconstitution of particular traditional forms of life are also occurring. Archer's view is clear, namely 'globalisation of *society* means that *societies* are no longer the prime units of sociology' (ibid.). The idea of society as the primary focus of sociological inquiry, frequently conceptualized as a social formation synonymous with the geopolitical unity of the modern nation-state, has been disputed by a number of analysts, as I have already noted. The increasing internationalization of economic and cultural life has effectively rendered the received image of society problematic. But if this means that we encounter a new social reality, is global or world society an appropriate designation? If we accept that 'globalisation effectively means that societies now cannot be seen as systems in an environment of other systems', does it follow that they are appropriately conceptualized as 'sub-systems of the larger inclusive world society (Albrow, 1990: 11)? One implication of the view that 'the peoples of the world are incorporated into a single world society, global society' (Albrow,

1990: 9) is that sociology needs must be international if it is to effectively address its object. In short a particular form of international sociology is deemed necessary to make sense of an increasingly global society. The implication is that because we live in 'one world' our 'theoretical assumptions and frameworks' need to be overhauled or revised, in short it is suggested that we need 'a new variety of social theory' (Archer, 1991: 133, 139). However, the idea that globalization is simply creating a single world society remains contentious: in particular such a notion masks the forms of ethnic and cultural fragmentation that have become an increasingly prominent feature of global reality (Friedman, 1990). The idea that processes of globalization may have *both* homogenizing and diversifying consequences does not threaten to undermine the prospects for international sociology, rather such consequences represent the inescapable parameters within which contemporary sociological analysis is situated.

If contemporary social theory and analysis have become international and cosmopolitan enterprises, it is also evident that distinctive national-cultural differences remain within sociology. In short there continue to be distinctive local sociological configurations distinguished by language and cultural differences in particular. And both international and local or regional forms of sociology are necessary for understanding the complex articulation of global processes with local or regional conditions.

The social, cultural, political and economic frictions which arise from the articulation of global processes with local institutions, customs and conditions have an analytic corollary, namely the tensions and misunderstandings which can arise in dialogues between different national sociological configurations in an international context. Here, amongst other things, we confront the question of language and translation, and the problem of cultural differences as they bear on the practice of sociology. Language and cultural differences, and associated problems of translation, are intrinsic features of contemporary social life, and although they constitute problems for the second order discourse of sociology they do not prevent the possibility of international sociology.

Social Worlds – Language and Cultural Difference

The idea that we now live in one world remains sociologically controversial. Ecologically and geopolitically the notion of one world is understandable. But what does it mean in sociological terms to talk of living in one world? The observation 'that global processes are now partly constitutive of social reality everywhere' (Archer, 1990: 134) is relatively uncontentious, but the extent to which and the respects in which they are constitutive varies considerably, for localized forms of life continue to select, absorb and transform the variety of instruments of homogenization that are a feature of the globalization of culture (Appadurai, 1990). Globalization does not necessarily mean that we all live in one *social* world, to the contrary, as the survey of 'The Global News Agenda' (Malik and Anderson, 1992) reveals, local priorities and interests continue to constitute the social world(s) that we know of and live within. And in so far as new forms of cultural heterogenization are as much a consequence of processes of globalization as manifestations of cultural homogenization, the argument that 'globalisation has nullified many of the good reasons for emphasising *diversity*' (Archer, 1991: 134) is difficult to sustain, as is the related observation that we encounter a 'progressive "integration of diversity"'. In consequence the pronouncement of the end of the 'anthropological order' appears premature, for processes of globalization not only connect distant localities and contribute to their transformation through an 'intensification of worldwide social relations', but also strengthen 'pressures for local autonomy and regional cultural identity' (Giddens, 1990: 64, 65). To that extent it might be argued that the notion of society is itself now inappropriate for conceptualizing the forms of sociality that have been constituted through the articulation of global processes with local forms of life.

Contemporary social theory has not retreated from international endeavour, on the contrary it has become increasingly preoccupied with the complex and uneven consequences of the globalization of modern institutions, practices and experiences. One of the consequences identified has been the emergence of a condition designated as 'postmodern' (Harvey, 1989; Featherstone, 1991; Bauman, 1992a). The description of such a condition as limited in relevance, at best, to the First World or the West is inadequate, for it overlooks the broader global deployment of the term, demonstrated for example in analyses of transnational migration circuits and 'the implosion of the Third World into the first' (Rouse, 1991: 17), misunderstandings and confrontations between the West and Islam (Ahmed, 1992), 'the oppositional potential of black cultural practices' (West, 1989: 95), consumer culture in Malaysia (Lee, 1992), and transformations in the international capitalist economy (Harvey, 1989). The consequences of the globalization of modernity, including experiences of conditions designated 'postmodern', are not confined to the West, or the First World.

The call for an internationalized sociology to address global processes is merited and to a degree it is being answered in the only way possible, namely through an increasing frequency of exchanges between localized forms of sociology, that is through contacts between 'sociologists from diverse cultural traditions and national origins' (Cardoso, 1986: 1). In a world of differences, of cultures, languages, customs, beliefs and political systems, the enterprise of international sociology is bound to be a difficult one. It is an enterprise that, of necessity, feeds off localized or regional forms of sociology, an enterprise that has to cope with the difficulties and misunderstandings that may arise from differences in the political systems, cultural traditions and languages in which sociology is practised.

Significant differences in the conception and practice of sociology may also arise within a specific socio-cultural context, for example between advocates of different philosophies, intellectual traditions and political affinities. One of the problems that continually plagues sociology, and disrupts communication, is the tendency for such differences to become exaggerated, or over-polarized, in the course of an argument. The debate which has developed around the postmodern constellation provides an appropriate illustration. For example, the comments that postmodernism has 'jettisoned reason', announced an 'epochal Great Break . . . between the "modern" and the "post-modern"', and pronounced the 'fall of . . . modernity' (Archer, 1991: 141, 137, 142) over-dramatize and misrepresent important issues and differences rather than clarify them. In consequence the 'postmodern' positions set up are hard to take seriously, which is a pity because there are important issues to be addressed as a number of analysts have demonstrated (Bauman, 1987, 1991; Lash, 1990; Hekman, 1990).

If appropriate forms of cross-cultural sociological communication, on which the enterprise of international sociology surely depends, are to be cultivated, it is necessary to promote effective communication about significant differences of perspective within and across sociological constituencies. The objective of rendering different cultures intelligible to one another is widely shared and recognized to be increasingly necessary as we encounter the re-emergence of seemingly 'traditional' ethnic communities and witness a rekindling of attendant social and political conflicts. How intelligibility between cultures is to be enhanced, what contribution sociology is able to make, or perhaps more accurately, what kind(s) of sociology can make an appropriate contribution, are potentially more contentious matters.

Does interlocution between cultures depend upon commensurability and common ideas about human nature and reason? Or is it perhaps that through dialogue cultures come to an appreciation of their differences, their *almost* indefinable incommensurabilities? Should the 'integration of diversity' be the objective of international sociology, or is the *interpretation* of diversity a more appropriate aim, one more likely to contribute to an enhanced understanding of diversity and a growth of tolerance and solidarity between different cultures and communities? An unqualified notion of international sociology, or global sociology, implies that a degree of commensurability between cultures already exists. In a sense there is an implied assumption of precisely that which needs to be explored.

The critical issue is the terms on which a sense of commensurability might be achieved and forms of difference and diversity accommodated. Scepticism about the 'linear spread of modernity and . . . blind faith in the modernisation process' (Archer, 1990: 2) has important implications for the practice of sociology, bound up as it has been with the project of modernity. The globalization of modernity is not a neutral process, indeed for Heidegger it raised the prospect of the 'complete Europeanisation of the earth and man (1971: 15). There now seems to be no possibility of avoiding modern technology and industrialization; no effective alternative but to accept that the language in which communication generally occurs is European, that discussion is 'forced over into the sphere of European ideas'; and that there is an almost irresistible temptation to 'rely on European ways of representation and their concepts', a tendency that confirms and lends weight to the 'dominance of . . . European reason'. Notwithstanding the above, communications between cultures remain disturbed and troubled by the sense that the language in which communication takes place has a powerful impact on (mutual) understanding and may prevent 'the possibility of saying what the dialogue is about' (Heidegger, 1971: 13–16, 5). In so far as the languages of cultures are not simply different but in some instances are 'other in nature and radically so', then interlocution between cultures will continue to be subject to interference, to misunderstandings and misinterpretations, no matter how 'universal' our assumptions might be, or rather, particularly when we *assume* the existence of universality.

The difficulties identified by Heidegger and explored further by critics of Western modernity remain, but there have been important changes. European or Western modernity is no longer unchallenged, for there are now a number of contending 'civilisational, continental, regional, societal, and other definitions' of global conditions and possibilities (Robertson and Lechner, 1985: 111). These remarks are not intended as, and do not represent, a challenge to the idea that contemporary sociology needs to extend the focus of its inquiries beyond the forms of social life nurtured within the geopolitical boundaries of the modern nation-state, to encompass transnational and/or global forms of sociality. Indigenization and what has been termed the 'postmodern' diversity of cultures do not undermine the enterprise of international sociology, they make it more necessary (Albrow, 1987). However, they do simultaneously alert us to problems of interpretation and translation which international sociology cannot evade.

Interpretation/Translation

All forms of sociology confront a problem of translation between what Schutz (1971) described as the first order constructs which we routinely employ in our everyday lives and the second order constructs of sociological abstraction. In the sociological interpretation of our own native culture(s) we confront a problem of translation. Cross-cultural sociological interpretation and communication is no less problematic, if anything the difficulties of translation are exacerbated. So what is the implication for international sociology of the view that the 'experience of other cultures . . . is ultimately irremediably different' (Albrow, 1987: 10)? Is it something like Benjamin's notion of translation, namely that an 'instant and final, rather than a temporary and provisional, solution of this foreignness [of languages] remains out of the reach of mankind' (1973: 75)? In which case the fate of international sociology is to continually encounter a lack of correspondence between languages, to continually run up against the fact that

'there remains in addition to what can be conveyed [in translation] something that cannot be communicated' (Benjamin, 1973: 79). What is at issue
here is the question of differences in 'modes of intention' between words
and the contextual character of meaning; it is a symptom of what Rorty
(1989) calls 'the contingency of language'. But such matters do not
necessarily prevent translation or stop communication, as Heidegger (1971)
demonstrates in a dialogue on language that explores differences between
Western aesthetics and the Japanese notion of *Iki*. Communication may
serve to establish or exemplify difference, but it also offers the prospect of
an understanding of the same.

There is, however, a related but more contentious issue which I have yet
to address, an issue that an internationalized sociology aiming to 'respect
humanity' has to face. The issue is that of the inequality of languages, the
fact that translation and the choice of the language in which dialogue or
communication is to take place is 'governed by institutionally defined
power relations between the languages/modes of life concerned' (Asad,
1986: 157). Sociology has its roots in the Enlightenment, in European
civilization and culture. The formative texts are in French, German, English
and, to a lesser extent, Italian and Spanish, and there is a continuing
concern over the question (and problem) of translation even within this
'family' of languages. The enterprise of international sociology is broader in
scope and more ambitious, and its field is populated with a multiplicity of
cultures and languages, but the language in which dialogue generally takes
place is English (Wallerstein, 1995). Languages are not equal, some are
'"weaker" in relation to Western languages (and today, especially to
English), [and] they are more likely to submit to forcible transformation in
the translation process than the other way around' (Asad, 1986: 157–8). In
short, particular languages, Western languages, and especially English, are
privileged in translation.

The privileging of Western languages is a corollary of the socio-cultural
and politico-economic forms of hegemony which have been exercised by the
West. The privileged status of Western languages also reflects the fact that
they 'produce and deploy *desired* knowledge more readily than [for
example] Third World languages do' (Asad, 1986: 158). This does not
constitute a denial of the necessity of translation, rather that the direction
of exchange or transfer is predetermined and loaded, that the tendency is to
interpret 'alien' cultures and civilizations through the conceptual prism of
Western modernity. The implication is that translation 'is inevitably
enmeshed in conditions of power – professional, national, international'
and that international sociology needs to be more reflexive, needs to
address the question of 'how power enters into the process of "cultural
translation"' (ibid.: 163).

Contemporary sociology has already begun to extend the focus of its
inquiries beyond the forms of social life nurtured within the geopolitical
boundaries of the modern nation-state to encompass transnational and/or
global forms of sociality. However, rather than invoke the notion of a

'global sociology' which assumes that 'the peoples of the world are incorporated into a single world society, global society' (Albrow, 1990: 9), it is more appropriate to explore the ways in which global transformations have led simultaneously to the dispersion of some common forms, commodities and ideas and yet, in so far as these are received, interpreted, adapted and utilized in potentially radically different cultural contexts, have contributed to the (re)production or (re)constitution of difference and diversity. In short rather than assume the existence of 'global society' as a rationale for a global or international sociology, conduct sociological analyses of processes of globalization and explore the problems of representation which arise when sociology is internationalized.

International sociology can not avoid engaging with a series of difficult questions concerning representation, questions which other disciplines concerned with cross-cultural analysis, for example anthropology, have also had to face. 'Who is speaking, for what, and to whom?' Such questions continue to matter in a context where 'there is no vantage *outside* the actuality of relationships between cultures, between unequal imperial and nonimperial powers, between different Others, a vantage that might allow one the epistemological privilege of somehow judging, evaluating, and interpreting free of the encumbering interests, emotions, and engagements of the ongoing relationships themselves' (Said, 1989: 217). There is no neutral space or terrain from which international sociology can operate. But that does not undermine the enterprise, it simply represents one of the critical conditions on which such a sociology has to reflect and within which it has unavoidably to operate.

The objective of international sociology is not to invent a 'universal Esperanto-like culture', a more credible and important task exists, one it shares with the discipline of social anthropology, namely 'to enlarge the possibility of intelligible discourse between people quite different from one another in interest, outlook, wealth, and power, and yet contained in a world where, tumbled as they are into endless connection, it is increasingly difficult to get out of each other's way' (Geertz, 1988: 131). Living amidst the signs of increasing global disarray and disorder, the enterprise of international sociology is more and more necessary. It is important to remember that difference and diversity exist not only in the social worlds sociology attempts to interpret and understand, but also within the discipline itself. To that extent the need is for an 'interpretive' rather than a 'legislative' internationalized sociology, one which attempts to offer a translation service between different cultures and communities. And that is precisely what the more lucid, politically and morally engaged contributions to the debate around the notion of the postmodern have sought to achieve.

There is now a pervasive sense that the context in which we are reflecting on the practice of social inquiry is radically different. For example, recall the references which have been made by analysts to 'new times'; 'late' or 'disorganized' capitalism; 'risk society' and 'reflexive modernization'; the consequences of processes of globalization; and the impact of the revolution in information technologies upon socio-spatial structures. It is in this context that a notion of the postmodern has been invoked to describe prominent features of the changing times in which we live. But whether the various issues and symptoms outlined above are to be described as 'postmodern', or are to be regarded as signs of a radically transformed, reflexive or hyper modernity is not to my mind particularly crucial or decisive, more important are the detailed diagnoses of existing conditions, our understanding of the complex processes and circumstances we encounter, and the ethico-political responses subsequently offered to the issues and symptoms identified.

Sociology as a Vocation

In his critical reflections on 'science as a vocation' Max Weber asks who still believes the findings of science can 'teach us anything about the *meaning* of the world?' (1970: 142). The reference is to natural science, but as subsequent comments confirm, Weber takes the view that whether it is physics, chemistry, astronomy, aesthetics, jurisprudence, the historical and cultural sciences, or the disciplines closest to him, notably 'sociology, history, economics, political science, and those types of cultural philosophy that make it their task to interpret these sciences' (ibid.: 145), the vocation of the analyst is confined to the generation of understanding through the revelation and interpretation of 'inconvenient facts'. Science is not equipped 'to answer the question: "What shall we do, and, how shall we arrange our lives?"' (ibid.: 152–3).

Weber's text was presented at Munich University in 1918 and published the following year. Its immediate focus is university life in Germany, loosely compared to the United States of America, but there is also a broader concern with the difficulty of facing up to the 'fate of our times', of living with the uncertainty which is a corollary of the processes of rationalization and intellectualization which have precipitated an increasing 'disenchantment of the world'.

Weber's comments on the state of university life in Germany after the First World War bear comparison with more recent reflections on the state of higher education, with what, following Lyotard (1984a), might be termed the current 'postmodernization' of higher education. Elaborating on the ways in which German universities were developing in the direction of their American counterparts, Weber noted how research institutes were becoming enterprises, increasingly requiring a 'very considerable' level of funding, and how universities were increasingly engaging in 'a most ridiculous competition for enrollments' (1970: 133), and the income from fees which is a corollary. In Weber's view such transformations were making academic life a 'mad hazard'. The 'hazards' with which Weber was preoccupied have subsequently increased in scale and scope, and have become a much more prominent part of higher education around the world.

In his reflections on the changing condition of knowledge production and distribution since the end of the 1950s Lyotard identifies a number of related developments, including the impact of the 'mercantilization of knowledge' on the prominent role formerly enjoyed by nation-states, the de-legitimation of totalizing rationales for the pursuit of knowledge and the emergence of 'legitimation through performativity', and an erosion of the status and place of the teacher or professor. Whereas, for Weber, one symptom of the Americanization of German university life was the way in which research institutes were becoming 'state capitalist enterprises', for Lyotard one of the more significant recent transformations in higher education is the increasing marginalization of the state 'which goes hand in hand with the commercialization of knowledge' (1984a: 5) and the associated increasing influence of 'multinational corporations'. In discussing the emergence and impact of new forms of the circulation of capital, as well as the potential consequences of the development of 'computer technology and telematics', Lyotard draws attention to transformations in knowledge, including the possibility that learning may circulate 'along the same lines as money, instead of for its "educational" value or political (administrative, diplomatic, military) importance' (ibid.: 6). Implied here, and in a subsequent discussion of the increasing emphasis being placed upon performativity criteria in education, is a sense that institutions of higher education are becoming increasingly subordinate to 'existing powers', and, in turn, that the vocational dimension of science is being steadily undermined and eroded. The primary objective of higher education is no longer to encourage recognition of 'inconvenient facts', or to 'bring about self-clarification and a sense of responsibility' (Weber, 1970: 152), rather it increasingly has as its main aim 'improving the system's performance' (Lyotard, 1984a: 49).

Increasingly knowledge is no longer valued as an end in itself and the idea of university autonomy has come to have little, if any, real meaning, for 'nowhere do teachers groups have the power to decide what the budget of their institution will be; all they can do is allocate the funds that are assigned to them, and only then as the last step in the process' (ibid.: 50). The increasing utilization of computer technology is continuing to transform the learning process and, in turn, threatens/promises to replace the traditional teacher. Paralleling the 'partial replacement of teachers by machines' there has been a concomitant shift from a preoccupation with the 'truth' of knowledge to a concern with its exchange value and efficiency. In such a context the 'grand narratives of legitimation' seem to be no longer so appropriate for understanding the process of knowledge acquisition, or more accurately, the process of acquisition of operational knowledge, skills and techniques. The conventional disciplinary-differentiated organization of knowledge is increasingly being challenged by de-differentiated or inter-disciplinary approaches relying on teamwork and performativity criteria. And there is a growing division emerging between two types of knowledge institution, one oriented primarily towards an economical transmission of vocationally related knowledge, training and certification – 'the selection and reproduction of professional skills' – the other, more oriented towards the production of knowledge through research – 'the promotion and "stimulation" of "imaginative" minds' (ibid.: 53).

Students in the early 1960s felt that they were living in an 'age of anxiety' (Zweig, 1963), subsequent developments in higher education are making it likely that students, and perhaps not only students, will be inclined to look back on that confusing, uneven, and much derided era with a degree of nostalgia. However, analytically it is not a question of lamenting or cele-brating the range of developments discussed by Lyotard, but rather of recognizing the existence of a continuing process of transformation in the conditions of knowledge production and distribution, and perhaps, closer to home, of considering the possibility that 'the process of delegitimation and the predominance of the performance criterion are sounding the knell of the age of the Professor' (Lyotard, 1984a: 53). What are the implications of the range of transformations identified above for the practice of sociology? In particular, is it appropriate to continue to talk, in the terms employed by Weber, of the practice of science as a 'vocation' or a 'calling'?

The implications of a postmodern condition of knowledge for the practice of sociology are explored by Bauman (1992a). The central issue to which Bauman's discussion is directed is where sociology stands in 'a new world, strikingly dissimilar from that in which its orthodox goals and strategies had gestated', and whether the discipline's status as 'a *privileged* discourse, as a supplier of rational models of social reality and managerially useful knowledge of its processes, [can] be rescued and retained?' (1992a: xxv). The answer given is that the legislative, social engineering ambitions which have been a feature of modern sociology, ambitions which had once been blessed with relatively generous funding by a centralized state seeking 'expert social-management knowledge', have been called into question on a number of counts and that there is now a 'need for a radical reorientation of the tasks and the strategies of social study' (ibid.: 104, 105). Sociology has been called to account analytically because its ability to deliver managerially useful knowledge has been found wanting. No less significant has been a marked decline in the demand for social-management knowl-edge, and an associated reduction in the availability of state funding, following a series of significant socio-economic and political transforma-tions, including in particular a 'gradual substitution of "seduction" for "repression" as the paramount weapon of social integration, [and the] shifting of responsibility for integration from the state bureaucracy to the market' (ibid.: 105). It is in this context that a number of alternative 'postmodern' strategies for sociology have been identified by Bauman, two of which are worth noting here. The first represents a response to the widely recognized pluralism of contemporary social life and acknowledges the existence of different 'forms of life', 'life-worlds', 'traditions' and 'language games', differences which can not be reduced to a single hegemonic universal form, without the risk of a significant loss of meaning; differences which Bauman suggests constitute the analytic focus of an interpretive 'postmodern' sociology, a sociology which represents a translation service between and across different traditions.

The objective of an 'interpreting sociology' is however broader and more socially relevant than Bauman appears to allow when he suggests that its purpose is confined to the '"enrichment" of one's own tradition' (ibid.: 107). An interpreting sociology aims to do more, it aims to illuminate differences, to draw attention to areas of incommensurability, and to attempt to translate between different forms of life in order to facilitate understanding and communication between self and other in an increasingly globalized yet pluralistic world. Rather than burying differences under conceptions and explanations assuming the status of unproblematic universals, an interpreting sociology is oriented to the cultivation of dialogues around and about differences. In so far as its objective is to interpret rather than integrate difference or diversity, an interpreting sociology stands on much the same terrain as those forms of ethnographic inquiry in social anthropology which have also been designated 'postmodern' (Tyler, 1986). Furthermore, given the ways in which knowledge about social processes and phenomena circulates in and out of what it is about, such an interpreting sociology may contribute to the (re)making of differences.

The second postmodern strategy identified by Bauman, and worthy of note here, is one which while it retains the 'two-pronged ambition of modernity', namely the hope of achieving an improvement in both the individual and general human condition through the power of reason, acknowledges that there are no teleological guarantees or secure foundations on which to rest a case, merely assumptions, values, and purposes. Bauman argues that, given the 'drying up of state interest in all but the most narrowly circumscribed sociological expertise' (1992a: 109), the emphasis in the second strategy is increasingly on the provision of knowledge which is likely to enhance the prospects of increasing 'the sphere of autonomy and solidarity' available to individuals, and that seems to mean knowledge about the 'new times' to which individuals increasingly find themselves subject. This is described as an analytic strategy which continues with '*modern* concerns under *postmodern* conditions' (ibid.: 111), one that is really only distinguishable from more orthodox modern forms of sociological inquiry by its focus on a 'new' object of inquiry. Once again I think there is more at issue here than Bauman is prepared to allow and that, in addition to knowledge about various 'new' socio-economic and political conditions which individuals encounter, another kind of knowledge is necessary to enhance the prospects for increased autonomy and solidarity, namely knowledge about the cultural assumptions and understandings through which subjects have come to understand themselves as particular individuals moved by 'desires', possessing 'interests', and experiencing 'embodiment'. In short, knowledge to facilitate the possibility of reason-led forms of reflexivity which may allow subjects to recognize that 'the self is not given to us' (Foucault, 1986a: 351) and that there is frequently more scope than we allow for reconstituting or recreating ourselves anew. In so far as this is the case, not only does the distinction between the two strategies outlined above appear much less pronounced, but the idea that the second strategy is only distinguished by its focus upon a 'new' object of investigation is undermined, for at least equally necessary to the objective of enlarging the 'sphere of autonomy and solidarity' is an interpretive understanding of the de-centred character of human subjectivity.

What then of the 'vocation' of sociology? Bauman's sociology has as its primary focus a critical interpretation of the ongoing transformations and associated forms of knowledge which constitute our conditions of existence, as well as an analysis of the possible consequences, including the scope for appropriate responsible courses of action, for individuals and collectivities. The analysis offered bears some comparison with Freud's turn of the century reflections on civilization and its discontents, in so far as it might be argued that a shared aim is to bring individuals to an awareness and understanding of things as they are, a potentially uncomfortable awareness, unqualified by the consolation of optimistic prophecy. In Freud's case this is achieved through psychoanalytic practice and an 'ethic of honesty', through what Rieff (1965) describes as an archaeology of the psyche. It is a practice which facilitates a 'working-through of illusions' associated with prevailing systems and symbols of authority, a challenging of systems of restraint and inhibition, but it 'leaves us with the anxiety of analysis' (Rieff, 1965: 320, 328), and confronting the necessity of making choices in a context where there remain few, if any, rules to guide conduct. The context is now a little different, the repressions and restraints with which Freud was so preoccupied have been displaced, to a substantial degree, by forms of seduction, but the 'moral irresoluteness fostered by the decline of religion' has not been compensated for by 'a new theoretic resolution' (ibid.: 306), to the contrary, confidence in secular scientific culture has itself been undermined by increasing evidence of the limits and limitations of the modern project.

It is to an identification and critical exploration of the limits and limitations of the modern project that Bauman's sociological work has been directed. The modern quest for order and certainty is destined to remain unrealizable because it is effectively self-undermining, the pursuit of order and certainty simultaneously producing disorder and uncertainty. As Bauman remarks,

> The passage from uncertainty to certainty, from ambivalence to transparency seemed to be a matter of time, of resolve, of resources, of *knowledge*. It is an entirely different matter to live with the postmodern awareness of no certain exit from uncertainty; of the escape from contingency being as contingent as the condition from which escape is sought.
>   The discomfort such awareness brings about is the source of specifically post-modern discontents: discontent against the condition fraught with ambivalence, against the contingency that refuses to go away, and against the messengers of the news . . . What the recipients of the news find difficult to accept is that whatever they resolve to do would lack the comfort of having the truth, or the laws of history, or the unambiguous verdict of reason on its side. (1991: 237)

Once again the likely outcome of analysis is unease and anxiety, an anxiety which follows from a recognition of the need to face up to the inescapability of living with contingency. An anxiety borne of the realization that agents confronted with responsibility for making choices and taking decisions are forced to do so without the security of guarantees, and that the absence of clarity is 'a permanent condition rather than a temporary (and in principle rectifiable) irritant' (Bauman, 1992a: xxii). In this postmodern setting the vocation of sociology is to enhance understanding of the slippery conditions within and under which conduct is constituted and interpreted, and reflexively reconstituted and reinterpreted, and thereby to simultaneously bring about both a realistic accommodation to (but not necessarily an acceptance of) the way things are – frequently order-defying and organization-denying – as well as an appreciation of the opportunities (and problems) which remain for making choices and taking decisions, for acting with consideration for others, and for exercising moral responsibility.

The question of the appropriate self-understanding of the discipline has been an important issue in the sociological replay of the modern-postmodern debate. Reinterpreting sociology in the early 1980s Berger and Kellner argue that its earlier self-confidence based on 'Enlightenment optimism' has proven unwarranted, its expectations misguided, but that 'demoralization' is not an appropriate response. Their argument is that 'sociology must return to the "big questions"' (Berger and Kellner, 1982: 16), questions which by their very nature can never be finally resolved. Their call is for a return to sociology as a moral science, for sociology to nurture its moral dimension by being 'attentive to the meanings of other people's lives' (ibid.: 17). This does not constitute a claim for sociology being able to offer guidance for conduct, but it does emphasize the moral relevance of sociology, or to be more precise it suggests 'moral qualities' which have not perhaps been accorded the importance or prominence they really warrant. Elaborating on the potential moral status of sociology Berger and Kellner suggest that the discipline has a 'curious relation to . . . a particular kind of ethics' (ibid.: 77). What Berger and Kellner have in mind is Weber's notion of an 'ethics of responsibility', an ethics which is guided by 'the consequences of . . . conduct' (1970: 127). In so far as sociology can offer insight into the range of possible consequences of conduct, as well as draw attention to the likelihood that intentions will frequently be compromised by the presence of unintended and unanticipated outcomes, then, Berger and Kellner argue, '"the spirit of sociology" . . . is akin to an ethics of responsibility, to a moral calculus of *probable* gains and *probable* costs' (1982: 78).

Directed as it is to an uncovering of 'inconvenient facts', to an exploration of the frequently underestimated complexity of social and cultural life, sociology is likely to reveal that things are not as we had formerly understood them to be, and that things as they are *here* and *now* is not how they are *there* or were back *then*. Such knowledge can not help but

contribute to the 'modern crisis of relativity' identified by Berger and
Kellner. Sociology does indeed inadvertently contribute to the 'progressive
disintegration of an order of objective certainty' (ibid.: 62) by drawing
attention to the existence of socio-cultural and historical differences, that is
to the variety of systems of meaning which are constitutive of, and which
receive expression in, human conduct. Sociology both reveals and contributes to the constructed character of social reality; it explores the complex
processes, the forms of action and interpretation, which are constitutive of
the context within which our conduct is formed and shaped, carried out,
rendered meaningful, or not, and found to have consequences, intended or
unintended. The social world is already, in itself, a precarious construction,
fragile and contingent, continually in a state of becoming, of coming into
being; the relativizing effect of sociology adds to the feeling of
precariousness, to the deepening sense of contingency.

   While Berger and Kellner emphasize the extent to which sociology is
bound up with relativity – 'a *product* of the same relativity that has always
been one of its objects of study' – they nevertheless seek to preserve the
prospect of comparative analysis by suggesting that '*all* human societies
and meanings systems have some things in common' (ibid.: 61, 75). Quite
what this 'human commonality' amounts to is not spelt out, in fact it is
passed over, held to be a matter which borders on 'philosophical anthropology and on the phenomenological analysis of the life-world' (ibid.: 75).
But is it necessary to assume a *condition humaine* in order to engage in
comparative analysis? A form of comparative analysis, which operates in
terms of a notion of the potential radicality of cultural difference, might
allow us to (better) come to an appreciation of the diversity of the forms in
which human being is expressed. Ironically, one of the 'moral' or 'proto-
moral' aspects of sociology identified by Berger and Kellner, namely
'respect for the immense variety of human meanings' (ibid.: 76), could itself
be argued to be threatened by the very idea of a common humanity, as
Readings demonstrates in a discussion of the fate of the indigenous people
of the continent of Australia. Readings argues that the idea of a common
human condition is a 'product of that very epistemological arrogance that
the Enlightenment celebrated' and that it erases 'rootedness and difference,
. . . [and] reduce[s] everyone to a blank abstract humanity, a bleached-out
indifference' (1992: 171, 184). In place of the assumption of a common
humanity Readings proposes thinking in terms of 'multiplicity and difference'. Such a proposal would seem to be not only more appropriate to the
moral aim attributed to sociology by Berger and Kellner, namely of
respecting 'the immense variety of human meanings', but would, in turn, be
less likely to increase the precariousness of the latter. The 'calculus of
probable consequences' identified with an ethics of responsibility has also to
include the consequences of thinking in terms of a 'common, abstract,
universal humanity', consequences which include the silencing or sub-
mersion of difference(s) within 'identity', the potential victimization and in
some cases terrorizing of otherness which may arise through imposition of

the universalizing meta-languages of modernity. Rather than thinking in terms of 'the identity of an abstract human nature' and assuming that all differences may be overcome, Readings argues that it is necessary for social analysts 'to think the multiplicity and diversity of culture without recourse to totalitarian notions of the universal' (ibid.: 186).

In so far as sociology is successful in both directing attention towards, and promoting respect for the diversity of meaning systems, it simultaneously induces perspectivism and reveals socio-cultural forms and processes, and associated stocks of knowledge, to be 'highly relative in terms of space and time' (Berger and Kellner, 1982: 61), and contributes thereby to what has been termed the crisis of modernity, in particular the rootlessness, disorientation and disintegration which has been identified as a corollary of modern social life. The reflexivity of modernity, to which sociology makes a substantial contribution, leads individuals to 'think about what before they did unthinkingly'; it promotes an increasing awareness of the relativity of forms of life and transforms values and norms from intrinsic, taken-for-granted aspects of everyday life to virtually optional features, that is features which it is appreciated could be different. Elaborating on the 'ambivalent fruits of the sociological perspective' (ibid.: 142) Berger and Kellner argue that as the features appropriate and necessary for social scientific inquiry, notably a degree of detachment and/or a 'debunking and relativizing thrust', have found an increasing resonance in everyday life, then the plausibility of values and beliefs has been impaired, at times undermined, and both the risk and incidence of disillusionment and normative disintegration have increased. If, as they suggest, sociological diagnosis is part of the social dis-ease, what form of response is required?

Sociology offers not one perspective on 'individual and collective existence' but a series of perspectives, a series of angles on social life, which when 'diffused (by teaching, writings, electronic media and what-have-you) beyond the scientific "community of investigators" to a broader public' (ibid.: 157) contribute to the relativization of values and beliefs, to the tendency towards de-institutionalization which is associated with the high degree of reflexivity identified as a defining feature of modernity. In response to the possible exacerbation of processes of de-institutionalization, disillusionment and normative disintegration, brought about in various ways as sociological knowledge infiltrates and transforms, relativizes and perhaps de-legitimates that which it is about, Berger and Kellner argue that there is an ethical matter to which it is necessary to draw attention, namely that the radical sociological analytic challenging, or suspicion, of value commitments and dilemmas in everyday life should not be considered the 'last word'.

In so far as sociology is necessarily subject, knowingly or not, to reflexivity and concerned with understanding the salient features of the present the question of where it ultimately stands can not receive a definitive answer. The question is destined to continually return, for it constitutes an exemplification of sociology's necessary reflexivity. Forty years after

T.H. Marshall's discussion of sociology's location at a crossroads Kurt
Wolff asked: 'Is there a place, a role, a function, is there any justification
for sociology? If so at all, for what kind of sociology?' (1989: 322). It is
the posing of the question, the implied advocacy, as Wolff puts it, of the
'suspension . . . of received notions' which is sociologically all important. It
is precisely this epistemic suspicion which constitutes the hallmark of
critical social analysis, and it is a feature which is intrinsic to the respective
works of the 'archaeologists of modernity', the works of Foucault, Derrida,
Lyotard, Baudrillard and Vattimo that have come to be identified with the
contentious idea of the postmodern and to which I turn in the following
chapter.

2

POSTMODERN IN(TER)VENTIONS

Theorizing 'the social' as a distinctive order or form of reality constitutes a modern preoccupation, a preoccupation which can be traced back to the formative influence of a series of eighteenth-century discourses, the writings of the *philosophes* of France and Scotland, writings which inaugurated what has become known as an 'Age of Enlightenment'. It is in this context that the social was first constituted as an object of abstract knowledge or reasoning, a focus for theoretical reflection and systematic analysis, as well as a target of technologies aiming to exercise control over the vagaries to which everyday life is subject. And it is from this complex setting that social theory developed and began to find a place within, and subsequently began to reflect upon, the project of modernity.

The persistence of a continuing commitment to some version of scientific rationality, universalism and the pursuit of progress demonstrates that the aims and objectives of modern social theory continue, to a substantial degree, to be influenced by an agenda of ideas, assumptions and objectives which derives from the works of the *philosophes* (Bauman, 1987). But it is also evident that the modern project which derives from the Enlightenment, and with it many, if not all, of the assumptions and established objectives or ends of modern social theory and analysis, are increasingly being called into question and rendered problematic, either because they are now considered not to be amenable to realization or fulfilment on technical grounds (the epistemological problem), or worse, are deemed to be inappropriate, if not unacceptable, on moral-political grounds (the ethical problem). It is with the diagnosis of such limits and limitations to the modern project that various interventions ambiguously identified as 'postmodern' have come to be associated.

The modern project has been problematized in and through a long-standing tradition of critical reflection and inquiry, a tradition which has sought, in various ways, to explore the complex, uneven and unpredictable consequences of modernity, a tradition which is virtually coterminous with modernity itself. It is here in a longstanding body of social and philosophical thought that a number of early 'postmodern' traces have been located. For example, in so far as a prominent concern in the respective works of Nietzsche, Heidegger, Simmel, Weber and Adorno is to take issue with modern reason and its consequences, then these analysts have been credited, albeit *avant la lettre*, with initiating 'postmodern' interventions. Simmel, the analyst of the crisis of modern culture and the exhaustion of modern cultural forms, has not only been described as 'a most (perhaps *the* most) perceptive analyst of modernity' (Bauman, 1991: 185), but is also regarded as 'the first sociologist of post-modernity' (Stauth and Turner, 1988: 16). Weber, critical of the prospects confronting a humanity subject to the charisma of modern reason, effectively challenges us to reconsider 'which *kinds* of charisma and rationalization will shape the "postmodern" world?' (Roth, 1987: 89). Nietzsche and Heidegger, founders of a 'philosophy of difference', secularize the metaphysical foundations of modern thought by undermining the notions of progress and overcoming and, thereby, 'provide the basis for at least some further steps toward the definition of what a postmodern philosophy might be' (Vattimo, 1988: 176). And in so far as Adorno outlines a radical critique of modern philosophy, of 'identity thinking' and the very possibility of conceptualizing the totality, it has been suggested that his work 'anticipates many postmodern motifs' (Best and Kellner, 1991: 225), that in '*Aesthetic Theory, Negative Dialectics*, and *Minima Moralia* . . . one senses the element of an anticipation of the postmodern . . . even though it is still largely reticent, or refused' (Lyotard, 1993: 28). One clear implication of these remarks is that the current preoccupation with the limits and limitations of modern reason can not be dismissed or explained away as simply a symptom of a 'disillusioned' generation of contemporary intellectuals, as some critics have attempted to suggest (Callinicos, 1989; Berman, 1992), for the concerns identified and the criticisms outlined are longerstanding. In brief, the implied scepticism about the Enlightenment equation of increasing rationality with progress in respect of 'justice, virtue, equality, freedom, and happiness' (Bernstein, 1991: 34) is by no means confined to those analyses which have relatively recently been designated 'postmodern'.

If these remarks appear tentative it is because the question of the postmodern remains riddled with ambiguity and controversy. Ambiguity follows from the fact that the notion of the postmodern may be read as implying sequentiality, something which comes after the modern, and that indeed is how some analysts continue to employ the term. But postmodern does not necessarily signify that we have taken leave of the modern, to the contrary, the term may be employed to refer to a critical relationship with the modern and as such it appears closely, if not inextricably, articulated with the modern (Vattimo, 1988). For example, the modern/ postmodern has been characterized as a single constellation in which 'reconciliation/rupture' are irreducible elements (Bernstein, 1991: 309); in response to the question 'What, then is the postmodern?', Lyotard has answered 'It is undoubtedly a part of the modern' (1984a: 79); and in another instance postmodernity has been portrayed as 'the modern mind taking a long, attentive and sober look at itself . . . [as] modernity coming of age . . . a self-monitoring modernity' (Bauman, 1991: 272). In turn controversy has followed from the fact that virtually all of the cherished analytical and political assumptions of modern social thought, namely that knowledge is progressive, cumulative, holistic, universal and rational, have been problematized by a radicalization of the reflexive potential of modernity, a radicalization which has served to alert us to both the limits and the limitations of the modern project, a radicalization which sometimes goes under the name 'postmodern'.

What then is at issue in the complex and confusing debate over the modern/postmodern? It is more than simply a question of the impossibility of completing the modern project, although that is certainly an important part of the story. It is increasingly evident that there has been a serious lack of appreciation and/or a fundamental misunderstanding, if not a self-defeating occlusion, of the complex and uneven 'reality' of modernity. It is a question of recognizing that the practical consequences of modernity seem to have been persistently at odds with its programmatic promise, that the modern social sciences and associated political technologies 'informed of *contingency* while believing themselves to narrate *necessity*, of particular *locality* while believing themselves to narrate *universality*, of tradition-bound interpretation while believing themselves to narrate the extraterritorial and extratemporal truth, of undecidability while believing themselves to narrate transparency, of the provisionality of the human condition while believing themselves to narrate the certainty of the world, of the *ambivalence* of man-made design while believing themselves to narrate the *order* of nature' (Bauman, 1991: 231–2). And it is precisely this possibility of being able to take stock of modernity, that is to be able to critically reflect upon its central assumptions, practices (including analytic practices), and accomplishments or consequences, which has been identified as symptomatic of the emergence of a postmodern condition.

Controversy not only surrounds the very idea of *postmodern* social and philosophical thought but also, as I will endeavour to show below, the designation of a range of analytic positions and figures as quintessentially *postmodern*. Explicit conceptions of the postmodern have been employed in various fields of inquiry during the course of the twentieth century, for example, in literary criticism, historical analysis, architectural description, theological narrative, and social and philosophical discourse (Smart, 1990, 1993a). Within the field of social theory a concept of the postmodern is first explicitly introduced by Wright Mills in the course of a discussion of the collapse of the grand narratives of liberalism and socialism 'as adequate explanations of the world and ourselves' ([1959]1970: 184). Echoing earlier critical engagements with modern reason to be found in the works of Weber and Adorno and Horkheimer respectively, Wright Mills argues that modern assumptions about the intrinsic relation of reason and freedom can no longer be sustained, for 'these two values, reason and freedom, are in obvious yet subtle peril' (ibid.: 186). As the modern age is being transformed so, Wright Mills continues, we find that our conceptions of society and self are inappropriate and unhelpful for making sense of emerging new realities and that 'too many of our old expectations and images are, after all, tied down historically: . . . too many of our standard categories of thought and of feeling as often disorient us as help to explain what is

happening around us; . . . too many of our explanations are derived from
the great transition from the Medieval to the Modern Age: and . . . when
they are generalized for use today, they become unwieldy, irrelevant, not
convincing' (ibid.: 184). Time indeed for 'enlightened thought' and for
exercising the sociological imagination.[1]

Archaeologies of Modernity

The attempt made by Wright Mills to salvage the sociological imagination
from the analytical, political and moral sterility to which it had succumbed
under the sway of an instrumental modern reason very broadly anticipates
a number of the themes which have been addressed by a diverse group of
analysts whose works are frequently equated with the postmodern, because
either they are regarded as formative influences in the generation of
postmodern social and philosophical thought, or they are considered to
contribute to a theory of postmodernity (Huyssen, 1984). It is here, in the
reception accorded to the respective works of a number of French analysts,
notably Barthes, Baudrillard, Deleuze and Guattari, Derrida, Foucault,
and Lyotard, particularly in the first instance in America, that the question
of postmodern theory has been posed. Implied here are a series of related
controversial issues concerning cross-cultural differences in the classification of forms of intellectual inquiry as 'poststructuralist' or 'postmodern',
issues already carefully documented in Huyssen's (1984) attempted
mapping of the contrasting trajectories of the postmodern in America
and Europe.
    The attribution of a common 'poststructuralist' orientation to Barthes,
Derrida, Foucault, and Lyotard, amongst others, is intended to draw
attention to the presence in their respective works of a shared critical
concern with a number of issues, notably: (i) the crisis of representation and
associated instability of meaning; (ii) the absence of secure foundations for
knowledge; (iii) the analytic centrality of language, discourses and texts;
and (iv) the inappropriateness of the Enlightenment assumption of the
rational autonomous subject and a counter, contrasting concentration on
the ways in which individuals are constituted as subjects (Smart, 1993a: 20–
3). The constitution of a postructuralist critique is held, in turn, to prepare
the ground for, to intersect, overlap or mesh with the development of
postmodern analyses (Lemert, 1990). Indeed, notwithstanding the existence
of a number of attempts to distinguish between poststructuralism and
postmodern forms of analysis, it is evident that the latter are now
considered 'to include poststructuralist work in literary theory, philosophy
and history' (Boyne and Rattansi, 1990: 10). In a sense it might be argued
that aspects of an allegedly 'dead tradition' of poststructuralist thought
(Giddens, 1987) have been resuscitated within what has come to be known
as postmodern social and philosophical theorizing.

It has been argued that we are living in 'new times' or in 'an interregnum' (Hall and Jacques, 1989) and simultaneously that in such circumstances it is not enough to simply recycle, as Jameson (1991) acknowledges, 'cherished and time-honoured' conceptions. If a justification for 'postmodern' theorizing is sought it is perhaps to be found here, that is in the idea that existing modern conceptions and analyses of social life have, as Wright Mills warned, increasingly begun to seem deficient, inappropriate, if not simply wrong. I have already suggested that the ideas of new times, new experiences, or new forms of thought are themselves by no means novel, to the contrary, they may be regarded as signifying the continuing presence of a modern preoccupation with the new, the persistence of a modern cult of the new. Also I have indicated that there are good grounds for being cautious about the status of both the times in which we live and the forms of social and philosophical analysis through which attempts are being made to make sense of the complex social conditions we now encounter. In particular, it is perhaps worth recalling in this context Huyssen's argument that 'we must begin to entertain the notion that rather than offering a *theory of postmodernity* . . . French theory provides us primarily with an *archaeology of modernity*, a theory of modernism at the stage of its exhaustion' (1984: 39). It is a notion that receives a substantial degree of support from the concerns expressed and the approaches deployed in the writings of a number of analysts designated as postmodern, analysts who, for the most part, appear completely bemused by such an ascription. For example, Foucault (1983) expresses confusion about the very idea of the postmodern and Baudrillard, another figure closely associated with postmodern social and philosphical thought questions whether there is any such thing and comments that '(e)verything that has been said about postmodernism was said even before the term existed' (Gane, 1993: 22). So what are we to make of the idea of postmodern theory?

Four contemporary figures in particular have come to be closely identified with the controversial notion of postmodern social and philosophical thought. And in so far as the notion of the postmodern constitutes a radical analytic challenge by drawing attention to problematic features of modern forms of social inquiry, Foucault, Derrida, Lyotard and Baudrillard have become virtually apocalyptic figures, the bearers of dark tales portending the end of man; 'Il n'y a pas dehors-texte'; the loss of the grand-narrative's credibility; and the death of the social and, along with it, an erosion of the Enlightenment assumption that the end of theory is to be a reflection or critical negation of the real, respectively.[2] At the risk of oversimplifying their different and, in some respects, contrasting positions, it might be argued that what emerges as a common denominator in their respective works is a sense that we are living at, and with, the closure of Western metaphysics, which is 'dominant throughout the world in its final form, scientific and technical rationality' (Schirmacher, 1984: 607). Or to put it differently, what seems to emerge from their respective analyses is a conception of modernity as 'the last phase of metaphysics', and by implication the contentious notion of postmodernism then becomes 'simply a metaphorical expression of this end, after which there will be no new beginning' (ibid.: 605).

Foucault

For Foucault, the modern Enlightenment *episteme* 'has constituted, under the name of man, a being who, by one and the same interplay of reasons, must be a positive domain of *knowledge* and cannot be an object of *science*' (1973: 366–7). A figure who is constantly unmade by the 'counter-sciences' of psychoanalysis and ethnology, and who, with the re-emergence of language, is destined to 'come to an end'. In Foucault's view 'as the being of language continues to shine ever brighter upon our horizon' (ibid.: 386), so the modern *episteme* begins to crumble. It is here in an archaeological analysis of the human sciences that analysts have suggested early traces may be found of Foucault's gradual evolution 'toward a postmodernism that is not adversarial toward reason and enlightenment' (Hoy, 1988: 20; see also Hekman, 1990). In short, a form of analysis which, *contra* Habermas (1987b), does not constitute a celebration of irrationality but rather attempts to provide an exploration of the question of enlightenment and the 'development and establishment of forms of rationality and technique' (Foucault, 1986b: 95), and their associated complex consequences, a form of analysis which it has been argued reveals postmodern traces. However, it is with the subsequent adoption of Nietzschean genealogy, which does not claim to have a privileged access to the unthought, that Foucault's work has been considered to more clearly display a postmodern orientation. Reflecting on Foucault's later work Hoy argues that 'we are no longer engaged in the modern enterprise with its metaphysical assumptions about the nature of man and its epistemological assumptions about a priori and invariant categories. The postmodern method is critical genealogical history. What genealogy describes is simply how we have come to be what we are. . . . If the postmodern genealogy counts at all as self-knowledge, then the self that is thereby known turns out to be not single, unified, complete, and whole, but complex, disseminated, fractious, and fragile' (1988: 36–7). With the turn to genealogical analysis there is a recognition of the problematic consequences of trying to find a foundation for modern morals in 'so-called scientific knowledge of what the self is, what desire is, what the unconscious is, and so on' (Foucault, 1986c: 343). It is in the context of the absence of such a foundation that the subject of ethics and the associated idea of something like an 'aesthetics of existence' – that 'the self is not given to us' and that 'we have to create ourselves as a work of art' (ibid.: 351) – becomes an increasingly prominent feature of Foucault's work. With the explicit address of questions concerning ethics and relations to self and others in the later works, and the associated generation of a foundationless conception of 'politics as an ethics', it is argued that Foucault's 'postmodern' credentials receive further confirmation (Richters, 1988). Such an interpretation is however open to challenge, for a closer reading of Foucault's reflections on the subject of ethics suggests the continuing presence of a characteristically modern preoccupation with the self, the corollary of which appears to be a relative moral indifference towards the other.

The idea that there is a necessary connection between analysis and ethical conduct, or in more familiar terms that 'correct' theory will ensure 'good' ethical and political choices and practices, is not endorsed by Foucault. Just as Lyotard argues that there is no meta-language or theoretical discourse 'to ground political and ethical decisions' (Lyotard and Thébaud, 1985: 28) and that modern intellectuals have wrongly claimed a legislative privilege in matters political, so in a comparable manner Foucault argues that it is 'not at all necessary to relate ethical problems to scientific knowledge' (1986c: 349) and, in turn, that the modern intellectual no longer represents the 'bearer of universal values'. However, while their role may have been reduced, Foucault (1980: 132) argues that intellectuals may continue to make a significant contribution to ethical and political concerns by engaging in specific 'interpretive' struggles over both the rules through which 'the true and the false' are constituted and differentiated and the effects of power which are a corollary of regimes of truth. To what extent Foucault's relatively late explicit engagement with the subject of ethical responsibility exemplifies a contribution to such concerns is a matter to which I will return below (see Chapter 4).

Subsequently the interpretive analytic intellectual strategy employed by Foucault, one which implicitly takes issue with the modern 'legislative' world-view and the power/knowledge syndrome intrinsic to it, has been designated postmodern (Bauman, 1987). Notwithstanding the admission that he did not comprehend what was meant by the terms postmodern or poststructuralist, Foucault is now widely regarded by critics and proponents alike as a key figure in the postmodern canon (Best and Kellner, 1991; Callinicos, 1989; Hoy, 1988; Hekman, 1990).

Derrida

Like Michel Foucault, Jacques Derrida has been associated with postmodern social and philosophical thought, primarily because he portrays Western metaphysics as literally undoing itself. Derrida's view is that Western thought is characterized by a 'metaphysics of presence', that is a desire to overcome occluding circuits of signification and interpretation and to gain direct or immediate access to reality. But this is unrealizable, for reason is necessarily burdened with language and cannot achieve pure, self-authenticating truth. There is no possibility of an unmediated access to reality, for the logic of analysis is itself constituted through various spatial

and visual metaphors. Reason then cannot dispel the opacity of intertextuality, and this is one of the ways in which Derrida's much celebrated,
derided, and misunderstood observation 'Il n'y a pas dehors-texte' (1967:
227) has been read. But such an interpretation does not exhaust the
meaning of this disputed phrase, indeed it constitutes, at best, a limited
reading.

The comment that there is nothing outside the text has licensed all
manner of wildly extravagant responses, particularly from critics eager to
consign Derrida's philosophy to a metaphysical dustbin. But if we are to do
something more than simply lend our voice to the chorus of derision which
has greeted the idea that there is 'nothing beyond the text' it is necessary
to abstain from premature judgement and to give careful consideration to
Derrida's notion of *text*. When this is done it becomes clear that the notion
of text and the associated practices of deconstruction are not confined to
books, discourses and conceptual and semantic contents alone. Rather the
concept of text is recast and extended 'almost without limit' to encompass
not only systems of thought but also the social and political institutions
with which they are articulated, that is why 'there is nothing "*beyond* the
text"' (Derrida, 1986: 167). Our understandings of the world, associated
forms of knowledge and their respective social and political contexts are
unavoidably 'textual', they represent matters of interpretation which in turn
(re)generate texts; evoke and/or constitute further texts. For Derrida,
conventional distinctions between text and interpretation, or between representations of the world with the status 'reality' and other representations
or forms of knowledge with the status of 'accounts' (for example scientific
and artistic narratives) are fraught with ambiguity, for the customary
dividing line through which the world and our forms of knowledge of it
have been constituted as distinct is erased by the notion of intertextuality.
Such a clarification of the notion of text makes possible a recognition of the
frequently neglected political character of deconstructive practice. As
Derrida remarks, 'because it is never concerned only with signified content,
deconstruction should not be separated from this political-institutional
problematic and should seek a new investigation of responsibility, an
investigation which questions the codes inherited from ethics and politics'
(1984: 42).[3] In short, deconstruction is necessarily political, it constitutes an
ethical-political critique which takes issue with assumptions intrinsic to the
Western metaphysical tradition, for example the notions of 'centered structure', 'fundamental ground' and the possibility of a 'reassuring certitude'
(Derrida, 1978).

As I have indicated above it is with the deconstruction of metaphysics
that Derrida's work is generally identified, with the provision of a series of
complex deliberations on the aporetic metaphors and assumptions through
which Western metaphysics has been, and continues to be constituted. This
should not be confused with a transcendance of metaphysics, for it is
necessary to draw upon the language of metaphysics as one engages in
deconstructing this very language, and to that extent we are always

encountering an ineluctable 'risk of metaphysical reappropriation' (Derrida, 1982: 58). In consequence, deconstruction may be described as a strategy of intervention by means of which metaphysical assumptions are subjected to exposure, question and marginalization.

Derrida portrays Western metaphysics as based upon a series of metaphorical binary oppositions in which one element is accorded a privileged status, the most pertinent to his argument being the writing/speech opposition intrinsic to the metaphysics of presence or 'logocentrism'. Deconstruction works to unravel Western metaphysics by challenging the primacy accorded to speech and promoting the claims of *writing* as effectively the precondition of language. In short, Derrida takes issue with the idea that speech is closer to 'psychic interiority (that itself reflects things in the world by means of natural resemblance)' (Kamuf, 1991: 31) and that writing is merely a mirroring of speech, is simply phonetic transcription. After identifying a series of metaphors which serve to privilege speech and to draw attention away from the signifying system through which it is constituted and sustained, Derrida proceeds to develop a more radical sense of writing to refer to the element of undecidability intrinsic to communication, 'to the endless displacement of meaning which both governs language and places it for ever beyond the reach of a stable, self-authenticating language' (Norris, 1982: 29). As with the notion of text, Derrida produces a new concept of *writing*, one which is 'not limited to the paper which you cover with your graphism' (1986: 167).

At issue here is the model of phonetic writing and the Saussurean exclusion of writing from the field of linguistics. Given, as Derrida demonstrates, that there is 'no purely phonetic writing . . . then the entire phonologist or logocentrist logic becomes problematical' (1982: 25–6). It is in the context of working to overturn and displace the privileging of the phonic (temporal) over the graphic (spatial), that Derrida argues that a simple inversion of the dissymmetry which privileges writing still leaves us within the binary opposition speech/writing and, in consequence, is itself no less problematic. It is in acknowledgement of the play of differences and 'economy of traces' which are intrinsic to all processes of signification that Derrida introduces the concept of writing as *différance*. No conceptual element signifies by itself, rather 'an element functions and signifies, takes on or conveys meaning, only by referring to another past or future element in an economy of traces' (ibid.: 29). Hence the idea that it is through *différance*, that is the 'systematic play of differences', that the process of signification is possible, and endless.

In sum the position taken by Derrida is that 'the medium of the great metaphysical, scientific, technical, and economic adventure of the West [phonetic writing], is limited in time and space' (1978: 10), indeed is drawing to a close. Taking issue with the logocentricity of Western metaphysics Derrida, like Foucault, identifies the (re-)entry of language as the moment at which Western metaphysics begins to unravel, the moment when it became necessary to recognize that no fixed, permanent centre, or fundamental ground is available. Indeed, more than that, that there never was a centre or foundation which could offer the reassurance of certitude to which modern forms of analysis seem perpetually to aspire, even as they operate to destabilize prevailing certainties. An appreciation of the complexity of language, and in particular the impossibility of defining an impermeable boundary between words and things, signifiers and signifieds, forms of knowledge and the worlds they claim to apprehend as they constitute them, causes Derrida to draw attention to the perpetual problem of meaning, to the always potentially contestable, and frequently contested, character of meaning. It is precisely the implied processes of deferral of meaning and endless interpretation – the 'play of differences' – which the notion of *différance* so effectively captures.

As I have implied above, Derrida's manoeuvres do not portend a break with metaphysics. Metaphysics has not become a negative pole within a binary couplet in which another *post*-metaphysical pole is privileged; on the contrary it continues to be necessary to work within the language of metaphysics. The only way to proceed is to engage in a 'vigilant textual practice aware of its own metaphysical liabilities' (Norris, 1982: 67). In Derrida's words the aim is 'to avoid both simply *neutralizing* the binary oppositions of metaphysics and simply *residing* within the closed field of these oppositions, thereby confirming it' (1982: 41). Whether this is more appropriately described as a reflexively modern or postmodern stance is however debatable.

Whilst both Foucault and Derrida have been closely identified with postmodern social and philosophical thought there is no sustained address of the postmodern in their respective works, and to that extent perhaps they constitute less significant figures than Lyotard and Baudrillard, both of whom have engaged directly, albeit in different ways, with the question of the postmodern. Because his report on transformations in the condition of knowledge has had such an impact upon contemporary debates the figure of Lyotard is frequently equated with the notion of the postmodern. However, Baudrillard's claims to postmodern status are no less significant, particularly if the frame of reference is broadened beyond the confines of the academy to embrace contemporary culture, communications, and the proverbial signs in the streets.

Lyotard's Postmodern Condition

In so far as Lyotard is concerned with the process of increasing rationalization of knowledge and its consequences, then his text *The Postmodern Condition* (1984a) bears comparison with the works of many other analysts who have been critical of the impact the development of modern reason has had on social and political life. For example, as I have noted, the outline of a 'postmodern' condition of knowledge, while not explicitly presented, is, in broad terms, anticipated in Wright Mills' late 1950s references to the problematic articulation of modern reason and freedom and associated collapse of the grand narratives of liberalism and socialism. The basic hypothesis at the heart of Lyotard's report is that 'the status of knowledge is altered as societies enter *what is known as* the postindustrial age and cultures enter *what is known as* the postmodern age' (1984a: 3, emphasis added). How knowledge has been altered and what the consequences might be are the issues to which Lyotard's analysis is directed. It is worth emphasizing that this particular project has a quite specific focus, namely to comment on the 'state of the sciences in the advanced societies', and that, unlike subsequent works, its preoccupations are not explicitly philosophical but rather sociological, historical and epistemological (Lyotard, 1988b). Subsequently Lyotard has moved away from a sociological elaboration of the postmodern condition of knowledge to a more explicitly philosophical address of reason and associated problems of justice and politics, matters to which I return in Chapter 6.

The familiar central premise of Lyotard's thesis on the postmodern condition is that the 'grand narrative has lost its credibility, regardless of what mode of unification it uses, regardless of whether it is a speculative narrative or a narrative of emancipation' (1984a: 37). Critics have been quick to respond to Lyotard's thesis, remarking that, on the one hand, the incredulity associated with meta-narratives might be argued to be 'at least as old as the Enlightenment' (Callinicos, 1989: 10) and, on the other, that not only does the thesis itself betray the traces of a master narrative, a criticism which Lyotard appears ready to acknowledge in asking 'Are "we" not telling, whether bitterly or gladly, the great narrative of the end of great narratives?' (1988a: 135), but also that it might be necessary to distinguish between different orders of grand narrative (Best and Kellner, 1991).

The idea that incredulity towards meta-narratives is as old as the Enlightenment itself, if not older, is not particularly contentious, unlike the equation of Lyotard's analysis with Romantic idealizations of a pre-modern past (Callinicos, 1989). There is a clear acknowledgement in Lyotard's work that 'the grand narrative of decadence was already in place at the beginning of Western thought, in Hesiod and Plato. It follows the narrative of emancipation like a shadow' (1992: 40–1). Certainly there can be little doubt, as I have noted above, that a critical preoccupation with the dark side of the Enlightenment has been a persistent feature of European thought since at least the end of the nineteenth century, a feature that has become more prominent of late. However, Lyotard is primarily concerned with the loss of trust and faith in grand narratives since the Second World War, with their accelerating decline and virtual irrelevance to contemporary conditions. It is worth noting in this regard that although Lyotard emphasizes the 'effect of the blossoming of techniques and technologies . . . which has shifted emphasis from the ends of action to its means' (Lyotard, 1984a: 38), an effect which it is speculated may be bound up with an 'obscure desire towards extra sophistication . . . [or] complexification' (1989c: 21–2),

and which draws attention to the continuing importance of the 'redeploy-
ment of advanced liberal capitalism' (1984a: 38), the idea that such factors
alone can account for transformations in the status of knowledge is
categorically denied. Rather it is argued that we need to ask why contemporary science has become vulnerable to such factors and the answer
given is that 'the seeds of "delegitimation" and nihilism were inherent in the
grand narratives of the nineteenth century' (ibid.: 38). Signs of the turning
back of modern reason upon, or against, itself – early traces of what has
subsequently been theorized as the development of a reflexive modernity
(Giddens, 1990; Beck, 1992) – can certainly be identified in the respective
works of Nietzsche, Heidegger, Weber, Simmel and Adorno, as I have
noted above.

But what of the objection that there are different orders of grand
narrative between which it is necessary to distinguish? Best and Kellner's
objection that 'Lyotard tends to lump all large narratives together and thus
does violence to the diversity of narratives in our culture' (1991: 172) and
parallel suggestion that distinctions need to be made between master
narratives synonymous with totalizing theory, grand narratives telling a
'Big Story', and meta-narratives on the foundations of knowledge, and so
on, confuses rather than clarifies matters. Lyotard's concern is with the
decline of particular grand or meta-narratives which have marked
modernity, narratives which have sought legitimacy by invoking a 'future
to be accomplished', a universal 'Idea to be realised' (1992: 29–30). The loss
of trust in and concomitant decline of such grand narratives does not, as
Lyotard remarks, 'stop countless other stories (minor and not so minor)
from continuing to weave the fabric of everyday life' (ibid.: 31). Indeed
Lyotard's own narrative on the postmodern condition has been acknowledged to be one of those 'not so minor' stories that paradoxically comes
close to being a 'grand narrative of the decline of the grand narratives'
(ibid.: 40).

Modern thought and action has been preoccupied with the 'Idea of
emancipation', an Idea which has been articulated through philosophies of
history or grand narratives. But since the Second World War grand
narratives of emancipation have been steadily invalidated. Lyotard
contends that the Holocaust refutes the speculative narrative's equation
of the real with the rational; the struggles of the peoples in Eastern Europe,
the former Soviet Union, and the Republic of China against oppression
exercised by Communist Parties in the name of 'the proletariat' tarnish, if
they do not radically refute, the emancipatory claims of historical
materialism; the events of May 1968 and its aftermath effectively undermine parliamentary liberalism; and the recurring crises of capitalism
invalidate the doctrine of economic liberalism and its 'post-Keynesian
modification' (Lyotard, 1988a: 179). It is the way in which each of these
narratives of emancipation have been discredited that leads to the
conclusion that 'an irreparable suspicion is engraved in European, if not
Western, consciousness: that universal history does not move inevitably

"towards the better", as Kant thought, or rather, that history does not necessarily have a universal finality' (Lyotard, 1992: 62). The modern project has not so much been abandoned or forsaken by the tide of history, by the passage of events, as substantially devalued, if not 'liquidated', by the very development of modernity itself. The erosion of confidence, of trust and faith, in its core assumptions and objectives has been a direct consequence of modern practices and their uneven effects. In effect it has been reflexively undermined by the persisting presence of its 'other', what has been described as 'the grey area of ambivalence, indeterminacy and undecidability' (Bauman, 1992a: xvi).

Reflexive Modernization

There are some interesting parallels between Lyotard's analysis and contemporary discussions of the process of reflexive modernization, specifically the contradictory character of techno-scientific development and, in particular, the consequences of the application of 'scientific skepticism to the inherent foundations and external consequences of science itself . . . [namely] that . . . both its *claim to truth* and *its claim to enlightenment* are *demystified*' (Beck, 1992: 155, emphasis in original). One crucial difference however is that whilst arguing very powerfully that the production of risks is now an intrinsic feature of modernity, and that it is techno-scientific development itself which is primarily responsible for the dramatic acceleration in both the scale and the gravity of risk production, Ulrich Beck ironically ends up advocating a regeneration of the project of modernity, hoping that the unpredictability of the consequences of techno-scientific development might be reduced, if not avoided altogether, through the generation of an alternative techno-scientific practice oriented towards self-control and self-limitation. But given the persistence of the institutions of modernity it is difficult to envisage how such an outcome might be realized.

The necessity of a radical humanizing of the modern techno-scientific 'imperative' has been acknowledged, but according to Giddens (1990) the realization of such a possibility would require a transcendence of modern institutions, the qualitative transformation identified above representing one of the dimensions of a potential *post*-modern social future. In contrast, for Beck such a transformation is equated with the emergence and development of a 'new modernity', a prospective alternative techno-scientific practice which is portrayed as possessing the potential to revive enlightenment, and to contribute to the freeing of the project of modernity from its 'rigidification in the industrial understanding of science and technology' (1992: 157). However it is only a possibility, one that is bound up, in turn, with a prescribed, and continuous, radical transformation of the political, a transformation which needs to take the form of a growing disempowerment and unbinding of formally constituted politics, and a simultaneous politicization of society. In effect, a legislative reference is made to the

possible development of a new political culture, following an irreversible
unravelling of centralized politics, which is depicted as already in train.
Tentative signs of a possible new political culture, identified by Beck,
include the emergence of 'different partial arenas of cultural and social sub-
politics' (ibid.: 198). It is suggested that with the development of a
'different epoch of modernization' an increasingly de-centred politics is
emerging, one which is characterized by reflexivity, de-differentiation and
flexibility, one which, it is worth noting, has also been described by a
number of other analysts as postmodern (Lash and Urry, 1987; Harvey,
1989; Soja, 1989).

After having argued so convincingly that modern solutions have become
the source of our problems, that the 'project of modernity needs first aid [as
it] threatens to choke on its own anomalies' (1992: 179–80), Beck's return
to modern science and, by implication, a version of modern rationality in
pursuit of a solution is curious. Demonstrating a continuing commitment
to, and faith in, a modern, legislative intellectual role, Beck argues that in
so far as most things can be considered to be a product or outcome of
human activity, then there can be no excuses, everything is now controllable, or at least potentially so. This represents little more than a
recycling of one of the central myths of modernity, in response to which it
might be argued that the reality of what has been called 'reflexive modernization' continues to be that we find ourselves living not with certainty or
control, but with contingency, a condition which has been increasingly
acknowledged to be a corollary of modernity *per se* (Giddens, 1990;
Bauman, 1991). The paradox of modernity is that the pursuit of control
and order continually reveals objects and processes which remain beyond
control and/or in a state of disorder. Indeed, in so far as the form of life we
know as modernity continues to prevail the prospects for an alternative
techno-scientific practice, one which will be conducive to adequate and
effective forms of self-control and self-limitation, needs must remain a
chimera. Many aspects of our lives remain far from controllable. Human
efforts continue to produce both more and less than planned, anticipated,
or desired, and the age of excuses endures, the difference now being that
excuses are frequently articulated in terms of direct or indirect references to
'errors' in respect of risk calculation and management. Acknowledgements
of miscalculation of risk; changes both within and of the stock of knowledge accepted as legitimate for risk calculation; failure to adequately and/or
appropriately publicize the level of risk believed to be associated with a
product, process, or form of conduct; as well as deliberate concealment of
risks serve as reminders that the age of excuses is far from over.

Self-control and self-limitation, Beck argues, must be 'supplemented by
opportunities for self-criticism' (1992: 234). The opportunities implied seem
however to be precisely those conventionally ascribed to the practice of
modern science – 'Only when medicine opposes medicine, nuclear physics
opposes nuclear physics, human genetics opposes human genetics or information technology opposes information technology can the future that is

being brewed up in the test-tube become intelligible and evaluable for the outside world. Enabling self-criticism in all its forms is . . . probably the *only* way that the mistakes that would sooner or later destroy our world can be detected in advance' (ibid.: 234). In so far as self-criticism is already regarded as a central feature of the practice of modern science it is not clear how implementation of Beck's proposal promises to improve our prospects. Moreover, it by no means follows that self-criticism 'in all its forms' will prevent mistakes being made, for opposing paradigms and counter-sciences are themselves no less vulnerable to error.

The elaboration on the subject of scientific self-criticism offered by Beck ultimately raises more questions than it resolves. Beck comments that the 'right to criticism within professions and organizations . . . ought to be fought for and protected in the public interest' and that the *'institutionalisation of self-criticism* is so important because in many areas neither the risks nor the alternative methods to avoid them can be recognized without the *proper technical know how'* (ibid.: 234 emphasis added). However, the process of institutionalization involves the selection, organization and ordering of particular forms of activity in 'recognizable and predictable patterns' (Berger and Kellner, 1982: 110), and as a corollary the exclusion, silencing or non-institutionalization of other forms of activity. What is, in any particular community at any particular time, recognized to constitute acceptable and/or appropriate self-criticism, or is regarded as 'proper technical know how', are precisely the potentially variable (and contentious) matters that will have a bearing on risk recognition and assessment, and public awareness. Institutionally protecting the right to criticism is one necessary element, but in and of itself it will not reduce 'the dominance of professionals or operational management' (Beck, 1992: 234) which is predicated on a longstanding monopoly of 'proper know how'. What is also required, if knowledgeable decision-making is to occur, is a radical opening up of access to information, a matter briefly broached by Lyotard (1984a) in a comment on the risks associated with the computerization of society and addressed in more depth by Illich (1978: 1985) in a discussion of the negative consequences and risks encountered in modern industrial society in general, and the problems which arise from 'disabling professionalism' and an associated monopolization of knowledge in particular (Smart, 1992).

In a subsequent essay Beck has implicitly acknowledged the limitations of his earlier discussion of reflexive modernization, in particular by accepting that it is necessary for people to say 'farewell to the notion that administrations and experts always know exactly, or at least better, what is right and good for everyone', in short that a 'demonopolization of expertise' (Beck, 1994: 29) is required, and also by recognizing that if reflexive modernization has given rise to a new modernity it is an 'ambivalent modernity'. I will return to the idea of reflexive modernization and the notion of an ambivalent modernity in a wider-ranging discussion of reflexivity in the next chapter.

Lyotard's Philosophical Politics

In contrast to Beck's call for 'the universal self-reformation of a previously fatalistic industrial modernity' (1994: 51–2) and associated invocation of a new (and better) modernity, Lyotard argues that intellectuals today 'are no longer able to take up obvious and pellucid positions; they cannot speak in the name of an "unquestionable" universality' (1988b: 301). The decline of the grand meta-narratives of emancipation has meant that intellectuals have lost authority, that they are no longer able 'to say publicly "Here is what you must do"' (ibid.: 301). Such a transformation in the status of both the figure and the practice of the intellectual, a significant theme in the work not only of Lyotard but also, as I have already noted, of Foucault (1980, 1988c) and, in a more extreme form, Baudrillard (1989a,b), has been identified as one of the key markers of the postmodern condition (Bauman, 1987). One implication of which is that the era of the universal intellectual, a figure who analyses the conditions of existence and speaks for 'a subject endowed with a universal value', is over. Indeed, given that thought now lacks 'universality' or a 'totalizing unity' the very notion of the intellectual itself is portrayed by Lyotard (1993: 5–6) as in jeopardy. However, it does not necessarily follow from this that critical thought or political activity has been irretrievably compromised, neutralized or silenced, or that because reason is being subjected to critical analysis that 'irrationalism' is being courted (Callinicos, 1989; Best and Kellner, 1991). Both charges fail to acknowledge the transformed circumstances and new responsibilities and opportunities which are a corollary of the 'postmodern condition'. If there has been an erasure of both the 'great figure of the alternative' and the 'great founding legitimacies', there has also been an associated freeing of 'thought and life from totalizing obsessions' (Lyotard, 1993: 169, 7).

Acknowledging the crisis of foundations to which his own work has contributed, Lyotard concludes that 'the crisis of reason has been precisely the bath in which scientific reason has been immersed for a century, and . . . this continual interrogation of reason, is certainly the most rational thing around' (1988b: 280). To continue to critically interrogate reason, to show that it is not 'a question of *one* massive and unique reason', but rather that there are only reasons or a plurality of rationalities, is a vital analytic task, one endorsed by both Foucault and Derrida. There is no justification for equating such an activity with advocacy of 'irrationalism', to the contrary it constitutes a rational challenge to established thought, to orthodoxy, to accepted opinion and it is intrinsic to a critically reflexive intellectual politics, an intellectual politics of resistance, which continues to be not merely a possibility but a necessity after the devaluation of the grand emancipatory narratives – a politics conducted in and through writing which offers resistance to 'what has already been done, to what everyone thinks' (Lyotard, 1988b: 302). However, such a politics does not simply stop at the practice of writing, rather it encompasses the implications of the transformation of language into a commodity, and the social, economic and political impact of the introduction of language machines within production in particular (Poster, 1990). It is a politics which follows from the postmodern realization that it is inappropriate to regard language simply as an 'instrument of communication'. Language constitutes a complex configuration of heterogeneous phrase regimens and a phrase from one regime cannot be simply translated into a phrase from another (Lyotard, 1988a: xii, 1993: 27–8). In short, there is no warrant for deriving a prescription concerning the 'good' or the 'just' from a description concerning the 'true', for they are incommensurable.

The (re)turn to language, and devaluation or decline of universalist discourses and rules of judgement associated with the erosion of 'the metaphysical doctrines of modern times', coupled with an increasing 'weariness with regard to "theory", and the miserable slackening that goes along with it (new this, new that, post-this, post-that, etc.)' leads Lyotard to argue that it is time to philosophize. Time to 'set up a philosophical politics apart from the politics of "intellectuals" and of politicians' (Lyotard, 1988a: xiii). A politics which recognizes both the absence of any possible redemptive or emancipatory end of the political (as well as epistemological grounds from which to generate authoritative forms of political calculation and critique) and the perpetual presence of the problem of the relation between phrases. In brief a critical politics of heterogeneity which bears witness to *différends*.

The question of difference, posed in various forms, has been one of the prominent features of the debate over modern and postmodern conditions. But references to otherness, plurality, *différance*, *différend* and fragmentation are not only a feature of debate, they constitute, in turn, 'reflections of what has become a fact of "modern/postmodern" forms of life' (Bernstein, 1991: 312). Just as the notion of *différance* is employed by Derrida to take issue with Western metaphysics and its ethical-political implications, so the notion of the *différend* allows Lyotard to elaborate on an earlier sketch of 'a politics that would respect both the desire for justice and the desire for the unknown' (1984a: 67); that is to raise the question of politics, and in particular to address the problem of 'the conflict of phrases and their judgement' (1988a: 141).

Identification of the decline of the grand narratives of legitimation constitutive of Western modernity need not, and does not in practice, prevent Lyotard from offering a number of narratives on, for example, the continuing contribution of Marxism to our understanding of techno-scientific complexification and the development of capitalism – 'Marxism has not come to an end', the question is 'How must we read Marx today?' (1988a: 171, 1989c: 23); the politics of modern democracies; and the problem of justice and the crisis of reason (1988a, 1988b; Lyotard and Thébaud, 1985). The central thesis outlined does not inhibit the generation of narratives on the contemporary situation, rather it describes a condition, a reality, that has become increasingly difficult to deny, namely that whilst the *rhetoric* of emancipation may persist, the modern Enlightenment *ideal* has been irreparably tarnished. The idea intrinsic to the philosophy of the Enlightenment that progress in science, technology, art and politics would produce an enlightened and liberated humanity, a humanity freed from the degradations of poverty, ignorance and despotism remains not only unrealized, but increasingly in question, for the 'progress' that has been a corollary of modernity has brought with it a series of new difficulties, 'the possibility of total war, totalitarianisms, the growing gap between the wealth of the North and the impoverished South, unemployment and the "new poor", general deculturation and the crisis in education (in the transmission of knowledge)' (Lyotard, 1992: 98). The question is, does this cast doubt on progress, or merely draw attention to the difficulty of achieving it? And when Lyotard (1984a) invites us to activate differences, does it mean 'all forms of otherness and difference are to be celebrated' (Bernstein, 1991: 313)?

Finding straight answers to such questions in Lyotard's work is difficult. For the most part Lyotard is concerned to draw attention to the difficulties and differences with which we have to cope, for example the growing fragmentation of community which leads, within the modern polity, to an increasing 'uncertainty about the identity of the *we*' (1992: 60). However, whilst Lyotard challenges universals and identifies cultural differences, as well as 'signs of the defaillancy of modernity' (Benjamin, 1989: 318), there is nevertheless a strong implication that the desirability of a *universal* tolerance of 'incommensurable vocabularies and forms of life' (Bernstein, 1991: 313) is a necessary corollary. Moreover, in so far as Lyotard considers 'the penetration of capitalism into language', embodied in the increasing deployment of relatively inexpensive language machines which are unable to 'soak up the enormous overcapitalization with which we are burdened', to be reducing the demand for wage labour, and thereby creating a situation in which the pursuit of justice in politics is going to make necessary 'an international accord on the concerted reduction of labor time without a loss of purchasing power' (1993: 28–9), a matter extensively explored by Andre Gorz (1989), is he not coming close to deducing a prescription from a description? As well as, perhaps, implying that there might, after all, be a prospect of an international social(ist) alternative to the barbarism of the global capitalist marketplace. Such remarks certainly suggest that the figure of the intellectual is not yet ready to be consigned to the 'tomb'.

Baudrillard

Of the four analysts identified as archaeologists of modernity, or founding figures of postmodern discourse, Baudrillard is perhaps the most controversial. Virtually a postmodern icon, Baudrillard is a cultural celebrity, a figure fêted in the media, and an increasingly enigmatic analyst whose work, quite deliberately, is made to overflow and defy all disciplinary boundaries. Baudrillard might once have been a sociologist, but his work no longer readily admits of any reconciliation even with that most fragmented and internally diverse of the social scientific disciplines (Baudrillard, 1984a).

Not suprisingly it is Baudrillard's work which has come to be most closely associated with the postmodern and, for some critics, with its apocalyptic tone in particular (Callinicos, 1989). Baudrillard has been described as 'the author of postmodern culture and society' (Kroker et al., 1989: 265), as the figure who 'has developed the most striking and extreme theory of postmodernity', and, possibly with unintended irony, as the 'great postmodern prophet' (Best and Kellner, 1991: 111, 141). Three quite different claims, the first implying that Baudrillard's prose exemplifies, rather than captures, the experience of the postmodern; the second that there is a systematic analysis of a specific social and cultural configuration – postmodernity – in his work; and the third, for this reader at least, that his own analysis has ultimately proven to be vulnerable to the 'fatal and enigmatic bias in the order of things' (Baudrillard, 1990a: 191; Smart, 1993b).

Baudrillard's work ranges widely across a number of intellectual, sociocultural, economic and political concerns. I do not propose to offer a detailed trace of Baudrillard's trajectory from the early discussions of consumer society, through a critical engagement with Marxist political economy, analyses of the advent of a new era of simulation and hyperreality, down to the more recent works (Kellner, 1989; Gane, 1991a, 1991b). My main concern will be to address the question of Baudrillard's relation to postmodern social and philosophical thought, but to that end it is necessary to give some consideration to the development of his analytic approach.

Baudrillard's work begins with relatively conventional premises and, like many other contemporary forms of French social thought, reveals the influence of Marxism, psychoanalysis, structuralism and semiology (Poster, 1988; Gane, 1991a). After a series of neo-Marxist analyses of aspects of consumer society and an attempt at grafting a radical theory of language on to Marxism, *The Mirror of Production* (1975) reflects Baudrillard's critical move away from Marx. In this work Baudrillard argues that the critique of political economy 'sustains an unbridled romanticism of productivity . . . [and] does not touch the *principle* of production' (1975: 17). As the title of the study suggests, Marx's critique is argued to do no more than reflect the productivist assumptions of Western capitalism and the discourse of political economy, to simply provide yet another productivist discourse which is in consequence limited to reproducing the 'roots of the system of political economy' (ibid.: 65). Baudrillard argues that Marxism does not submit either the form production or the form representation ('the status of the sign, of the language that directs all Western thought') to critical analysis and further, that it reads the complex histories of all hitherto existing societies in terms simply of a history of modes of production. Bound up with the moral philosophy of the Enlightenment, Marxist thought relies upon concepts which 'depend upon the metaphysics of the market economy in general and on modern capitalist ideology in particular. Not analysed or unmasked (but exported to primitive society where they do not apply), these concepts mortgage all further analysis' (ibid.: 59). Indeed Baudrillard proceeds to argue that it is not only a matter of drawing attention to the inappropriateness of the assumption of universality associated with Marxist discourse, but that Marxist categories and concepts are no longer meaningful for understanding the 'passage from the form commodity to the form sign' (ibid.: 121) in Western capitalism.

Baudrillard is concerned not only with the limitations of Marxist thought, but more broadly with the way in which, since the Enlightenment, the West has constituted itself as 'a culture *in the universal*' and all other cultures have been 'entered in its museum as vestiges of its own image' (ibid.: 88–9). Concepts and analyses developed to make sense of modern Western capitalist social formations have been deployed beyond the field in which they were produced. Attempts to understand pre-capitalist or non-Western societies through conceptions of the mode of production (Marxism), or the unconscious (psychoanalysis), constitute for Baudrillard incontrovertible examples of the 'self-fetishization of Western thought' (ibid.: 50). In short, they represent a serious miscomprehension of their subject matter, and as Baudrillard suggests, 'a culture that is mistaken about another must also be mistaken about itself' (ibid.: 107). To proceed, 'the *mirror of production* in which all Western metaphysics is reflected, must be broken' (ibid.: 47) and for Baudrillard this means taking leave not only of Marxism, but also of structural linguistics and semiology, a leave-taking that leads to the development of a series of more radical deliberations on sign structures and successive orders of simulacra, as well as associated analyses of the implications of the obscene ecstasy of communication, which is a corollary of 'the perpetual interconnection of all information and communication networks' (Baudrillard, 1988a: 27). It is here, that is to say in Baudrillard's turn away from Marxism, psychoanalysis and structuralism, and towards an exploration of a new (third) order of simulacrum that analysts have identified the emergence of specifically postmodern preoccupations (Poster, 1988; Best and Kellner, 1991; Smart, 1992).[4]

Whether Baudrillard's work warrants the description 'postmodern' has been a source of disagreement and debate. On the one hand his work has been classified and criticized as 'postmodern theory' which offers an 'analysis of postmodernity' (Best and Kellner, 1991), yet on the other hand it has been presented as a new and challenging form of theory which is 'anti-postmodernist' (Gane, 1991b). Baudrillard certainly does offer a radically different style of analysis and there are a number of significant references to postmodern forms in his writings, but whether his work constitutes 'postmodern social theory' (Kellner, 1988) is questionable. When asked in some later interviews what he thinks of his status as a 'theoretician of the postmodern' or 'high priest of postmodernism', Baudrillard has responded coolly and critically, stating that, 'I can do nothing against this "post-modern" interpretation' and again, 'before one can talk about anyone being a high priest, one should ask whether postmodernism, the post-modern, has a meaning' (Gane, 1993: 157, 21). Such remarks suggest that Baudrillard is, at best, ambivalent about his 'postmodern' status, and at times he seems to be positively antagonistic to the very idea of the postmodern – 'there is no such thing as postmodernism . . . Everything that has been said about postmodernism was said even before the term existed . . . [A]s soon as it is clear that the term adds nothing new it is best to let go of it' (ibid.: 22). However, it is evident that Baudrillard himself found it hard throughout the 1980s to let go of the postmodern, for there are several significant references to the term, not only in interview responses but also in his other writings.[5]

A notion of the postmodern certainly has had a place in Baudrillard's approach to cultural analysis. For example, in a short statement, 'On Nihilism', Baudrillard draws a distinction between the 'true revolution of the 19th Century, of modernity, . . . the radical destruction of appearances, the disenchantment of the world and its abandonment to the violence of interpretation and history' and a 'second revolution, that of the 20th Century, of post-modernity, which is the immense process of the destruction of meaning, equal to the earlier destruction of appearances' (1984b: 38–9). Baudrillard comments that he notes, accepts, assumes and analyses this second revolution. Likewise, in a subsequent interview Baudrillard distances himself from modernity and declares that 'there are quite a few things which interest me in the post-modern . . . [although] I don't know exactly what a post-modern culture would be' (1984a: 20). But not knowing exactly what a postmodern culture might be did not prevent Baudrillard from continuing to employ the term in subsequent texts. For example, when Baudrillard elaborates on an earlier conference discussion of the 'state of excess' in which we find ourselves (Baudrillard, 1989b) and discusses the consequences associated with the extension of the '"modern" movement . . . beyond its own limits', he makes reference to 'the law which is imposed on us by the situation itself . . . the law of the confusion of genres and genders [the transpolitical, the transsexual, the transaesthetic]', a law which he states 'we can call *postmodern*' (1992a: 10, emphasis added). The argument advanced by Baudrillard is that we are living in the wake of various modern movements of liberation, 'after the orgy', and all that we can do is replay the scenarios. He remarks that we live 'in the indefinite reproduction of ideals, of phantasms, of images, of dreams, which are, from now on, behind us and that we must, nevertheless reproduce in a sort of fatal indifference' (1992b: 22). Implied here is the failure of modernity, the emptying out of all the great ideals; 'progress carries on, but the Idea of Progress has vanished. Production carries on, always faster and faster, but the Idea of Production as a source of wealth has disappeared. Such is the banal destiny of all great ideals in what could be called *postmodernity*' (ibid.: 236, emphasis added).

The social world described by Baudrillard is indifferent, aleatory, indeterminate and narcissistic; it is a world in which the real has given way to simulations, codes and hyperreality. It is a place where meaning, significance, the message and the referent 'circulate so quickly that they are made to disappear'; where the proliferation of media and information has, as a direct corollary, the constitution of 'silent majorities', for whom a strategy of inertia or neutralization is the only possible response; and where, in the absence of 'exact images' or mirrors of the world, theories simply 'float around one another' (Baudrillard, 1984a). It is this situation, of attempting to 'live with what is left', of 'playing with the pieces', which Baudrillard has described as postmodern. Whether or not it is appropriate to regard Baudrillard as a postmodern theorist, it is indisputable that he has employed a notion of the postmodern in a significant number of his critical analytic reflections on contemporary social life, and as such it is hard to accept the declaration that 'he has "nothing to do with postmodernism"' (Gane, 1991b: 158), and it is equally difficult to concur with the assessment that '[f]ar from embracing postmodernism, Baudrillard's *whole effort* is to combat it' (Gane, 1991a: 55, emphasis added). Baudrillard's views on the subject of the postmodern are much more ambiguous than such responses acknowledge or allow.

It is evident that Baudrillard is far from consistent in his observations on the modern and the postmodern. In one essay on the subject of modernity he suggests that to 'speak of modernity scarcely has meaning in a country without tradition or Middle Ages, like the United States' (Baudrillard, 1987: 64). A year or so later in a more substantial work, Baudrillard repeatedly describes America as the very exemplification of modernity, and Europe, handicapped by its past, by its traditions, as only 'very reluctantly . . . [becoming] modern' (1988b: 97). Comparable inconsistencies, as I have attempted to demonstrate above, can be found in Baudrillard's references to the postmodern. But such observations still leave open the question of Baudrillard's status as a 'postmodern analyst', a question that, if it can be resolved at all, can not be answered satisfactorily through selective textual references and interview responses. If there is any foundation to the identification of Baudrillard's idiosyncratic analytic approach with a notion of the postmodern it probably arises from his attempt to cultivate an alternative form of theorizing, theory as challenge, 'fatal theory' (Smart, 1993b).

The conception of the end of theorizing which has been accepted since the Enlightenment, namely that theory can represent the truth of the real, can no longer be sustained in Baudrillard's view, for given the precession of simulacra no privileged appeal can be made to an independent external referent or objective reality. In a context where 'the real is not only what can be reproduced, but *that which is always already reproduced*' (Baudrillard,

1983a: 146), that is the 'hyperreal'; where there is no objectivity to the world, which theory can claim to capture, no deep truth that it can claim to uncover, then theory can have 'no status other than that of challenging the real' (Baudrillard, 1987: 125). Given Baudrillard's speculation, that 'our "society" is perhaps in the process of putting an end to the social, of burying the social beneath a simulation of the social' (1983b: 67), and his views on the associated transformation of theory, the objective of social theory becomes problematic. Baudrillard's response is to argue that the function of theory must now be 'to seduce, to wrest things from their condition, to force them into an over-existence which is incompatible with that of the real' (1988a: 98). Theory must emulate its object and its strategy, and become an 'event in and of itself' (1987: 127). Living in a world in which there is no more transcendence because '[e]verything is exposed to transparency', it is argued that it becomes necessary to substitute fatal theory for critical theory. Fatal theory constitutes a form of theory which forces things to their extremity, and beyond, theory which defies the world to be 'more objective, more ironic, more seductive, more real or unreal' (Baudrillard, 1988a: 54, 100). Reflecting on Baudrillard's analytic response to the hyperreal order of simulation and its complex consequences, Gane concludes that 'he is forced into fiction-theory' (1991b: 94), into 'a change of register, from social analysis to a rich inmixing of metaphysics, ethics, literature and poetry, as well as cultural criticism' (Gane, 1991a: 194). Where then does Baudrillard stand as a theorist?

The change of register identified signifies a radical break with the philosophy of the subject and the associated tradition of Western metaphysics. In so far as the world has continually resisted the orderly designs of the sovereign subject, Baudrillard advocates overturning the metaphysical postulate of the pre-eminence of the subject and instead recognizing, if not submitting to, the 'objective irony that lies in wait for us . . . the ironic presence of the object, its indifference and indifferent connections, its challenge, its seduction, and its disobedience to the symbolic order' (1990a: 182). In short, theory is to take the side of the object, but where does this lead us? It takes us beyond the dialectic, for the world is not dialectical but sworn to extremes and radical antagonism rather than reconciliation and synthesis, and into what Best and Kellner call a 'postmodern metaphysics', that is a metaphysics which has abandoned the philosophy of the subject and the notion of an independent real; a 'metaphysics . . . saturated with irony and . . . influenced by . . . pataphysics' (1991: 129).[6]

In answer to the question 'Why Theory?' Baudrillard has argued that to reflect the real or 'to enter into a relation of critical negativity with the real' can no longer be the end of theory (1988a: 97). No longer can theory derive its legitimacy from established facts. The value of theory now lies 'not in the past events it can illuminate, but in the shockwave of the events it prefigures' (1990b: 215). Fiction-theory, defying the world to be more, tearing itself from all referents and taking pride only in the future, exemplifies, albeit ironically, a conception which might, after all, be considered the very epitome of the *post*modern.

Weak Thoughts on the End(s) of Modernity

A number of the themes intrinsic to Baudrillard's provocations on contemporary culture reappear in Gianni Vattimo's more coherent attempt to think through the problems of 'late modernity'. For example, where Baudrillard (1984b) talks of a 'nihilism of transparency', 'the simulated transparency of everything', and the absence of any theoretical and critical foundation, Vattimo explores the respective works of Nietszche and Heidegger as prefiguring a postmodern form of social and philosophical analysis and draws attention to the 'dissolution of the category of the new', the end of the idea of history as a unitary process, the erosion of our sense of reality as an 'objective given' by the proliferation of a multiplicity of communications media generated 'images, interpretations and reconstructions', and wraps this all up within a continuing deliberation on the 'crisis of metaphysics'. One significant difference, however, is that whereas Baudrillard ultimately appears to lose his fascination with the postmodern, Vattimo develops a powerful case for the relevance and importance of deploying a notion of the postmodern by arguing for the virtues of 'weak thought', 'accomplished nihilism' and an 'ethics of interpretation' (1988, 1992).

A preoccupation with the closure or unravelling of Western metaphysics runs through the work of each of the 'archaeologists of modernity' and it constitutes a key theme in Vattimo's 'postmodern' elaboration on the social and philosophical thought of Nietszche and Heidegger. Given modernity is dominated by the idea of 'progressive "enlightenment" which develops through an ever more complete appropriation of its own "foundations"', and further is 'defined as the era of overcoming' 1988: 2, 166), then a critical overcoming of Western metaphysics becomes a contradiction in terms. In so far as we continue to be subject to, as well as subjects of, modernity then there is no alternative system of thought, or language, available to us through which we can overcome the errors of modernity; no alternative, more true foundation from which we can mount a criticism of Western thought and its assumed foundations, 'stable structures' and 'solid certainties'. In consequence, Western metaphysics can not be 'abandoned like an old, worn out garment, for it still constitutes our "humanity" . . . ; we yield to it, we heal ourselves from it, we are resigned to it as something that is destined to us' (Vattimo, 1988: 52). But whilst we are not able to abandon our metaphysical heritage, our relationship to it has been radically transformed. Postmodern philosophy constitutes a coming to terms with the 'errancy of metaphysics, recollected in an attitude which is neither a critical overcoming nor an acceptance that recovers and prolongs it' (ibid.: 173). In short, postmodern philosophy represents a weakening of metaphysics, hence the notion of 'weak thought' (*il pensiero debole*), and it is in this sense, and this sense only, that it may be described as 'post-metaphysical'.

Implied in Vattimo's notion of weak thought are a series of associated notions, namely nihilism, hermeneutics and difference. An 'accomplished nihilism' is at the heart of the questioning of metaphysical truth. The highest values (our grand narratives) have lost legitimacy and to that extent have largely disappeared – not however to be replaced by other privileged narratives or values – and it is in this context that reference has been made to a growing sense, or experience, of the end of history and/or end of modernity. Our unitary, linear sense of history has been displaced by a plurality of histories; the idea of progress intrinsic to modernity has been secularized – 'depriving progress of a final destination, secularization dissolves the very notion of progress itself' (ibid.: 8); and finally recognition that the idea of a unitary history is a fiction, a story, draws attention to the rhetorical strategies through which all histories are constituted. The world has indeed become a fable (Nietzsche, 1968).

The transformation of the world into a fable is articulated with a weakening of 'reality', with a dissolution of the idea of a unilinear sense of history, an undermining of the ideal of progress and, as a corollary, the prospect of the end of modernity as a project. The process of transformation, as Vattimo (1992) cautions, is not confined to theory and analysis alone, on the contrary, the undermining of the hegemony accorded to European ideals and assumptions following the diverse forms of resistance and rebellion of colonized peoples ('the end of colonialism and imperialism'), along with the growth of information technology and electronic media of communication ('the advent of a society of communication'), have dramatically transformed conditions of existence.

In contemporary capitalist society the distinctive characteristics of existence, 'ranging from commercialization in the form of a totalized "simulacrization" to the consequent collapse of the "critique of ideology", . . . gesture toward a possible new human experience' (Vattimo, 1988: 26), a potentially bewildering experience of the proliferation of world-views and an associated 'irresistible pluralization' of interpretations, within which the assumption of a correspondence between information media generated images or simulations and a real world can no longer be sustained. As Vattimo comments, 'the increase in possible information on the myriad forms of reality makes it increasingly difficult to conceive of a *single* reality. It may be that in the world of the mass media . . . the true world becomes a fable (1992: 7). Or more appropriately, a series of fables, for the post-metaphysical world is a world of differences, a world of interpretations, a world in which hermeneutics constitutes 'the thought of modernity and its consummation' (ibid.: 115).

While the world may be regarded as a source of contrasting and conflicting interpretations or differences, it is important to recognize that differences are from the outset compromised and lacking in innocence. It is not simply a matter of critically mapping the way in which discourse and dialogue has tended to be 'forced over into the sphere of European ideas' (Heidegger, 1971: 14), but rather of recognizing that the global diffusion of the values, assumptions, practices and institutions of Western modernity has constituted a process through which the idea of the 'radical alterity of cultures' has itself been rendered problematic. However, if cultures have long since lost their 'authenticity' they have not completely disappeared under the weight of Western modernity, on the contrary we now encounter a 'range of hybrid formations' (Pieterse, 1994: 167). In Vattimo's terms we experience a 'mixed reality', 'a condition of widespread contamination', 'an immense construction site of traces and residues' (1988: 158–9). Having drawn attention to the complex consequences of the diffusion of the institutions of modernity, and in particular to hybridization – that is the unpredictable patterns of articulation of global processes with local and/or regional practices, customs and traditions – Vattimo concludes that 'the texts belonging to our tradition . . . progressively lose their cogency as models and become part of the vast construction site of traces and residues, just as the condition of radical alterity of cultures that are other is exposed as an ideal which has perhaps never been realized, and is certainly unrealizable for us' (ibid.: 161). It is this condition, a condition in which critical reflections on the modern have begun to undermine the idea of the modern as '*the* fundamental value to which all other values refer' (ibid.: 99), which has been identified as symptomatic of the postmodern.

Like Baudrillard, Vattimo places considerable significance on the impact of the mass media. Indeed it is the emergence of a diversity of means of mass communication which is considered to be decisive in precipitating a proliferation of world-views and a concomitant 'dissolution of centralized perspectives, of what . . . Lyotard calls the "grand narratives"' (Vattimo, 1992: 5). From this standpoint the implied increase in information and communication has not rendered society 'more "transparent", but more complex, even chaotic' (ibid.: 4), yet it is here, in the disorientating excesses of chaos, that Vattimo seems to find hope for 'emancipation'. The notion of emancipation invoked requires clarification; the sense of freedom implied is not to be confused with the classical notion of emancipation which is 'strictly linked to the destiny of the universal' (Laclau, 1992: 132), on the contrary, Vattimo's conception of emancipation is equivalent to a freedom *from* the principle of a universal reality, or, to put it another way, it refers to the 'liberation of differences'. With the collapse of 'the idea of a central rationality of history' (Vattimo, 1992: 9) local elements, rationalities and constituencies are rediscovered and reactivated and it is in this complex pluralistic setting that Vattimo suggests a 'postmodern' experience, or opportunity, of emancipation may become a possibility. Following the realization that there are different cultural universes, that we live in a multicultural world, and that all forms of life, including our own, are marked by an acute sense of 'historicity, contingency, and finiteness', there is the possibility of recognizing the existence of an opportunity to be different, to be, as Foucault (1986c) suggests, other than we are. In such circumstances emancipation becomes a possibility which arises from our fluctuating experiences of 'belonging and disorientation', of the familiar and the strange, but its realization is contingent upon our response – on how we respond. The unanswered question is whether we can overcome our individual and collective 'deep-seated nostalgia for the reassuring' and respond positively to contingency 'as an opportunity of a new way of being (finally, perhaps) human' (Vattimo, 1992: 11). It is this question which has simultaneously troubled modern sensibilities and stimulated postmodern imaginations (Heller and Feher, 1988; Bauman, 1991; Smart, 1993a).

Theorizing After Postmodernity

One of the curious features of the discussion which has developed around the controversial idea of postmodern social and philosophical thought is that the analysts most closely identified with the idea of the postmodern might be described as, at best, reluctant participants. Indeed the idea of postmodern theory or postmodern social and philosophical thought seems to owe more to the consuming interests and constitutive powers of troubled critics than it does to the presence of any distinctive, consistently shared innovatory *theoretical* strategy, or project, in the respective works of the analysts who have been burdened with the ambiguous status postmodern. This is not to deny that the postmodern is an issue in the works of Lyotard, Baudrillard and Vattimo, rather it is to leave open the question of the status of their respective contributions. It is to pose the question, in what respects, if any, is it analytically appropriate to designate the analysts considered in this chapter 'postmodern'.

One of the defining features of modernity is its reflexivity. Reflexivity is not confined to everyday social life, to routine social practices, to mundane forms of thought and action, or to 'non-intellectual' practice, to the contrary it might be argued that it is precisely in the context of the practice of abstract social and philosophical analysis that reflection has become most pronounced, and has turned on modernity itself. The world described by Giddens as one 'which is thoroughly constituted through reflexively applied knowledge' (1990: 39) is a world in which it is increasingly difficult, if not impossible, to draw radical distinctions between representations (social knowledge) and social realities (the processes and contexts analysed). The circularity of the relationship between social knowledge and social realities, the fact that social knowledge constitutes a resource which unavoidably, and unpredictably, contributes to the transformation of the social contexts analysed, has meant that knowledge is of necessity continually subject to revision, and in consequence no longer to be characterized by certainty.[7] And in so far as the nature of reflection itself has become subject to reflection it too has become increasingly uncertain. It is precisely in this complex context that the contributions of the analysts discussed above belong, that is to say their critical reflections on the central assumptions, practices and consequences of the modern project have drawn further attention to the problematic character of Western metaphysics and, simultaneously, have contributed to the widely shared understanding that we are encountering its closure or end; an understanding which is experienced, or lived, as contingency.

In the analyses of modernity conducted by Foucault, Derrida, Lyotard, Baudrillard and Vattimo assumptions intrinsic to modern forms of thought and politics are questioned and challenged, unsettled, through a process of 'wholesale reflexivity', a process which does not treat a particular set of analytic themes and political beliefs as simply given, beyond question or privileged. Unlike their critics, the archaeologists of modernity, for the most part, exemplify a radical reflexivity in their analytic practices; they submit the complex assumptions, conceptions and procedures intrinsic to modern forms of analysis to a process of unremitting critical reflection. And in so far as this is the case their respective interventions may be regarded as significant, albeit controversial, contributions to the regeneration, if not radicalization, of 'the attitude of modernity' (Foucault, 1986d). It is in relation to just such a practice, a radically reflexive analytic challenge to received ideas, forms and assumptions, that Lyotard has invoked a notion of the postmodern, arguing that it undoubtedly constitutes a part of the modern, that it exemplifies the modern in its nascent state, and that 'this state is constant' (1984a: 79). Whilst such a clarification of the relationship between the modern and the postmodern may dispense with the pointless diversions created by critics preoccupied with setting up a banal notion of the postmodern as superseding or transcending the modern, merely in order to be able to knock it down again, and thereby live more easily with their unquestioned analytic assumptions and political prejudices, it does not conclude matters.

One of the concerns which has been articulated in the course of the debate which has developed around the modern/postmodern constellation is that of the prospects for critical thought and politics. Given the critical interrogation of both modern social thought and the related assumption of a close articulation between theoretical discourse and political strategy and ethical decision-making, it is understandable that the prospects for taking a critical position, making distinctions, and taking a stand have become subject to reconsideration. However, these are by no means novel considerations or concerns, they have, in one form or another, accompanied the development of social thought throughout the century, and have been particularly prominent within the Marxist tradition of social analysis.[8] The difference now is that a number of epistemological and socio-political developments have placed not simply this or that variant of radical modern social thought and politics, but prevailing modern forms of progressivist discourse per se in question (Jay, 1988). The absence of any epistemological vantage point from which to mount a convincing claim to totalistic knowledge; a series of crises of representation in respect, not only of questions of epistemology and aesthetics, but also 'the political articulation of

social "interests"' (Boyne and Rattansi, 1990: 13); the emergence of a
'multiplication of antagonisms' and socio-political struggles, a virtual
corollary of the end of the era of 'normative epistemologies' and 'universal
discourses' (Laclau and Mouffe, 1985); coupled with an undermining of the
conventional universalizing intellectual role, and associated legislative
strategy, and concomitant emphasis on a more specific intellectual role and
an associated interpretive strategy (Bauman, 1987), have eroded the old
certainties, or have revealed them to have been, perhaps all along, merely a
product of the unwarranted assumption of privileged analytic and political
positions.

What emerges strongly from the debate over the modern/postmodern
constellation is that there are 'no more assured foundations arising out of a
transcendent order' (Laclau and Mouffe, 1985: 187) and that in consequence ethical and political convictions can only find false comfort in
metaphysics (Bernstein, 1991). With the application of the powers of
reflection to the process of modern reflection itself the old certainties have
indeed collapsed. We find ourselves abroad in a world in which social
theory and analysis is no longer able, with any credibility, to provide a
warrant for political practice and ethical decision-making. But this does not
signal either the end of theory, or for that matter the end of an analytic
interest in politics or ethics. On the contrary, questions concerning political
responsibility and ethical decision-making, the difficulties of adjudicating
between the expression and pursuit of self-interest and the promotion and
adequate provision of the public domain, as well as the problems encountered in everyday social life of making a choice or taking a stand, have if
anything become analytically more significant, and it is in this broad
controversial context that reflexive forms of social theorizing have come to
occupy a more prominent position. The end towards which such forms of
theorizing are directed is not the provision of legislative programmes which
attempt to achieve an assimilation of 'the Other' to 'the Same', but the
cultivation of self-reflexive processes of 'interpretation and reinterpretation'
(Bauman, 1992a) which, notwithstanding the realization that pluralism – 'a
plurality of traditions, perspectives, philosophical orientations' (Bernstein,
1991: 329) – is a constitutive feature of what Bauman calls our 'postmodern
habitat', have as their endless task the nurturing of understanding and
dialogue between and across different, at times radically different, interests,
traditions and cultures, as a condition necessary for the constitution of a
form of responsible subjectivity conducive to the cultivation of relations of
tolerance and solidarity between 'self' and 'other'.

Notes

1 Variations on the general criticisms articulated by Wright Mills have continued to be a
feature of reflections on sociological discourse. Consider, for example, Stein and Vidich's
(1963) comments on sociology's loss of its 'critical sense'; Horowitz's view that 'the prevailing
tendency in American sociology during the past two decades between 1940 and 1960 has put

this discipline into a *cul de sac*' (1965: 3); Gouldner's (1972) warning of a growing crisis in sociology and proposal for a radically reflexive sociology; the observation offered by Giddens that we 'live in a world for which the traditional sources of social theory have left us unprepared – especially those forms of social theory associated with liberal or socialist politics' (1987: 166); and the cryptic remark with which Castells has concluded a series of observations on the experience of vertigo associated with contemporary processes of transformation, namely that 'the grand theories which explicitly and implicitly have produced the categories with which we still, inadequately, think our world, . . . have proved to be completely obsolete' (1992: 94–5). A series of related attempts to rescue sociology from the legislative impasse to which it has become subject by drawing upon and assimilating 'Heideggerian, Wittgensteinian, Gadamerian and other "hermeneutical" themes and inspirations' (Bauman, 1988: 229) offer the prospect of a different direction for inquiry, one which leads to analytic emphasis being placed upon 'the shared world of social meanings through which *social* action . . . is generated and interpreted' (Filmer et al., 1972: 4). It is here in the development of interpretive modes of sociological inquiry that Bauman (1988) has subsequently identified the possibility of a *postmodern* sociology, a form of sociology which attempts to provide a translation service between a plurality of traditions and communities. These matters are discussed in Chapter 1.

2 It is worth emphasizing that a radical questioning of modern forms of inquiry and analysis is not confined to these particular figures, nor to post-1968 French social and philo-sophical discourse alone. For example, in philosophy (Rorty, 1991), anthropology (Rabinow, 1986 and Tyler, 1986), literary criticism (Hassan, 1987), politics (Derian and Shapiro, 1989) and sociology (Denzin, 1986) modern approaches have been subject to various forms of postmodern intervention.

3 The text is a translation of the French original: 'parce qu'elle n'a jamais concerne seulement des contenus de sens, la deconstruction devrait ne pas être separable de cette problematique politico-institutionnelle et réquerir un questionnement nouveau sur la responsabilité, un questionnement qui ne se fie plus necessairement aux codes herites du politique ou de l'éthique'.

4 Baudrillard initially identifies three orders of simulacra:

(i)   based on the natural law of value is the order of counterfeit. '*Counterfeit* is the dominant scheme of the "classical" period from the Renaissance to the industrial period.'

(ii)   serial production based on the commercial law of value. '*Production* is the dominant scheme of the industrial era.'

(iii)   operational simulation based on the structural law of value. '*Simulation* is the reigning scheme of the current phase that is controlled by the code' (1983a: 83).

In a subsequent paper Baudrillard has added a 'new particle to the microphysics of simulacra', a fourth order of simulacra which corresponds to the 'fractal stage of value'. Whereas in the third order 'a code and value unfurls itself in reference to an ensemble of models' in the fourth order there is no referent at all (Baudrillard, 1992a: 15).

5 See for example, references to postmodernism/postmodernity in Baudrillard, 1984a, 1984b, 1989b, 1990b, 1992a and 1992b.

6 Baudrillard describes pataphysics as a 'science of imaginary solutions, a science of the simulation or hypersimulation of an exact, true, objective world, with its universal laws' (1983b: 33–4).

7 Elaborating on the reflexive character of modernity Giddens adds that '[t]he point is not that there is no stable social world to know, but that knowledge of that world contributes to its unstable or mutable character' (1990: 45). It might not be the precise point that Giddens wishes to make in this context, but it is one of the conclusions to which his analysis of the juggernaut-like character of modernity irresistibly leads. And it is precisely this constellation of uncertainty, of contingency, or rather a pervasive self-consciousness of the same, which Bauman (1991) has described as postmodern.

8 Appropriate contemporary examples of the way in which the prospects for critical thought and radical politics have continued to be addressed within the Marxist tradition can be

found in the analyses of processes of transformation to which modern forms of life have been subject offered by Frederic Jameson (1984, 1988, 1989, 1991) and David Harvey (1989) respectively. Jameson has no doubt that we are now living '*within* the culture of post-modernism' (1984: 63) and he appears to accept the need for theoretical innovation and development with an admission that languages which 'have been useful in talking about culture and politics in the past don't really seem adequate to this historical moment' (in conversation with Stephanson, 1988: 12–13). However, in practice there is a continuing unquestioning commitment to a Marxist analytical and political framework and vocabulary throughout his work. And although Harvey recognizes that there is a danger 'our mental maps will not match current realities' (1989: 305) a comparable reluctance to reflect on the possible implications of postmodern conditions for Marxist analysis and politics is evident in his work.

3

REFLEXIVITY, MODERNITY AND SOCIOLOGY

Reflecting critically on the erosion of values arising from processes of economic and cultural transformation associated with the development of modernity, Max Weber was moved early in the twentieth century to lament that 'this nullity imagines that it has attained a level of civilization never before achieved' (1976: 182). At the close of the century, concern continues to be expressed over the erosion of values, a significant difference now being that, in the wake of so many sombre historical moments and proliferating signs of apparent social malaise, there seems to be much less confidence and much more ambivalence about the level of civilization attained. Modern civilization, 'our' civilization, that form of life which now appears global in scale and scope, is increasingly recognized to be a source of costs (direct and indirect; some known to and borne by present generations, some unknown, some lying in wait for future generations) as well as benefits, risks as well as securities, and there is broad agreement that all is not as well as it might, should, or perhaps could be. However, diagnoses of the state and fate of the modern condition vary enormously and whereas for some analysts evidence of limitations testifies to the possible limits of the modern project itself, perhaps to a crisis of modernity, possibly the advent of a new condition of 'postmodernity', for others current problems constitute evidence not so much of an insuperable crisis of modernity as of the need to modernize modernity itself.

Increasing evidence of the limitations of modernity are taken by Zygmunt Bauman as markers of the modern project's intrinsic limits and as grounds for introducing a notion of the postmodern to describe the distinctiveness of a disorderly or Rhizomatic culture, a world-view which is 'irreducibly and irrevocably pluralistic' (1992a: 35), as well as associated forms of social and cultural analysis which place emphasis on interpretation and translation rather than legislation. Contesting the idea that aberrant forms can simply be (dis)counted as symptoms of a modernity in crisis, a modernity which it is frequently assumed will in due course rid itself of its pathological forms, Bauman comments that 'postmodernity (or whatever other name will be eventually chosen to take hold of the phenomena it denotes) is an aspect of a fully-fledged, viable social system which has come to replace the "classical" modern, capitalist society and thus needs to be theorized according to its own logic' (ibid.: 52). In marked contrast, Andre Gorz has argued that, while it might be appropriate to regard existing problems and difficulties as constituting a crisis, it is not acceptable to talk of a crisis of modernity. In this instance, difficulties are not regarded as intrinsic limitations which betray the limits of modernity; it is not a question of the process of modernization having 'reached an impasse', rather in Gorz's opinion what we are encountering is evidence of the need to 'modernize the presuppositions on which modernity is based' (1989: 1). Gorz argues that what has been (mis)taken as 'the end of modernity and the crisis of Reason is in reality the crisis of the quasi-religious irrational contents upon which the selective and partial rationalization we call industrialism – bearer of a conception of the universe and a vision of the future which are now untenable – is based' (ibid.: 1). However, if industrial modernity is to be regarded as no longer tenable, the introduction of a notion of the postmodern to account for contemporary conditions is, in turn, regarded by Gorz as totally unnecessary. Embracing Ulrich Beck's analysis of the problems of 'industrial society' and the possible emergence of a new form of modernity, Gorz argues for 'rationality itself to be rationalized' (ibid.: 1), which effectively constitutes a call for reflexivity, for a more reflexive form of modernity.

While there may be differences between analysts in their respective conceptualizations and diagnoses of the current condition of modernity there does appear to be a considerable degree of agreement that reflexivity constitutes a distinctive and significant feature. For example, it is has been argued that what distinguishes our modernity is 'a very high degree of reflectiveness' (Berger and Kellner, 1982: 153); its inclusion 'reflexively in its own sphere of action' (Gorz, 1989: 1); that it is 'becoming *reflexive*, it is becoming its own theme' (Beck, 1992: 19); and finally that there is a 'presumption of wholesale reflexivity – which of course includes reflection upon the nature of reflection itself' (Giddens, 1990: 39). Giving appropriate weight to the implications of the doubling hermeneutic circuits of 'interpretation and reinterpretation, of interpretation fed back into the interpreted condition only to trigger off further interpretive efforts', makes necessary in Bauman's view (1992a: 204) the introduction of a notion of the postmodern to clearly distinguish a habitat, *our* habitat, in which a 'self-reflexive process of reinterpretation' is never-ending. But whether prevailing conditions are considered to be more appropriately wrapped up by a notion of the 'modern', qualified in different ways as radical, risk-ridden, hyper, or disorganized, or the 'postmodern', with whatever qualifications, reflexivity is now widely acknowledged to be a significant feature of present conditions.

Modernity and Reflexivity

In so far as modernity constitutes a form of life in which a questioning reason is central, then it might be argued that from its inception modernity has tended to be reflexive. Anticipating the potential objection that all forms of human action may be regarded as reflexive, to some degree, in so far as monitoring the grounds, performance and consequences of action is virtually routine in human affairs, Giddens argues that the reflexivity of modernity is of a qualitatively different order. With the development of modernity 'thought and action are constantly refracted back upon one another . . . social practices are constantly examined and reformed in the light of incoming information about those very practices, thus constitutively altering their character' (Giddens, 1990: 38).

What we experience and know as modernity is formed through endless processes of reflexive structuring, de-structuring and restructuring in which forms of knowledge are generated and adopted or applied, and as they contribute thereby to the complex unintended as well as intended transformation of the processes and practices which have constituted the focus or object of inquiry, they are simultaneously exposed through reflexivity to the necessity of revision. Giddens argues that 'high' or 'late' modernity is characterized by 'extreme reflexivity', by which he means that the 'entry of knowledge into the circumstances of action it analyses or describes creates a set of uncertainties to add to the circular and fallible character of post-traditional claims to knowledge' (1991: 29, 28). It is precisely this sense of uncertainty and fallibility which Bauman has identified as constitutive of the postmodern habitat, a habitat in which there is 'an incessant flow of reflexivity' (1992a: 204), to which the social and human sciences in both their informal populist and more formal academic guises continue to make a substantial contribution.

As Michel Foucault notes in his discussion of the emergence and distinctive features of the social and human sciences in *The Order of Things*:

> In modern experience, the possibility of establishing man within knowledge and the mere emergence of this new figure in the field of the *episteme* imply an imperative that haunts thought from within; it matters little whether it be given currency in the form of ethics, politics, humanism, a duty to assume responsibility for the fate of the West, or the mere consciousness of performing, in history, a bureaucratic function. What is essential is that thought, both for itself and in the density of its workings, should be both knowledge and a modification of what it knows, reflection and a transformation of the mode of being of that on which it reflects. (1973: 327)

Foucault adds that there is 'something here profoundly bound up with our modernity' (ibid.: 327). The social and human sciences which emerge with the formation of the modern epistemological configuration provide knowledge which is always linked to ethics and politics, always articulated with action, always modifying what it knows, although not always in accord with design, and in consequence, through reflection, such knowledge is itself necessarily subject to perpetual modification.

The reflexive character of modernity involves the actual or potential modification of processes and practices in the light of, but by no means in line with, new knowledge, as well as the corollary, the continually necessary revision of forms of knowledge in the light of transformed processes and practices. The social and human sciences, as both Bauman and Giddens note, play a basic role in the reflexivity of modernity, challenging existing forms of knowledge and associated understandings of social conditions and processes by providing new knowledge, which itself is continually vulnerable to doubt and exposed to revision. Elaborating on the uncertainty which has been a corollary of the reflexivity of modernity, Giddens remarks that the radical doubt which is a companion of modernity is 'not only disturbing for philosophers but is *existentially troubling* for ordinary individuals' (1991: 21). Such an appreciation of the pervasiveness of uncertainty has led Bauman to identify ambivalence as a corollary of modernity and to describe recognition of the inescapability of the same as symptomatic of a condition of postmodernity. Acknowledgement of and accommodation to ambivalence as a necessary corollary of modernity, rather than as a temporary anomaly which may be rectified through further rounds of knowledge generation and associated forms of social engineering, exemplifies the postmodern condition of 'self-conscious contingency' (Bauman, 1991: 246). In short 'living with ambivalence' constitutes for Bauman our *post*modern condition.

A New Modernity?

While recognizing many of the symptoms of uncertainty and ambivalence noted above, Beck finds evidence of the emergence of a new form of modernity. Rather than signs of a *post*modern condition, Beck initially argues that the evidence indicates a process of 'reflexive modernization' leading to the development of a 'risk society'. But, as I have briefly indicated in the previous chapter, the conception of such a new form of modernity begs a number of questions. Reflexive modernization may be an effective concept to describe the contradictory character of technological and scientific development in late modernity, and the notion of 'risk society' certainly does appear to resonate with the experiences of both professional and lay members of modern communities. However, the idea that a regeneration of modernity involving an alternative organization of techno-scientific practice, in which self-criticism 'in all its forms' within professions and organizations – albeit yet to be fought for and realized – will necessarily constitute an improvement on existing conditions represents, as I will explain below, merely an over-optimistic projection. Moreover, contrary to Beck's protestations, this 'new' prescription does look very much like more of the same – like the modern project reconstituted.

   In so far as 'proper technical know how' continues to be upheld as vital to the task of risk recognition and the generation of alternative methods to avoid them, then the consequences of forms of professional monopoly and associated questions concerning trust need to be critically explored. However, as will become apparent, in Beck's analysis there is a neglect of any sustained consideration of the existence and significance of inequalities of access to what Scott Lash has described as 'networks of *information and communication structures*' (1994: 121), inequalities that is which lead to some having both access to and a command over technical know how, including control over the criteria and certification processes which confer legitimacy, as well as the broader matter of the general relationship between expert systems and what Brian Wynne has described as 'the informal non-expert public domain' (1996: 46). Lash (1994) offers a salutary reminder that agents occupy different positions within the 'mode of information'. If the opportunity to participate in criticism within professions and organizations is bound up with possession of what Beck describes as 'proper technical know how', then position or standing in the mode of information will powerfully influence both the possibility and the terms of any participation in the 'institutionalization of self-criticism'.

Developing Scott Lash's criticism of Beck's unreflexive preoccupation with experts and associated 'relative neglect of the grass roots' (1994: 200), Brian Wynne proceeds to take issue with the relationship drawn between 'expert' and 'lay knowledge', arguing that public opposition and criticism, and associated withdrawals of trust, do not necessarily trail in the wake of expert dissent. Wynne argues that the idea of an earlier, simpler, industrial modernity in which reflection is absent and expertise is uncontested, and accorded trust, constitutes an imaginative fiction in so far as the status of the expert has always been open to contestation. Moreover, a relationship of dependency is not equivalent to, and should not be mistaken for, one of trust:

> Lack of overt public dissent or opposition towards expert systems is taken too easily for public trust. Yet there is ample sociological evidence supporting a different theoretical conception of this relationship, one which recognizes ambivalence and also the clustered problems of agency, identity and dependency. (1996: 50)

Elaborating on the need to revise understanding of the expert–lay knowledge dichotomy, Wynne draws attention to 'just how ambivalent public relationships with expertise are, and how deeply dependency relationships are enculturated into social habits and identities' (1996: 51). It is precisely the evidence of degrees of scepticism and uncertainty surrounding the issue of 'proper technical know how', and associated measures proposed to counter risks, which has led analysts such as Lash and Wynne to argue that ambivalence is intrinsic to risk society, a conclusion to which Beck (1994), in turn, has ultimately been driven.

In so far as reflexivity undermines certainties and promotes ambivalence about modern forms of life, Beck's new modernity, 'risk society', is clearly vulnerable to reinterpretation as the 'ambivalent society' – ambivalent about the direction in which it is heading and/or the goals to be pursued; the appropriateness and effectiveness of the means employed, as well as the associated direct and indirect, immediate and delayed, known (calculated and anticipated) and unknown consequences; not to mention uncertainty about the adequacy of possible responses and counter-measures. Risk society, an ambivalent society, appears virtually rudderless, or as Giddens (1990) would have it, like a 'juggernaut'. Apparently resigned to being unable to rationally determine the direction in which it is heading, a late, risk-ridden modernity has succumbed to the seductive yet unpredictable 'culture' of the marketplace, a culture which frequently receives expression and promotion (and strives for legitimacy) in terms of the proclaimed virtues of 'sovereign' consumer choice and an associated idea of the 'freedom of the individual' – that is through individualizing rationales which have contributed to the prioritizing of private interests and relative neglect and denigration of the public domain, which in its turn has been held responsible, in part at least, for the undermining of 'community' (Etzioni, 1994). As Mary Douglas has remarked in an analysis of 'the new concern with risk', the impact of increasingly globalized modern markets on individuals and communities has been profound. Drawn from small, local, communal settings into 'regional, national and international spheres', individuals find themselves simultaneously set free, from 'dull, local niches', yet left exposed and feeling vulnerable (Douglas, 1994: 15).

Risk Society – Thesis and Critique

The notion of risk society has undoubtedly found a place within the sociological lexicon and it has also made an impact on popular social commentary, as I have suggested in my earlier discussion of the public concern in Britain in the 1990s provoked by reports of a connection between BSE in cattle and the emergence of a new variant of CJD in humans, reports which raised critical questions about the relationship between science, industry, and government (Woollacott, 1996). As might be expected the high profile achieved by the thesis has stimulated a number of critical responses, some of which I have briefly noted above. However, of all the criticisms aimed at Beck's initial thesis a brief review offered by Bauman (1992b) seems to have had the most telling effect. At the heart of Bauman's criticism is a disbelief that further modernization of modernity, or rationalization of modern rationality, is going to offer any effective remedy for the catalogue of emerging risks and dangers identified by Beck to be a consequence of techno-economic development. If techno-scientific rationality has to be held responsible for the accumulation of modern civilizational hazards, and social awareness of the risks of modernization has had to counter a continual barrage of scientific denial and reassurance, in short has had to overcome resistance from the bearers of scientific rationality, in what respects, and under what conditions, can it be considered appropriate or feasible to (re)turn to modern science for a remedy?

Beck's position in *Risk Society* is that the unforeseeable effects of modernization, the unpredictability of the consequences of techno-scientific development, may be alleviated through the cultivation of an alternative *post*-industrial techno-scientific practice oriented towards self-control and self-limitation. An alternative practice of 'reflexive scientization' is presented as being able to make 'the self-imposed taboos of scientific rationality visible and questionable'. Beck adds that the 'suspicion is that "objective constraints", "latent side effects", which stand for the "auto dynamism" of the techno-scientific development, are themselves *manufactured* and thus are in principle *solvable*' (1992: 157). Reflexive scientization is promoted as promising a regeneration of the Enlightenment project of modernity, as offering a 'revival of reason' which will both overcome the 'rigidification' associated with industrial modernity and scientifically expose, and 'methodically and objectively' interpret, risks and dangers. As Beck would have it, '[w]here everything has become controllable, the product of human efforts, *the age of excuses is over*. There are no longer any dominant objective constraints, unless we allow them and make them dominate' (ibid.: 234). The problem with this scenario is that although it may now be plausible to argue that virtually everything is indeed directly or indirectly bound up with human effort and its consequences to varying degrees, that does not make everything controllable, either in principle or in practice. And the difficulties in this context can not be attributed simply to the absence of a willingness to intervene, or to attempt to assert control over our destiny. To the contrary, as Beck documents so effectively, it is precisely such an enthusiasm for intervention which has inadvertently led to the unintended manufacture of an accumulating catalogue of daunting risks and dangers. The implication here is not that nothing can be done about existing risks and dangers, rather that Beck's powerful depiction of the ways in which modernization is inclined to create unanticipated new risks and threats, gives no cause for confidence that a modernization of modernity, or a rationalization of rationality, in short the emergence of a reflexive modernization, will lead to a reduction in our exposure to risk and an exponential qualitative improvement in conditions of existence.

Much depends upon the extent of public awareness of risk and the scale and degree of organization of the criticism directed against scientific and technological practices. In turn, this set of factors requires the existence, as Beck readily acknowledges, of what is variously termed 'alternative expertise', '"counter-scientific" mediations', 'the scientization of protest against science', and again a 'demonopolization of science' (ibid.: 160–3). But beyond general references to the need to 'open up the political' and speculative scenarios of possible futures there is little in Beck's initial thesis to indicate how, or from where, an alternative techno-scientific practice oriented towards effective radical self-criticism and self-control is realistically likely to emerge. It is all very well stating that 'Science *can change itself* and revive enlightenment theoretically and practically through a critique of its historic self-conception' (ibid.: 180), but it is not clear how an alternative science will avoid a repetition of errors broadly comparable to those attributed to existing scientific practices. What Beck does make clear is that an appropriate transformation of science will require the realization of one of three possible social futures.

The three possible social futures outlined are; (i) *reindustrialization* to counter the risk of industrialization, that is 'back to industrial society', a future Beck decribes as 'probable' (ibid.: 224–5); (ii) *democratization* to make techno-economic decision-making accessible to public control through a centralized parliament, a possible future portrayed as one which has already had its day, one at odds with the emergence of an increasingly decentred politics or, in Beck's terms, 'the *unbinding* of politics' (ibid.: 231); and finally (iii) *dedifferentiations* of society and politics, a future which takes off from the de-centred character of politics, from the simultaneous existence and complex articulation of conventional or mainstream parliamentary political forms, which aside from the articulation of foreign and military policy, and responsibility for maintaining 'internal security', have an increasingly diminishing influence, and ostensibly 'non-political' forms of technocratic, corporate and pressure group activity, which Beck suggests are increasingly constituting an influential 'sub-politics'. Beck describes a steady drift, or migration, from a centred 'official' politics (parliament-government-political administration) to a de-centred political context in which the major influence increasingly rests with 'the sub-political system of scientific, technological and economic modernization' (ibid.: 186), alongside which there are a range of other 'sites and forms of sub-politics' introduced to limit the expression of political power (i.e. the judiciary and media publicity). Such developments occurring in the course of reflexive modernization, and signifying a dilution of the influence of the official institutions of the democratic political system, represent in Beck's view the outlines of an emerging 'new political culture', one which includes other 'arenas of cultural and social sub-politics' that have emerged with the decentralization of politics, notably 'privacy, citizens' initiative groups and the new social movements' (ibid.: 198).

It is the radical potential implicit in the fluidity and flexibility made possible by the unbinding of politics which leads Beck to talk of the prospect of opening a 'new page in the history of democracy' (ibid.: 196), one on which resistance to the unwarranted equation of technological and social progress is already being inscribed. However, if there is now less consensus about the virtues of techno-economic development and more awareness of, and unease about, consequent risks and dangers, it nevertheless remains the case that, as Beck notes, 'techno-economic sub-politics' is relatively immune to criticism, for 'unplanned, and closed to decision-making, [it] only becomes aware of itself as social change at the moment of its realization' (ibid.: 203). In consequence it is only after the event, 'lagging hopelessly behind', after the realization of a particular techno-economic development, and dissemination of information concerning its actual or potential social impact, that those in politics and the public sphere are in any position to express concern, should they wish to do so, through channels which may be available and open to them.

Notwithstanding the difficulties, the risks and dangers, which are a corollary of reflexive modernization, Beck detects in the uncertainty of risk society an opportunity 'to find and activate the increase of equality, freedom and self-expression promised by modernity, *against* the limitations, the functional imperatives and the fatalism of progress in industrial society' (ibid.: 232). It is an opportunity whose potential for realization is presented as being bound up with three other conditions, notably the existence of 'strong and independent courts' and 'strong and independent media' to exert 'sub-political controls', coupled with an 'institutionalization of self-criticism' within professions, to nurture expression of alternative views and implementation of alternative practices. How these first two preconditions are to be achieved, given continuing attempts to politicize the judiciary and evidence of an increasing concentration, or monopolization, of media ownership, as well as possible signs of a 'dumbing-down' in the quality of the contents communicated, is not clarified. However, it is the final pre-condition which is perhaps the most controversial, for scientific practice (with which Beck is primarily concerned) already embraces, advocates and promotes self-criticism. And if self-criticism is already a constitutive feature of the practice of a modern science identified as problematic, wherein will the difference(s) lie?

Beck's reference to the necessity of '[e]nabling self-criticism in *all* its forms' (emphasis added) invites a number of important questions. What does 'self-criticism in all its forms' include? What would scientific practice look like if self-criticism in all its forms were to be made possible and given a serious hearing? At what points in the scientific process would work be required to be open to such criticism? By what criteria are particular forms of self-criticism to be deemed more or less (in)appropriate, (ir)relevant, and/or (in)effective in relation to the objective of re-forming scientific practice? In addition there remains the continuing difficulty of trying to ascertain, or determine in advance, what the complex direct/indirect, immediate/delayed consequences of particular scientific initiatives are likely to be. Beck notes that 'the public sphere and politics are always and necessarily "uninformed", lagging hopelessly behind . . . developments' (ibid.: 208). But it might also be argued that while professional scientists are generally better informed, they too frequently find themselves lagging hopelessly behind the effects of their actions, only after the event, after implementation, and that is often too late, coming to appreciate the complex, and perhaps regrettable consequences of their conduct of scientific innovation and cultivation of forms of technological intervention. The observation, that self-criticism in all its forms is 'probably the *only way* that the mistakes that would sooner or later destroy our world can be detected in advance' (ibid.: 234), implies that the tarnished promise of modernity can be restored, that the fix that those credited with possessing 'proper technical know how' have got us into can be more than temporarily resolved by others bearing comparable credentials. What is to prevent new risks emerging and/or 'alternative methods' subsequently being identified as problematic or risky, in their turn, is not clarified. The implication of my remarks is not that self-criticism is unable to assist in the early detection of some potential or actual mistakes, but that it is not possible, in advance, to guarantee that subjecting present measures and initiatives to wide-ranging critical inquiry will prevent a future in which the subsequent detection of mistakes and/or unanticipated risks and dangers continues to be a prominent and disconcerting feature. To suggest otherwise is to offer false comfort. It is to succumb to the rhetoric of modernity, notably that everything is indeed controllable, and to neglect the reality of modernity, which is that the world, as Giddens remarks, is not 'subject to our prediction and control' (1990: 151). What is presented by Beck is indeed little more than an optimistic scenario, not an outline of a probable future; it is merely a possibility, paradoxically one which relies upon the very institutions which currently constitute the source of the problems we encounter being able to provide a lasting solution to the difficulties for which they are largely responsible.

In response to the criticism that his proposed solution simply promises, or more appropriately threatens, to produce new problems (Bauman, 1992b), Beck has subsequently been moved to clarify, if not radically amend, his position. The concept of reflexive modernization signifies a process in which modernity itself is held to be subject to modernization, it is a process which involves the transformation of industrial modernity, which is undercut by its own dynamism. Beck's conception of the process of reflexive modernization may appear to share some similarity with Daniel Bell's earlier forecast of a 'change in the social framework of Western society' (1973: 9), a change conceptualized in terms of the possible development of a 'postindustrial society'. But if Beck's new modernity is in an important sense 'post'-industrial, it shares few of the features of Bell's postindustrial society. Emphasizing the surreptitious and unplanned character of the transformation of industrial modernity, following 'auto-nomized modernization', Beck argues that it is necessary to distinguish between an earlier phase or stage, when industrial society is systematically producing 'effects and self-threats' which escape public concern, and a later phase where an awareness of such threats increasingly informs discussion and debate. It is with the former that the process of reflexive modernization is argued to begin, a process which is held to be unconscious, unintended and unplanned, a process which occurs 'undesired, unseen and compulsively', and represents a form of 'self-confrontation' (Beck, 1994: 5). Only somewhat later does it become appropriate to talk of 'self-reflection on modernity' or the 'self-referentiality of modernity' (ibid.: 6, 176).

But is the distinction offered between two historical phases or stages, first of an autonomized modernization which reflexively undercuts the basis of industrial modernity, and then of a later phase in which there is reflection on the risks and dangers thrown up by industrial modernity, appropriate? It might be argued, in contrast, that from the outset industrial capitalist modernity has been recognized to be a system which perpetually undercuts itself, one which is 'constantly revolutionizing . . . production, and . . . the whole relations of society' (Marx and Engels, 1968: 83) in an unplanned manner, and that a steadily growing volume of increasingly organized reflection on the accumulating evidence of attendant risks and dangers has been a corollary. In so far as this is the case the proposed distinction between two discrete phases or stages, an earlier one termed *reflexivity* in which there is an unseen transition from the industrial to 'the risk period of modernity', in the course of which the 'bases of modernization' come into confrontation with the 'consequences of modernization', and a later phase termed *reflection*, in which modernization and its consequences is deemed to be central to public, political and scientific inquiry, becomes unnecessary. Reflection, more or less conscious, and always subject to the limits of cognitive, moral and aesthetic dimensions, as well as the limits associated with particular disciplinary fields – not to mention the limitations on all forms of knowledge of not being able to anticipate the unintended consequences and/or take into account the complex side effects of courses of action – has always been a feature of modernization, although it has become a more prominent aspect as the momentum of reflexive modernization has increased.

The forced distinction between reflexivity and reflection is ultimately analytically unnecessary, for as explanations of the consequences of the reflexivity and ambivalence of modernity, offered by Giddens and Bauman respectively, already make clear, the institutions of modernity are destined to continually defy our attempts to exercise control. The disorder of unintended and unanticipated consequences remains an inescapable feature of modern life, and modern scientific reason, by definition, is continually exposed to the possibility of being reflexively undercut or challenged, and is thereby unable to provide us with the security of certain knowledge. The notion of the reflexivity of modernity advanced by Giddens already encompasses reflection, but not in the form Beck has subsequently criticized for being too optimistic. There is no sense in which Giddens implies that 'more reflection, more experts, more science, more public sphere, more self-awareness and self-criticism will open up new and better possibilities in a world that has got out of joint' (Beck, 1994: 177), ironically if such optimism is to be found it is present in Beck's initial thesis. A more direct counter to the optimism evident in Beck's (1992) idea that the institutionalization of effective forms of self-criticism, itself no mean task, would allow knowledge of risks and dangers to emerge in advance, and would thereby make possible the introduction of alternative measures and methods, is provided by Bauman's thesis on the ambivalence of modernity.

For Bauman contingency is a corollary of modernity rather than a 'temporary affliction', but it is a serious mistake to suggest that this thesis promotes a 'sit back and do nothing' mentality, or that it is infused with a 'pitch-black pessimism' (Beck, 1996: 38, 53n10). On the contrary, recognizing the intrinsic ambivalence of modernity constitutes a necessary first step towards a coming to terms with the consequences of what Beck has subsequently described as 'the unforeseeable side and after-effects of . . . [the] demand for control' and 'the new manufactured incalculability and disorder' (1994: 10, 11). It represents an important initial step, one which

allows different possible responses to living with ambivalence to be considered and explored. Drawing attention not only to the opportunities but
also to the problems which follow the restoration of moral choice and
responsibility to agents, Bauman notes that such agents are deprived 'of the
comfort of the universal guidance that modern self-confidence once
promoted' (1992a: xxii). What is offered is not pessimism, but a careful and
balanced analysis of existing conditions and possibilities, a sober
assessment of what is involved in living without guarantees, a survey of
the opportunities and dangers that are to be found on a site Bauman (1991)
identifies as 'postmodernity'.

Following Bauman's criticisms, Beck (1994) has made reference to the
uncertainty, lack of clarity, disorder and 'irreducible ambivalences' of risk
society. Rather than presenting the institutionalization of self-criticism and
the prospect of science (equipped with 'proper technical know how')
opposing science, as the appropriate path to take to detect and avoid
mistakes, Beck has subsequently appeared to place more emphasis upon the
'onset of ambivalence' and has even acknowledged that 'living and acting in
uncertainty becomes a kind of basic experience' (ibid.: 29, 12). Recognition
of the ambivalence of modernity leads Beck on to consider how to respond
and the answer given is that 'the model of unambiguous instrumental
rationality must be abolished' and our deepening dependency on experts
must be countered through a process of 'demonopolization of expertise'
(ibid.: 29). What this seems to involve is an alternative to existing forms of
scientific governmentality, notably the opening up of knowledge generation,
administration, and decision-making to non-specialists. In Beck's terms it
constitutes a 'different way of handling ambivalence . . . [which] presumes
that *experience* is once again made possible and justified in society – also
and particularly against science' (ibid.: 30). However, it soon becomes
apparent that this alternative 'experience' is to be elevated to the status of a
highly ambiguous alternative type of science. We are advised that on one
side:

> there is the old, flourishing laboratory science, which penetrates and opens up the
> world mathematically and technically but devoid of experience and encapsulated
> in a myth of precision; on the other, there is public discursivity of experience
> which brings objectives and means, constraints and methods, controversially into
> view. Both types have their particular perspective, shortcomings, constraints and
> methods. Laboratory science is systematically more or less blind to the
> consequences which accompany and threaten its successes. The public discussion
> . . . of threats . . . is related to everyday life, drenched with experience and plays
> with cultural symbols. It is also media dependent, manipulable, sometimes
> hysterical and in any case devoid of a laboratory, dependent in that sense upon
> research and argumentation, so that it needs an accompanying science (classical
> task of the universities). It is thus based more on a kind of science of questions
> than on one of answers. (ibid.: 30–1)

Beck argues that each represents 'a completely different type of knowledge' but the distinction drawn is problematic. One type is formally and
methodically constituted through processes and practices intrinsic to the

institution of modern science, while the other more ambiguous type appears to be closer to a 'lay' understanding, but paradoxically it too is portrayed as necessarily informed by a form of scientific research and argumentation derived from the universities, a form of science which it is implied does not share the deficiencies of laboratory science. On what grounds 'university' science is to be distinguished from 'laboratory' science, and the latter's limitations, is not explained and in consequence the distinction drawn is ultimately unconvincing. The concept of a homogeneous 'laboratory science' distinguishable from 'university science' is highly contentious, for it fails to take account of a range of complex transformations in the practice of scientific research. For example, the appropriateness of a distinction between 'laboratory' and 'university' science has been affected by the increasing emphasis placed upon the importance of industry as a partner for university science, a development embodied in the proliferation of university 'science parks' and research funding connections with industry.

The distinction outlined is also problematic in another respect, notably there is no recognition of the possible emergence of a new pragmatics of scientific knowledge which can not be equated with the pursuit of per-formativity (Lyotard, 1984a). It is no longer appropriate to simply equate 'laboratory' science with instrumentality, positivism or the pursuit of performativity, on the contrary, it might be argued that an increasingly important dimension of such science is the pursuit of paradox and the cultivation of counter-examples. Although there is an acknowledgement of transformations in the world of science in Beck's work, in particular a transformation conceptualized in terms of a shift from primary to secondary scientization, the uncertainty and associated absence of security which are deemed to arise with 'the reflexive self-doubt of the sciences' (1992: 172) appear to be regarded as, at least in principle, remedial features which may be alleviated by a reorientation or reconstitution of scientific practice. Compare this with the discussion of transformations in the condition of knowledge offered by Lyotard, who places the emphasis on rather different aspects and draws attention to the way in which 'science – by concerning itself with such things as undecidables, the limits of precise control, conflicts characterized by incomplete information, "fracta", catastrophes, and pragmatic paradoxes – is theorizing its own evolution as discontinuous, catastrophic, non-rectifiable, and paradoxical' (1984a: 60). Whether such a science warrants the description 'postmodern' is not at issue here, but what is worth noting is that for Lyotard modern techno-scientific practice is 'driven by a dynamic independent of the things which men might judge desirable, profitable or comfortable' (1992: 98). The modern world of growing complexity depicted by Lyotard is more one to which we are subject, rather than one over which we can exercise much control, but there nevertheless seems to remain a remote possibility that a democratization of access to information and knowledge, or a demono-polization of expertise, might offer a basis for critical reflection and for 'making knowledgeable decisions' (1984a: 67).

Critical reflection on the complexity of modernization and its consequences is also a key feature of the idea of risk society. Such reflection
undermines the 'fragile clarities and pseudo-certainties' of science and could
become, Beck argues, 'the standard for a new modernity which starts from
the principles of precaution and reversibility' (1994: 33). Beck alludes to the
possibility that doubt born of critical reflection offers the prospect of a
reconstitution of 'science, knowledge, criticism or morality', albeit in a form
more modest, tentative and open to the unanticipated, and with a tolerance
derived from an appreciation of 'the ultimate final certainty of error' (ibid.:
33). The description of such a possible transformation as 'rationality
reform' is not particularly contentious, however Beck's designation of an
associated potential social order as a 'new modernity' is more controversial.
As many analysts have observed, under modern conditions techno-scientific
innovation has a dynamism all of its own, it remains unchecked, and
appears to be continually accelerating. Innovations promoting, if not
provoking, interventions which promise to realize designs and/or increase
or enhance control seem to have a momentum all of their own. In short,
humanity's narcissism finds itself 'at the service of complexification'
(Lyotard, 1992: 100). In such circumstances, the scenario for a better
future, briefly outlined by Beck, requires a humanization of technology, but
if the institutions of modernity prevail such a reform does not look a
realistic prospect. Rationality reform, and the possibility of more knowledgeable decision-making being able to restrain or rein in 'unfettered
scientific and technological development', constitute features not of a new
modernity, but of an as yet unrealized, virtually utopian social order which
lies '"beyond" modernity' (Giddens, 1990: 163–70).

Reflexivity and Sociology

In the course of his discussion of the ways in which modernization has
overrun industrial society Beck argues that it is necessary to be open to
thinking about the possibility of something emerging which is 'as yet
unknown and yet to be discovered' (1994: 25). The advice, while not
original, is sound and timely, particularly given the talk of 'new times' (Hall
and Jacques, 1989). However, Beck's speculation that the transformation of
modern industrial society will open up paths to 'new types of modernity'
does not itself represent the best demonstration of thinking the as-yet-
unknown. Beck appears to already know what will emerge if 'modernization overruns even industrial society' (1994: 25), namely another modernity,
a variation on a seemingly continuous theme. All that appears to be
unknown is what 'face' of modernity will present itself. Ironically, in a
series of critical comments on the evident unwillingness of social analysts to
recognize that industrial society represents 'only one shape of modernity',
Beck argues that sociology needs to 'become a bit of an art, that is, a bit

playful, in order to liberate itself from its own intellectual blockades' (ibid.: 24). The assumption (itself not exposed to critical reflection) that the demise of industrial modernity will open up paths to new types of modernity might be argued to exemplify one of those intellectual blockades. I am not suggesting that we are inevitably witnessing the end of industrial modernity, or any other modernity for that matter, simply that in contemplating the range of transformations identified by Beck there is no warrant for assuming that all paths into the future are predestined to lead to a form of 'modernity'. Given the extreme reflexivity of modernity, the anticipation of a particular social future, which receives expression in forms of knowledge and courses of action that transform 'the environments about which such knowledge was developed', may well serve to confound expectations of its realization (Giddens, 1991: 29). A reflexive sociology has to be mindful of the fact that the consequences of the 'institutional reflexivity' of modernity necessarily include contingency and ambivalence, consequences which have potential epistemic and ethico-political implications for the conduct of social inquiry.

The issue of reflexivity has been opened up in a number of different ways within sociology, notably in rhetorical, epistemic, and ethico-political and moral terms. A largely rhetorical and programmatic sense of reflexivity is developed by Alvin Gouldner (1972) in the context of an analysis of an anticipated 'crisis of Western sociology'. Gouldner's reflexivity represents a personal commitment to a particular kind of sociology of sociology, one which cultivates the 'viewing [of] our own beliefs as we now view those held by others', one which aims at a transformation of both the sociologist's self and 'the sociologist's relation to his[her] work' (ibid.: 490, 495). This version of reflexive sociology appears to give priority to transforming the sociologist by raising the analyst's self-awareness; it poses the question 'not merely how to *work* but how to *live*' (ibid.: 489). However, the posing of questions which appear to favour a preoccupation with the persona of the sociologist should not blind us to the additional presence of an expressed concern with the institutional conditions under which sociology is practised. As Gouldner notes, 'Reflexive Sociology assumes that any sociology develops only under certain social conditions which it is deeply committed to know' (ibid.: 498). Unfortunately, beyond a few similar rhetorical flourishes which imply that the radical potential of sociology is contained and compromised by 'the dialectic between Welfare and Warfare policies, and . . . the liberal sociologist's role as market researcher on behalf of both' (ibid.: 502), Gouldner has relatively little of substance to say on the subject of the epistemic and political conditions under which sociological knowledge is constituted. The focus of Gouldner's reflexive sociology tends to fall on particular factors 'internal' to the sociologist – on the need to cultivate 'new sensitivities' and raise 'self-awareness' – rather than on the organizational features and conventional practices of the intellectual sub-culture. A critical analysis of the latter constitutes a distinctive feature of Pierre Bourdieu's attempt to construct a rather different sociology of sociology, one characterized by epistemic reflexivity.

Bourdieu's Reflexive Sociology

Bourdieu is without doubt a major figure in contemporary social science, a figure whose work overflows conventional disciplinary boundaries and ultimately defies classification in terms of the dualistic schema that too often structure 'disciplinary space' (Wacquant, 1993: 241). If there is a specific characteristic which distinguishes Bourdieu's contribution to contemporary social theory from those of his peers then it is likely to lie with 'his signature obsession with reflexivity' (Wacquant, 1992: 36).

Bourdieu's preoccupation with reflexivity manifests itself in a concern with the milieu of knowledge production, the aim being to draw attention to features which bear on and shape processes of knowledge production. At one level there is a concern with the ways in which academic institutions and disciplinary fields shape knowledge, at another deeper level there is a preoccupation with the analytic gaze itself. In both instances the objective is to provide knowledge of the social and cultural milieu in which social science is produced in order to facilitate a degree of control of 'the effects of the determinisms that operate in this universe' (Bourdieu and Wacquant, 1992: 67), thereby enhancing the scientificity of sociological inquiry. The process of objectivizing an 'institution socially recognized as founded to claim objectivity and universality for its own objectivations' exemplifes reflexivity and constitutes for Bourdieu 'a fundamental dimension of socio-logical epistemology' (ibid.: 67, 68). What is involved here is more than an acknowledgement of the effect the class, race, and/or gender characteristics of the analyst might have on the process of knowledge production, and more than an address of the forms of determination arising from the position occupied by the analyst in the field of cultural production. What needs to receive consideration in Bourdieu's view are the consequences of the analytic gaze or intellectual orientation, the fact that 'as we observe (*theorein*) the social world, we introduce in our perception of it a bias due to the fact that, to study it, to describe it, to talk about it, we must retire from it more or less completely' (ibid.: 69).

To avoid what he terms 'epistemocentrism', analyses of the social world need to take into account that they are the product of a particular limiting gaze or orientation. Acknowledgement of the limits and limitations of scientific analysis is important, but the particular features identified in Bourdieu's promotion of a reflexive sociology are hardly novel. The question of the consequences of adopting a theoreticist or intellectual orientation towards social phenomena has already been well explored in Alfred Schutz's (1971) phenomenological analysis of different provinces of meaning and associated structures of relevance. Art, religion, everyday life, and science constitute finite provinces of meaning with their own particular structures of relevance. A sociological analysis of art, religion, or anything else for that matter, will always be subject to limitations because of the problematic relationship, or likely lack of fit, between the 'secondary' constructs or abstractions necessary for sociological inquiry and the 'primary' constructs intrinsic to the act of creation or appreciation of art, involvement in religious experience, or participation in routine, mundane forms of interaction in everyday life. The structures of relevance for the artist producing, or a viewer aesthetically appreciating a work are quite different from an analyst seeking to account for the emergence of a particular artistic work attributed with particular properties. Likewise, as Schutz notes, the structures of relevance for the sociologist engaging in an analysis of everyday life are quite different from those routinely employed by people simply preoccupied with the mundane business of living rather than analysing everyday life. People engaged in the routines of everyday life employ taken-for-granted constructs through which a sense of order and predictability is constituted and conveyed in conduct. The sociological analyst, in contrast, has to forge constructs of constructs, has to generate a more abstract level of second-order construct(s) with which to make scientific sense of everyday social life. The relationship between the two orders of constructs remains perpetually problematic, not least of all because of the complex ways in which the 'discourse of sociology and the concepts, theories and findings of the other social sciences continually "circulate in and out" of what it is that they are about. In so doing they reflexively restructure their subject matter, which itself has learned to think sociologically' (Giddens, 1990: 43).

Bourdieu seeks to differentiate his version of reflexive sociology from others developed within the American sociological tradition (e.g. Garfinkel and Gouldner) by arguing for a focus on the intellectual process, and by suggesting that a 'truly reflexive and critical analysis' represents 'the condition of scientific progress' (Bourdieu and Wacquant, 1992: 72). Gouldner's contribution receives short shrift, and is quickly dismissed as offering no more than a 'programmatic slogan' and Garfinkel is accused of being more concerned with the general issue of reflexive monitoring of action by knowledgeable agents than with the practice of sociological inquiry. Bourdieu argues that sociology itself has to be subject to critical reflexive analysis, that it 'must use its own instruments to find out what it is and what it is doing, to try to know better where it stands' (ibid.: 191). In short, sociology has to put its own house in order, to reconstitute itself.

There are a number of issues which arise here. To begin with it might be argued that the history of sociological inquiry is replete with different attempts to explore what the discipline is about, what it is doing, where it stands, and what its impact might be. In this context it is difficult to understand the dismissal of phenomenological and ethnomethodological contributions to an understanding and reconstitution of the practice of sociology (O'Malley, 1971; O'Neill, 1972), for they exemplify many of the features which subsequently have been ascribed to reflexive sociology by

Bourdieu. It is also worth asking whether the objective, or intended effect, of critical reflexive sociological analysis is confined solely to the achievement of an increase in the quality and quantity of sociological knowledge, as Bourdieu's comments frequently imply, or whether more is at stake.

Sociology, Reflexivity and Ethics

The nub of Bourdieu's argument is that the practice of reflexivity offers the prospect of more and better science, but there is also the suggestion that with 'the progress of science and . . . the growth of knowledge about the social world, *reflexivity makes possible a more responsible politics*' (Bourdieu and Wacquant, 1992: 194). This represents a clear endorsement of the assumptions and main objectives of the modern project and suggests a possible parallel with the general position taken by Beck in his analysis of the prospects for a new modernity, notably that modernity is ultimately capable of putting itself to rights. Elaborating on the practice of reflexive sociology, Bourdieu argues that it 'can help free intellectuals from their illusions – and first of all from the illusion that they do not have any, especially about themselves' (ibid.: 195). Reflexive sociology is to function as a disoccluding practice, one which brings unthought elements to thought, unconscious contributions to consciousness. Such a sociology is identified as offering the prospect not simply of better science, but, in so far as the latter facilitates identification of sites for the exercise of responsible action, it could also be said to constitute, or contain, an 'ethic'. As science increases awareness of formerly concealed or unconscious determinations, so Bourdieu argues 'a form of freedom which is the condition and correlate of an ethic is [made] possible' (ibid.: 198). In this way reflexive sociology is credited with making possible a greater awareness of the circumstances in which we find ourselves, as well as the contexts and/or respects in which we may find a degree of freedom and thereby face up to the prospect of taking responsibility for our actions. Such a form of sociology opens up 'the possibility of identifying true sites of freedom, and thus of building small-scale, modest, practical morals in keeping with the scope of human freedom' (ibid.: 199). It is this claim which leads Wacquant to make reference to Bourdieu's 'ethical conception of sociology as a sort of *social maieutics*' (ibid.: 200). But there is relatively little further consideration of the ethical dimension of reflexive sociology. Reflexive sociology is to function as a form of analysis which facilitates a greater understanding of the context and practice of analysis, and in so far as it increases consciousness of the 'genesis of problems, categories of thought, and instruments of analysis' it may offer the prospect of a degree of freedom from social determinations, and may thereby produce a more rigorous science with the potential to achieve a 'liberating awakening of consciousness' (ibid.: 213–14, 215), a very familiar theme which has already informed several variants of critical sociological inquiry.

Unlike what Bourdieu describes as 'ordinary sociology', that is a form of sociology which neglects to question its ways of working and thinking about the social world, reflexive sociology is described as practising 'radical doubt'. Ironically it is precisely a distinction of the order outlined above – 'ordinary' ('traditional' or 'positivistic') v. 'reflexive' – which lies at the heart of phenomenological sociology and Garfinkel's ethnomethodology, forms of inquiry from which Bourdieu has attempted to distance himself by arguing that they neglect to address 'the conditions of possibility of . . . doxic experience' (ibid.: 73), a criticism which if it applies to some versions of phenomenological sociology certainly does not exhaust possibilities (cf. O'Neill, 1972). Furthermore, the issue identified by Bourdieu of the unwillingness of professional sociologists to investigate traditional socio- logical ways of working and thinking is also part of the problem to which phenomenological sociology has been directed through a process of 'suspension of belief', 'bracketing' or 'reduction', terms which signify the Husserlian practice of radical doubt employed against the 'natural attitude, which characterizes both the commonsense attitude of everyday life and the attitude of the naive natural and cultural sciences' (Filmer et al., 1972: 127, 128). Evidence of such shared concerns, to which others could be added, for example the common identification of the problem of language for the sociologist – 'an immense repository of naturalized preconstructions . . . that are ignored as such and which can function as unconscious instruments of construction' (Bourdieu and Wacquant, 1992: 241), as well as remarks on the danger of substituting a naive doxa of 'scholarly' common sense for the 'lay' equivalent (ibid.: 248) – radically reduce the distinctiveness of Bourdieu's conception of reflexive sociology.

However, it is not Bourdieu's apparent lack of appreciation of the existence of a considerable degree of common ground between the practice of reflexive sociology emanating from the auspices of phenomenological sociology and his own later version which I want to emphasize here, but the brevity with which the ethical dimension of sociology is addressed. Is the topic exhausted by brief references to the way(s) in which sociological knowledge of determinations may increase awareness of the respects in which we do, and do not, have degrees of freedom to exercise respon- sibility? Or are there other important ethical aspects of social analysis which need to be addressed? In so far as Bourdieu's priority is to promote the virtues of 'epistemic' reflexivity, the ethical dimension identified as a potential corollary is left largely unexplored. In particular, no considera- tion is given to the possibility that increases in awareness in everyday social life, arising from a diffusion of insights gained from more reflexive sociological practices, may contribute to the undermining of values and beliefs through which a 'sense of connection, shared fate, mutual respon- sibility, [and] community' (Bellah et al., 1996: xxx) is constituted. Or to put it another way, Bourdieu appears to be oblivious to the possibility that the features which may be appropriate to the scientific relevance structure of reflexive sociology may become 'highly problematic when transferred to the relevance structure of everyday life' (Berger and Kellner, 1982: 158).

In so far as modernity is indeed 'intrinsically sociological' (Giddens, 1990), it is inappropriate and irresponsible to address the question of sociological reflexivity primarily in epistemic or cognitive terms and to neglect associated ethical concerns. Directly and indirectly sociology plays a vital role in 'the organically self-reflective life, in which we all live' (Bauman, 1992a: 215), a role which includes an important ethical dimension. Charles Taylor has remarked that reflexivity is 'central to our moral understanding' (1989: 139) and although the primary focus of his analysis is the making of modern identity, his observation is no less relevant for the practice of sociological inquiry, for sociology plays a prominent part in the constitution of modern identity. An important responsibility of reflexive sociology is to attempt to provide an understanding of the moral difficulties and ethical dilemmas which have arisen with modernity, including in particular the various ways in which assumptions intrinsic to forms of social inquiry may inform, transform, or for that matter merely naively reflect and reinforce, expressions of subjectivity, patterns of conduct and rationales intrinsic to modern social life.

In the related terms employed by Mary Douglas, what is required of reflexive sociology is that it gives critical consideration to the problematic consequences of the late-modern 'cultural pressure to delegitimize control and to license ever more exploiting, escaping and expanding' (1994: 261), and that, in turn, it directs attention to the question of the kind of society that might curb such pressure. The immediate focus of the analysis provided by Douglas is the impact on the biosphere of the modern cultural pressure to continually expand and exploit, that is the problematic consequences of a form of life which has 'successfully presented a steady, cumulative argument in favour of expansion, individual freedom, [and] the sloughing off of chains and shackles' (ibid.). The absence of any effective response to the problematic environmental consequences of a globalized modernity leads Douglas to remark that 'we can only see one good society, our own culture' and that it is necessary to contemplate and appreciate other possibilities, other forms of life, if 'our long-established predatory and expansionary trend' (ibid.: 265, 266) is to be countered.

Although the argument Douglas presents for a reflexive sociology is concentrated on the environmental risks associated with modernity, the analysis offered opens up a wider range of ethico-political matters. Recognition of the possible virtues of other forms of life, Douglas suggests, may already be present 'informally and privately', the assumption being that individually we are 'capable of recognizing ourself in the Other and, without losing sight of the quality of otherness, we are individually capable of embracing the stranger' (ibid.: 262). However, the fact that individually we may possess a quality or ability does not mean that it is routinely expressed or employed in face-to-face encounters. We may be capable of recognizing ourself in the other, of appreciating the other, but nevertheless routinely neglect to do so. For Douglas the existence of an informal and private capability to appreciate others is important, for it raises the prospect of a more public and collective appreciation of the virtues of other forms of life, which in turn may provide something which is currently lacking in a world seduced by the imperatives of capitalist modernity, notably other models of the 'good society'. The critical question is how such 'potential' is to be realized.

In her concluding remarks on the risks of modernity and the virtues of reflexivity Douglas endorses the view that concern needs to be 'transmuted into responsibility' (ibid.: 268). However, standing in the way of the realization, or constitution, of a more responsible self, a self mindful of 'obligations of solidarity and community', is a culture of 'therapeutic con-tractualism' (Bellah et al., 1996: xxxv), a culture which Douglas identifies as the source of passive or blame-free 'modes of conceiving the person' (1994; 229–30). It is such modes of conceiving the person which have contributed to the distancing of modern subjects from moral responsibility.

4

RESPONSIBLE SUBJECTS

A rhetoric of responsibility, including pronouncements on the responsibility of agents of various kinds, and in particular the responsibility of *human* agents or subjects for their actions and conduct, has become a prominent and controversial feature of the contemporary political agenda. But if the question of responsibility has become prominent in contemporary social and political discourse, associated ethical implications have rarely been given the analytic consideration they warrant. The (ir)responsibilities of corporate and governmental agents for the production of risks with local and/or global implications have been identified as increasingly problematic features of a late or reflexive modernity, but the ethical dimension has, for the most part, remained implicit (Beck, 1992; Grove-White, 1996). The questioning, and in some cases the reduction, of forms of public provision of health, education and welfare services following the closer embrace of a market philosophy and the implementation of further rounds of economic restructuring, which includes a turn towards post-Fordist, more flexible forms of capital accumulation, is one of the contexts, if not for some the primary context, in which the idea, and the presumed necessity, of individuals looking after themselves, making choices, and thereby supposedly assuming more responsibility for their care and their fate, has been increasingly advanced. The implied distinction between 'public' and 'private', and the associated reality of a shift, or more appropriately off-loading, of responsibility from 'state' to 'individual' is one of the themes currently preoccupying the modern polity. This transformation has led, as Bauman observes, to 'a hard time for moral responsibility; not only in its immediate effects on the poor and unfortunate who need a society of responsible people most, but also (and perhaps, in the long run primarily) in its lasting effects on the (potentially) moral selves. It recasts "being for Others", that cornerstone of all morality, as a matter of accounts and calculation' (1993: 244). In circumstances where the *telos* of being has increasingly become the enhancement of self-interest, and the latter is closely identified with material wellbeing and obtaining value for money, 'the enterprise self' (Douglas, 1994) effectively becomes a consumer, for whom meaningful others are primarily the producers of commodities and the bearers of services. As an intrinsic concern for others has become more marginal, so the expectation of assuming or exercising moral responsibility has diminished.

I intend to respond to the question of responsibility implied in the above, to focus on the ethical dimension which a number of analysts contributing to the debate over the transformation of modernity have sought to retrieve (Jonas, 1984; Tester, 1993; Bauman, 1993), but to do so through a critical interpretation of Michel Foucault's reflections on power, freedom and subjectivity. Drawing on the work of Emmanuel Levinas, I will be trying to determine what, if anything, Foucault has to say on the subject of responsibility.

One of the key issues which has surfaced in discussions of the transformation of modernity is that of a relative shift of emphasis, from a subsumption of the 'moral regulation of conduct . . . under the legislative and law-enforcing activity of global societal institutions', to a situation in which rather than a singular authoritative source, to which one can turn or appeal for guidance, agents increasingly encounter a 'pluralism of authorities', and in turn are required to take responsibility and make choices for their 'self-constitution' (Bauman, 1992a: 201–4). The undermining of the prospect of outlining universally binding rules of conduct for agents and the concomitant necessary 'resumption by agents of moral responsibility', identified as a corollary of the increasing pluralism of authority, has led Bauman to conclude that ethical questions and problems can no longer be marginalized in the analysis of modern society.

It is precisely the identification of the human subject as a moral subject, as an active and creative subject, which has been recognized as a significant and distinctive feature of Foucault's later writings. It is to a number of matters which arise in relation to Foucault's analytic treatment of issues of subjectivity and responsibility that I will be attempting to address my remarks in this chapter. There are four particular concerns to be explored in the course of my discussion of Foucault's work, namely:

(i)   Conception of the subject.
(ii)   Government of conduct.
(iii) Care of the self and related conception of an 'aesthetics of existence'.
(iv)   Question of the responsibility of the (moral) subject.

The Question of the Subject

The late appearance in Foucault's work of an explicit address of the question of the subject has already been well-documented (Dews, 1989; Smart, 1991). Prior to Foucault's turn to the question of the subject, the focus of his work fell almost entirely upon the exercise of power through 'sovereignty-discipline-government' (Foucault, 1979). In a subsequent reconstitution of the project Foucault acknowledges that, in the examination of the specific technologies related to 'truth games' employed by human beings to understand themselves, too much attention may have been devoted to technologies of domination and power, that is technologies which 'determine the conduct of individuals and submit them to certain ends' (Foucault, 1988a: 18). Foucault then adds that he is 'more and more interested in *the interaction between oneself and others* and in the technologies of individual domination, the history of how an individual acts upon himself [herself], in the technology of self' (ibid.: 19, emphasis added). The turn to the subject, and in particular the way in which 'a human being turns him or herself into a subject' (Foucault, 1982: 208), represents a belated compensation for the earlier neglect of the active subject, the ethical subject, in Foucault's work.

What does Foucault's later work, that is the texts, essays and interviews which emerge with his final 'theoretical shift', tell us about his understanding of the subject? As I have implied above, in his work up to and including the first volume on *The History of Sexuality* the subject appears primarily as an effect of social practices of subjection. A constituting (and therefore potentially moral) subject is absent from Foucault's discourse at this stage. In the first volume on sexuality the issue of the constitution of forms of subjectivity is addressed, but it is through a consideration of objectifying confessional technologies, in which the truth and meaning of the subject is communicated by an interpreter/therapist who is an 'other', albeit a significant one. If there is any consideration of the subject's self-constitution it is in terms of the articulation of accounts, dreams, and fictions which constitute discursive material for investigation and interpretation by others who reveal the 'truth' of the tales and thereby the 'truth' of the subject. It is the silence over the question of the self-constituting practices of the subject which leads critics to equate a bleak politics of resignation with Foucault's work – no escape from domination and relations of power, resistance inevitably undermined, and so forth. As I have implied above, it is difficult not to regard Foucault's late re-direction of his project towards technologies of the self as constituting a response to his critics, as constituting an acknowledgement that there is indeed a case to answer.

Although Foucault says in the Vermont interview that he is more and more interested in 'the interaction between oneself and others', there are in practice few significant signs in his work of a serious consideration of social interaction; relatively few analytic explorations of the interactional contexts in which selves are socially constituted. In consequence it is understandable that critics should have concluded that 'his ethics privileges a notion of the self establishing a relation with the self, rather than understanding the self as embedded in and formed through types of social interaction' (McNay, 1992: 163–4). The impression which emerges from Foucault's work is of self-constitution, or self-stylization, as a relatively solitary or isolated process. Where we might ask is the interactional context actually addressed in the analysis; where is the interest in social interaction between oneself and others made manifest? And can an approach to the question of self-formation or self-stylization which appears to neglect social interaction provide a sound basis for the cultivation of a modern ethics of existence?

I am not implying here that the practices of the ancient Greeks constituted an attractive alternative or model for Foucault, indeed he goes out of his way to correct such a potential misunderstanding, commenting that Classical Antiquity 'is not anything to get back to' (1986a: 347).

However, there is a sense in which he does seem to be arguing, as McNay comments, that 'they provide important insights for a modern ethics' (1992: 164; Foucault, 1989: 311). In particular, it is through reflection on the moral world of ancient Greece that Foucault is able to reach the conclusion that there is no necessary link between ethics and other social structures and that we can therefore 'create ourselves'.

Governing Conduct: Political Technology of Individuals and Technologies of the Self

Notwithstanding the several attempts which have been made to read into Foucault's earlier works concerns which receive an explicit address in later writings, there is evidence of a significant change of analytic emphasis from a focus upon the government of individualization, achieved through a political technology of individuals, to a consideration of technologies of the self 'which permit individuals to effect *by their own means or with the help of others* a certain number of operations on their own bodies and souls, thoughts, conduct, and way of being, so as to transform themselves in order to attain a certain state of happiness, purity, wisdom, perfection, or immortality' (Foucault, 1988a: 18, emphasis added).

Foucault's turn to questions concerning self-constitution follows a series of observations on struggles against the government of individualization – 'against forms of subjectivity and submission' – and an overdue attempt to offer clarification of the ambiguous notion of power. The clarification is significant because it introduces the notion of a 'free' subject – that is 'individual or collective subjects who are faced with a field of possibilities in which several ways of behaving, several reactions and diverse comportments may be realized' (Foucault, 1982: 221) – in relation to whom power is exercised. But the clarification of power, specified as a 'set of actions upon other [possible] actions', or again as 'guiding the possibility of conduct and putting in order the possible outcome' (ibid.), does not lead, at this point at least, to an equivalent consideration of the subject, enigmatically identified as possessing a recalcitrant will, and as being intransigent about freedom. Indeed, Foucault admits to finding it necessary to undertake a theoretical shift 'to analyse what is termed "the subject" . . . the forms and modalities of the relation to self by which the individual constitutes and recognizes himself *qua* subject' (1987b: 6). It is a shift through which the question of relations of power is reformulated as a question about government, a question about the leading, guidance, or direction of conduct or action; a question about the structuring of 'the possible field of action of others'.

But rather than resolve matters, Foucault's clarification of relations of power raises a series of further questions. Relations of power for Foucault are synonymous with sociality. Power is held to be always present in human relations, 'whether it be a question of communicating verbally . . . or a question of a love relationship, an institutional or economic relationship' (Foucault, 1987a: 122). Power relations are relations in which influence is exercised over the conduct of free subjects, and as Foucault puts it, 'only in so far as they are free' (1982: 221). Such free subjects are considered to have the potential to block, change, overturn or reverse a relation of guidance, direction, or influence. Is there an implication here that the subject is, in part at least, responsible for his/her own fate, in so far as there is always the potential to transform a relation of power into an adversarial confrontation? And what of the responsibilities intrinsic to the exercise of power and associated relations of guidance and direction, the responsibilities which might be argued to be a corollary of actions which structure the field of other possible actions? It is not clear where Foucault stands on the question of the responsibility of the subject in this, or for that matter any other sense. Indeed it might be argued that there remains a significant silence in his work over the question of the extent to which the subject is, or can be, active and responsible, although his own practice as a politically active philosopher, as an engaged 'specific' intellectual, and in particular his brief reflections on intellectual practice, seem to tell a different tale. For example, in 'Truth and Power' (1980) and 'Questions of Method: An Interview' (1987c) Foucault appears to be quite categorical about the responsibility of the contemporary intellectual subject. The intellectual can no longer convincingly claim to be the 'bearer of universal values', rather the contemporary intellectual is considered to occupy a position which has a 'three-fold specificity' in respect of social class, 'his conditions of life and work', and most significantly according to Foucault, the 'politics of truth in our societies' (1980: 132). It is in relation to the latter that the function of the intellectual may 'take on a general significance', notably in a context where an implied responsibility to work to ascertain 'the possibility of constituting a new politics of truth' (ibid.: 133) is honoured. However, while it is primarily around the last of the three aspects noted above that Foucault chose to elaborate his conception of the contemporary intellectual's role, the second aspect, 'conditions of life and work', has become a matter of some importance in reflections on Foucault, *the man* and his work.

It is ironic that Foucault, the analyst who remarked on the 'disappearance or death of the author' (1977: 117), the man who in an analysis of the modern epistemological configuration commented 'that man would be erased, like a face drawn in sand at the edge of the sea' (1973: 387), should himself after death have become the object of a form of analysis which claims to find a close and telling affinity between the author's life and his work. Having sought to remove the face from discourse, literally to efface it, Foucault, cast as a Dionysian figure, has been summoned back to support a thesis claiming a unity and coherence to his life and work (Miller, 1993). The more voyeuristic biographical details of the private Foucault's pursuit of personal pleasures and experiences in the urban male homosexual sado-masochistic sub-culture of San Francisco, outlined by Miller, tell the tale of a subject seemingly oblivious to the *ethos* of care of self and others. The Foucault drawn by Miller is a figure in pursuit of limit-experiences, a figure intensely preoccupied with self-fashioning, a highly individualized self for whom the issue of responsibility for others appears to have little, if any, significance.

Foucault's reflections on the subject reveal a preoccupation with the idea of a freely chosen life, a preoccupation with the possibility of freely constituting oneself, and there seems to be no place for a sense of moral responsibility for the other in his articulation of the notion of a freely chosen 'aesthetics of existence'. As Alasdair MacIntyre remarks, 'we have good reason to be suspicious of any contemporary ethics of free choice, according to which each individual makes of her or his life a work of art. For something very like this aestheticization of the moral, which places the choices of each individual at the core of her or his moral life and represents these choices as an expression of that individual's creativity, is characteristic of advanced capitalistic modernity' (1993: 60), a form of social and cultural life which continually prioritizes the interest(s) of self over and above other(s).

Foucault seems to continually evade the issue of responsibility. For example, in addressing the issue of the self-constitution of the subject through technologies of the self Foucault is categorical – 'these practices are . . . not something that the individual invents by himself. They are patterns that he finds in his culture and which are *proposed, suggested, imposed on him by his culture, his society and his social group*' (1987a: 122, emphasis added). Whilst such an observation may seem relatively uncontentious it does leave open and unanswered the respect(s) in which subjects are, or can be, recognized as active and responsible, as opposed to being simply relays for the discharge of culturally given technologies of (self-) government. To be more precise, and to address directly one of Foucault's later preoccupations, in what sense is it appropriate, given the above, to talk of 'creating oneself', and if so on what basis does it become possible 'to create oneself'? Foucault takes the view that 'the self is not given to us . . . [and] that there is only one practical consequence: we have to create ourselves as a work of art' (1986a: 351). It is through a process of reflection on similarities and differences between the Greek world and the modern West that the conclusion that the self is not given to us is reached. Foucault argues that some of our main ethical principles 'have been related at a certain moment to an aesthetics of existence' and that an important conclusion can be drawn from this, namely that 'the idea of an analytical or necessary link between ethics and other social or economic or political structures' (ibid.: 350) is unfounded. There are two points to be made here. First, Foucault's view is simply asserted rather than convincingly demonstrated. Second, the idea that there is no 'necessary link' does not mean that the constitution of the self as a moral subject of action can be considered free of social, economic or political structures and processes.

Foucault's own references to cultural practices which are proposed, suggested and imposed draw attention to, but unfortunately neglect to explore, the complex social contexts in which forms of subjectivity are actually constituted, and within which subjects participate, along with others, in processes of mutual self-development. An acknowledgement of the formation of the self through social interaction is not entirely absent from Foucault's work, for example brief reference is made to individuals transforming themselves through the help of others and in addition attention is drawn to the importance in the development of care for the self of the role of a counsellor, guide, friend, master, 'who will tell you the truth' (1987a: 118), but no attempt is made to elaborate on such references, to explore the implied non-reciprocal relationship with the other which is at the very heart of social life, the ethical significance of which might be argued to be anterior to a relation with the self (Levinas, 1989; Bauman, 1993; Heller, 1994).

A further qualification needs to be introduced at this point concerning Foucault's notion of the subject. The discussion of the subject offered by Foucault for the most part appears to be confined to considerations of the constitution of particular forms of subjectivity – mad, sick, delinquent, sexual – and does not entertain any notion of the subject in general (Foucault, 1989: 313, 329–30). When questioned on this matter Foucault acknowledges that a rejection of an '*a priori* theory of the subject' was necessary to allow analysis of the relations which can exist between 'different forms of the subject and games of truth, practices of power and so forth' (1987a: 121). Questioned further on the implications of his position Foucault attempts to offer clarification. It is argued that the subject:

> is a form and this form is not above all or always identical to itself. You do not have towards yourself the same kind of relationships when you constitute yourself as a political subject who goes and votes or speaks up in a meeting, and when you try to fulfill your desires in a sexual relationship. There are no doubt some relationships and some interferences between these different kinds of subject but we are not in the presence of the same kind of subject. In each case, we play, we establish with one's self some different form of relationship. (Foucault, 1987a: 121)

The existence under modern conditions of different forms of subjectivity is not contentious. But do references to 'some relationships and some interferences' between different kinds of subject, and the discussion of the 'free subject' in particular, suggest something more, perhaps the presence of an unclarified sense of an auto-biographicalizing, albeit de-centred, subject? In Foucault's narrative there is an understanding of the self as reflexive and creative, that is a self aware of its constitution through social and cultural 'practices of the self', a self aware of the latitude such practices may allow and the possibilities they may provide for self-transformation, for being able to (re)fashion 'self'. It is such a Goffmanesque sense of the subject 'making out' which seems to inform Foucault's promotion of the virtues of an ethical stylization of the self as necessary for an era in which 'the idea of morality as obedience to a code of rules is now disappearing, has already disappeared' (Foucault, 1989: 311). Is there a trace here of something approaching a universalist normativity in Foucault's espousal of an ethical stylization of the self? Certainly critics such as Rochlitz believe that Foucault's discussion of the aesthetics of existence contains 'a normative content, even a virtually universalist normativity: referring to a requirement for the autonomy of the person and opposition to unjust suffering' (1992: 250). But, as I have already briefly suggested above, there is another more significant problem associated with Foucault's discussion of the subject, namely the absence of any consideration of the question of moral responsibility.

The idea of a progressive governmentalization of power relations 'under the auspices of the state' draws attention to the ways in which the exercise of action upon other possible actions has become increasingly 'elaborated, rationalized and centralized' (Foucault, 1982: 224) – in effect routinized. It is precisely through this process that moral responsibility for action has been argued to be undermined and usurped by legislation of 'universal rule-dictated *duties*' (Bauman, 1993: 54) associated with the formation of the modern state practising a pastoral form of power, that is exercising a 'government of individuals' (Foucault, 1981a: 240). Signs of increasing discontent with legal-rational intervention 'in our moral, personal, [and] private life' led Foucault to identify a possible parallel between the present and Classical Antiquity, namely the existence of a comparable concern with ethics, with relations to self and others. In effect, although Foucault does not use these terms, a comparable concern with the responsibilities of the subject in the absence of any secure foundations (see Foucault, 1986a: 343).

There are a number of questions which might be posed at this juncture. Is the parallel drawn by Foucault between the present and Classical Antiquity one that extends no further than similarities in respect of problems, or is there, notwithstanding denials to the contrary, a sense in which a way of approaching contemporary predicaments is being sought in Classical Antiquity? Foucault certainly implies that something may be learnt from the Greeks about the self, specifically that it has no truth, that there is no true self which analysis can decipher, rather that the self has to be continually created, hence the emphasis placed upon an 'aesthetics of existence' (1986a: 350) and the articulation of what has been described as 'an ethic for which freedom lies . . . in a constant attempt at self-disengagement and self-invention' (Rajchman, 1985: 38). And when reference is made to the need to be aware that 'everything is dangerous', and that as a corollary it becomes necessary to make ethico-political choices concerning 'the main danger', is Foucault (1986a: 343) not assuming the presence of that very form of subjectivity which he neglects to analyse and which may be argued to be in jeopardy, namely the morally responsible self, responsibly identifying and determining how to respond to the main danger?

An Ethic of Responsibility

Ethics constitutes a practice for Foucault, a mode of being, a way of relating to self and thereby others. Elaborating on his analyses of the Greco-Roman world, Foucault argues that caring for the self, to know and improve one's self, and to exercise mastery over passions and appetites, was fundamental to 'ethics, as a deliberate practice of liberty' (1987a: 116). In short, care for the self is depicted as taking moral precedence over care for others. In contrast, it is suggested by Foucault that for us a preoccupation with the self has generally been viewed with suspicion and that instead the tendency has been to place emphasis upon sacrifice of the self and care of others. While asceticism has undoubtedly contributed to the cultural formation of Western modernity, Foucault's viewpoint is hard to reconcile with the culture and politics of a late, increasingly consumer-orientated capitalism, one in which a preoccupation with the self and the promotion of self-interest is not only a commonplace, but is widely promoted and celebrated as a virtue. Suspicions concerning 'self' preoccupation have been largely suspended, if not dissolved altogether with the establishment of a culture of 'therapeutic contractualism' (Bellah et al., 1996), a culture in which a preoccupation with self and self-fulfilment has become the norm.

Care for the self, for the Greeks, involved the establishment of self-mastery, the embodiment of a mode of being in which self-control rather than passions and appetites was paramount. For Foucault such a care for self necessarily implies relations with others:

> Care for self is ethical in itself, but implies complex relations with others, in the measure where this *ethos* of freedom is also a way of caring for others . . . *Ethos* implies also a relation with others to the extent that care for self renders one competent to occupy a place in the city, in the community or in interindividual relationships . . . And the care for self implies also a relationship to the other to the extent that, in order to really care for self, one must listen to the teachings of a master . . . [T]he problem of relationship with others is present all along this development of care for self. (Foucault, 1987a: 118)

What then are we to make of Foucault's understanding? The precedence accorded to care for self is controversial, particularly if the relation to the Other, responsibility for the other, is to be placed, as Heller (1994) suggests, at the centrepoint in ethics. One implication here is that Foucault's interpretation of the Greeks is problematic. McNay remarks that it is highly selective, that although the ancient Greeks 'may have exercised a degree of liberty in the control of their daily lives, this liberty was nonetheless embedded in a network of social and political obligations. In other words, the ancient Greek sense of the self was always informed by those "analytical and necessary" links that Foucault wishes individuals in contemporary society to divest themselves of' (1992: 164). It is worth adding, as Caputo reminds us, that the cost of the constitution of a particular sense of the self was borne by marginalized, effectively faceless

others, 'the originary *ethos* . . . [being] constituted by an act of exclusion –
of whatever is not free, male, and Greek' (1989: 58).

Is an ethical relationship to the other implied in the contemporary search
for styles of existence affirmed by Foucault? Can such an ethical relation be
assumed in a context where promotion of the pursuit of self-interest on
behalf of the 'modern individual' has diminished, if not in some instances
erased, any sense of responsibility for the other? It is all very well talking
about creating ourselves as a work of art, but is such a preoccupation with
the self conducive to caring, or showing responsibility, for others? Differences identified between the ancient Greek culture of the self, in which
emphasis is placed upon aesthetics and the importance of 'exercising a
perfect mastery over oneself' (Foucault, 1986a: 362) through imposition of
'austerity practices' (effectively a government of the self which allegedly
simultaneously exemplified a responsibility towards others), and the
modern hedonistic cult of the self, in which the 'relationship to the self no
longer needs to be ascetic to get into relation to the truth' (ibid.: 371), on
the contrary 'truth' of the self is revealed through the practices of science,
suggest not. The modern subject is constituted through the human sciences
and associated normative disciplines, largely independently of ethical
concerns. And yet, as Levinas (1989), and subsequently Bauman (1990) and
Heller (1994) remind us, the ethical 'face' has not been entirely effaced, the
moral gesture has not been completely erased or lost. The significant
difference between the moderns and pre-moderns is that we 'rationalize
ethics'; we 'query and test the contents of most traditional moral customs
and virtues' (Heller, 1994: 52). The seemingly endless processes of questioning, interpretation, rejection and innovation which have become an
intrinsic feature of modern life risk 'discrediting moral gestures fully' and
lead Heller to the conclusion that '[m]oderns need to remind themselves
constantly of the transcendent, absolute character of the first gesture [of
taking responsibility for the other] to protect morals from being colonized
by sheer immanent/cognitive claims' (ibid.: 52). Is there any recognition of,
or place for, such a 'gesture' in Foucault's work?

Foucault's late preoccupation was to dwell on the question of how it
might be possible to free ethical concerns from dependence upon knowledge
– 'My idea is that it's not at all necessary to relate ethical problems to
scientific knowledge' (1986a: 349). We might go further, indeed we should
perhaps go much further, for subjecting ethical matters to scientific interrogation has tended to 'decentre the real moral questions' (Heller, 1994: 50)
and diminish the moral self. It has led to the present situation in which
the (potential) moral self 'has been dissembled into traits; the totality of the
moral subject has been reduced to the collection of parts or attributes of
which no one can conceivably be ascribed moral subjectivity. Actions are
then targeted on specific traits of persons rather than persons themselves,
by-passing or avoiding altogether the moment of encounter with morally
significant effects' (Bauman, 1993: 127). The question then becomes how
might it be possible to regenerate an ethic of responsibility which has been

undermined by the prevalence of a modern legislative coding of rules of conduct. While Foucault identifies and explores some of the influences which have contributed to the formation of particular modern forms of subjectivity (e.g. Christian asceticism and the renunciation of the self and subsequently the human sciences disclosure of the truth of the self and positive constitution of 'a new self' [Foucault, 1988a: 49]) he neglects to consider the implications for moral responsibility, for the moral self.

Foucault may not engage directly with the question of the responsibility of the subject, but is it perhaps implied in his critical reflections on the neglect of 'the question of an ethical subject . . . in contemporary political thought' (1987a: 125)? If so it needs to be addressed more directly, particularly in the light of enigmatic remarks on the need to 'search for styles of existence as different as possible from each other' (1989: 330). Although questions of ethics only receive an explicit address with Foucault's later writings on Classical Antiquity it has been argued that a concern with the moral implications of modernity is present throughout his work (Rajchman, 1985; Bernauer, 1992). For example, it might be noted that in an early work on mental pathology Foucault depicts the modern relationship to the self as becoming possible from the moment 'reason ceased to be for man an ethic and became a nature' (1976: 87). And in a subsequent analysis of the human sciences Foucault can be credited with making a series of observations on the inability of modern thought to be able 'to propose a morality', an inability that is bound up with the fact that modern thought is 'both knowledge and a modification of what it knows, reflection and a transformation of the mode of being of that on which it reflects. Whatever it touches it immediately causes to move' (1973: 327).

Notwithstanding the fact that it is only with a theoretical shift towards an analysis of the subject that the issue of 'self-formation as an "ethical subject" (Foucault, 1987b: 28) receives a sustained consideration, it has been suggested, as I have noted above, that a subterranean ethical concern runs through all of Foucault's writings. The ethic identified is for thought and it is described as 'a practice which educates . . . readers into an ethical responsibility for intellectual inquiry' (Bernauer, 1992: 269). It is an 'ethic for the intellectual' (Rajchman, 1985: 124), 'an ethic of responsibility for the truth one speaks, for the political strategies into which these truths enter, and for those ways of relating to ourselves that make us either conformists or resisters to those relations. It is a timely ethic *which assists in reclaiming thought's moral responsibilities*' (Bernauer, 1992: 271, emphasis added); a critical practice which attempts to open up new ways of thinking.

But does an ethic of responsibility for intellectual inquiry exhaust the possible ethical implications of Foucault's later works on the subject and technologies of the self? Is there, and/or ought there to be more? What bearing, if any, does such an ethic of the intellectual, an ethic of responsibility for the truth one speaks, have on the elementary, or perhaps a more appropriate term would be the primary ethical matter of care and responsibility for others? Are there ethical implications beyond those identified with intellectual inquiry and the sphere of pleasure? In short are there wider implications concerning the responsibility of the subject in relation to others, in relation to the question of how we might (should) live?

Reflecting on the Greek cultivation of the self Foucault notes that while it was articulated by philosophers, knowing 'how "to perfect one's own soul with the help of reason" is a rule "equally necessary for all"' (1988b: 48). On the question of care of the self Foucault notes that it constituted a 'true social practice' not an exercise in solitude. The activity of taking care of the self involved communications with others, with guides, advisers and confidants – 'the care of the self and the help of the other blends into preexisting relations . . . The care of the self – *or the attention one devotes to the care that others should take of themselves* – appears then as an intensification of social relations' (Foucault, 1988b: 53, emphasis added). And again – 'The care of the self appears therefore as intrinsically linked to a "soul service", which includes the possibility of a round of exchanges with the other and a system of reciprocal obligations' (ibid.: 54). If such references do suggest wider implications, and I believe they do, they also suggest that the idea of an ethical relation between care of the self and care for others is more contentious than Foucault seems to allow, as is the implied ethical linking of responsibility with reciprocity (cf. Bauman, 1993: 220). It is only possible for care of the self to encompass care for others if there is from the beginning, if there is *already*, a responsibility for the other, an unmeasured and unmeasurable non-reciprocal responsibility which is 'anterior to all the logical deliberation summoned by reasoned decision' (Levinas, 1987a: 111). A relationship of responsibility with and for the other characterizes our social life and it is a relationship in which, as Levinas argues, 'I have to respond to and for the Other without occupying myself with the Other's responsibility in my regard' (1987a: 137). It is from the initial moral bearing of being responsible, or taking or assuming responsibility for the other, that a particular ethical practice of caring for the self follows.

Responsibility for Others: Foucault and Levinas

In discussing the Greeks, Foucault makes reference to a close relationship between care of the self and care for others. Exercise of self-mastery or self-government is regarded as a necessary precondition for the government of others. Indeed 'rationality of the government of oneself' is held to be the same as the 'rationality of the government of others' (Foucault, 1988b: 89). Being concerned with oneself, taking care of oneself, is an activity, an activity which is accorded significance because caring correctly for the self is considered to promote correct behaviour 'in relationship to others and for others' (Foucault, 1987a: 118). Throughout there is an implication that potential parallels might be drawn between Classical Antiquity and our present in respect of the intensity of relations to self, but there are also, as I have already indicated, important differences. For example, whereas in Greco-Roman culture it was taking care of the self which led to knowledge of oneself, in modern Western society emphasis is placed upon the necessity of coming to 'know' in order to be able to 'take care of' the self.

In so far as our morality has been formed primarily through the combined influence of Christianity, with its notions of asceticism and self-renunciation, and a 'secular tradition which respects external law as the basis for morality' (Foucault, 1988a: 22), the idea that a rigorous morality might be based upon giving priority to caring for ourselves has been identified by Foucault as difficult to accept. Foucault argues that because we have inherited a social morality which 'seeks the rules of acceptable behaviour in relations with others' (ibid.: 22), the very idea of care of the self appears morally problematic, if not immoral. However, while accepting for the moment that 'our morality', the morality of Western civilization, may in the past have been articulated in terms of asceticism and self-renunciation, it is appropriate to question whether this continues to be the case, whether the inherited Christian tradition now has as much purchase on us, on how we think about ourselves and conduct our lives. In what respects, if any, do 'we' continue to be constituted as ascetic subjects? If it is true that within the Christian tradition knowing oneself has constituted 'the way to self-renunciation' (ibid.: 22), it might reasonably be argued that within a largely secularized late-modern therapeutic cultural setting knowing oneself has increasingly come to be equated with self-discovery, and thereby it has become much more of a route to self-realization or self-actualization than self-renunciation. Indeed, in the current cultural context Foucault's analytic preoccupation with the virtues of self-stylization effectively serves to promote further self-realization, to the neglect of any sustained consideration of relationships of responsibility to and for others. And it is precisely the absence of any consideration of relations with and responsibility for others which makes Foucault's repeated references to creating ourselves and the autonomy of personal ethics morally problematic. However, there is an additional potential objection which might be made to Foucault's premise, a different order of objection. We might question whether the idea of care of the self has indeed been as 'morally problematic' as Foucault contends. Philip Selznick has suggested to me that what is neglected in Foucault's narrative is an appreciation of the long history of concern for character and 'virtue ethics' in Western theology and moral theory.[1] From this standpoint a certain kind of 'care of the self' may be regarded as a 'prominent feature' of moral theory, albeit a feature which may from time to time have become marginalized or occluded, only to be subsequently rediscovered or retrieved.

For the Greeks caring for the self is said to take moral precedence over care for others 'in the measure that the relationship to self takes ontological precedence' (Foucault, 1987a: 118). But is it sufficient to uncritically represent this particular notion of ontological precedence? In contrast it might be argued that ontology, 'the intelligibility of being – only becomes possible when ethics, the origin of all meaning, is taken as the starting point' (Levinas, 1989: 231; see also Bauman, 1990: 16–18). Furthermore, given the significance already accorded to the thought of Classical Antiquity within the tradition of Western philosophy, and Foucault's concern 'to try to think something other than what one thought before' (1989: 256), is it appropriate to confine a genealogy of ethics to Greco-Roman culture? Do Foucault's (1981a) earlier undeveloped observations on the thematic presence of an individualizing political technology of pastorship in Hebraic texts perhaps suggest scope for a possible parallel ethical exploration around the question of responsibility for others? Such a concern with the question of moral responsibility for others is at the heart of the 'post-rational' ethics developed by Levinas.

A cautionary note before proceeding. Levinas, like Foucault, argues against conceptions of the universality of reason, the unity of truth, and human beings as self-conscious subjects, and places emphasis on 'disjunctions, differences, gaps, dispersions in time and knowledge which are refractory to unification or totalization' (O'Connor, 1988: 58). But if there are interesting similarities between the two philosophers on some issues there appear to be more important differences in their respective responses to ethical questions and relations (Salemohamed, 1991).

For Levinas, the ethical relation is an asymmetrical face-to-face relation. It is a relation governed by proximity; it is the fundamental relation. The ethical relation has primacy; it is prior to both logic and reason. The face-to-face relation is irreducible – 'the face before me summons me . . . The Other becomes my neighbour precisely through the way the face summons me, calls for me, begs for me, and in so doing recalls my responsibility, and calls me into question' (Levinas, 1989: 83). By the face Levinas does not mean a phenomenon whose mode of being is appearance, but the demand of 'the one who needs you, who is counting on you'. The face in the ethical sense invoked by Levinas is a 'notion through which man comes to me via a human act different from knowing' (1988a: 171). An act which is fundamentally and originally ethical; that for Levinas is the relation to the other.

Responsibility towards the other 'demands an infinite subjection of subjectivity', it constitutes a relation of proximity which is 'prior to any commitment . . . "older" than the a priori' (Levinas, 1989: 90). Responsibility for another, for the other, is according to Levinas 'human fraternity itself' (ibid.: 106) and it 'commits me . . . before any truth and any certainty' (ibid.: 110). The unlimited responsibility for the other comes, Levinas argues, 'from the hither side of my freedom, from a "prior to every memory", an "ulterior to every accomplishment" . . . The responsibility for the other is the locus in which is situated the null-site of subjectivity' (1981: 10). Or as Levinas expresses the relationship elsewhere, 'this attention to the Other . . . can be affirmed as the very bond of human subjectivity, even to the point of being raised to a supreme ethical principle' (1988b: 159). And as it is presented in yet another formulation, the alterity of the face constitutes an 'obligation that cannot be effaced' (Levinas, 1988a: 179).

Responsibility for the other is constitutive of subjectivity for Levinas – 'the very node of the subjective is knotted in ethics understood as responsibility' (1992: 95). But if subjectivity is addressed in ethical terms by Levinas, ethics in this instance is not a metaphysical 'what ought to be', rather it represents a critical disturbance of being, of the complacency of our being. In effect Levinasian ethics may be described as critique in so far as it is synonymous with a 'putting into question of the ego, the knowing subject, self-consciousness', a putting into question which is vested in a point of exteriority, a difference which 'cannot be reduced to the Same', in short 'alterity', the other, or the being of the face (Critchley, 1992: 4–5).

In his discussion of the ethical relation Levinas places the emphasis firmly and deliberately on care for others, rather than care for the self. In contrast Foucault continues to prioritize the self, to ask whether we can have an 'ethics of acts . . . able to take into account the pleasure of the other? Is the pleasure of the other something which can be integrated in our pleasure . . .?' (1986a: 346). Foucault certainly appears, albeit briefly, to acknowledge the other as a potential focus of our responsibility, but it is always secondary, and very much so, to a preoccupation with the self. In consequence his contribution to a regeneration of ethics as a 'manner of being' does not ultimately constitute an effective challenge to the modern cult of the self, to the contrary it reads more like an affirmation of the same. For care of the self to begin to embrace care of other(s) at the very least an ethics of self-limitation is necessary, and while that might have been a feature of the 'ethical work of the self on the self' (Foucault, 1988b: 91) in Classical Antiquity it seems to be largely absent from contemporary societies, 'in which an orderly conduct of life is possible without recourse to the innate human capacity of moral regulation' (Bauman, 1990: 29). While the Greek notion of 'taking care of one's self' constituted an ethical and aesthetic practice of self-mastery, a practice signifying the presence of 'ascetic themes', the modern context in which Foucault ruminates on the virtues of everyone's life becoming a work of art is quite different, one in which self-discovery and self-expression prevail and hedonistic themes continue to predominate.

Is the problem, as Foucault suggests, that we have lost virtually all trace 'of the idea in our society, that the principal work of art which one has to take care of, the main area to which one must apply aesthetic values, is oneself, one's life, one's existence' (1986a: 362), or is it that our modern preoccupation with oneself and an associated increasing rationality of human conduct, which has effected a technologizing of human existence, has virtually neutralized the moral impulse, such that taking care of the self too often seems to preclude any thought or possibility of taking care of the other? In short has the subject of responsibility for the other become a subject of indifference? It is precisely the dissipation of responsibility towards the other with which Emmanuel Levinas has been preoccupied and to which his ethical discourse constitutes a critical response.

Ethics and Politics

In an interview conducted in 1983, Foucault stated that what interested him was 'politics as an ethics', but aside from a series of critical distancing remarks on the limitations of 'forms of totalization offered by politics' and brief comment on ethics as a practice and ethos as a manner of being, there is relatively little, if any, positive clarification of the articulation of politics and ethics. And where the question of ethics does receive more con-sideration in his work, then as I have noted above Foucault tends to focus almost entirely on the self, presenting ethics virtually as self-first philo-sophy. Once again there is an informative contrast to be drawn with the work of Levinas for whom the question of the relationship of ethics and politics is pivotal.

In outlining his conception of ethics as first philosophy Levinas makes repeated reference to the face-to-face relationship, to the inter-human relationship. But what happens when two becomes three, when the face-to-face is dissolved within the turbulent sociality of social life? How does Levinas view the articulation of ethics and politics? What are the prospects for ethical responsibility given the complex politics of social life? As Levinas acknowledges, we live in a world where there are many others; we inhabit social worlds in which there are frequently more than two people, and in consequence the ethical perspective of alterity is generally encompassed, if not at times subverted, by the ontological perspective of totality. As the focus moves from the dyadic relationship of self and other with the entry of a third person, so the ethical relation is necessarily recognized to become political, to become subject to the 'totalizing discourse of ontology', and to the organizational forms and consequences of socio-political ordering. It is precisely in this context, that is with the consequences of a moral-political governing of social life, that the critical significance of 'the ethical norm of the interhuman' is identified (Levinas and Kearney, 1986: 30). The concern expressed by Levinas is that if the notion of an ethical foundation to the moral-political order is occluded or relinquished, then it will not be possible to effectively evaluate and chal-lenge problematic manifestations of social and political life, such as, for example, fascism and totalitarianism. Hence the emphasis placed on the notion of ethics as first philosophy, and the significance accorded to ethical responsibility as 'wakefulness' and as an 'incessant watching over of the other'. For Levinas it is necessary to be continually vigilant for 'the political order of the state may have to be challenged in the name of our ethical responsibility to the other' (ibid.: 30). Retrieval of a notion of ethical responsibility preserves the prospect of a critical questioning of politics and opens up the possibility of a disruption of totalitarian forms of political life. But does Levinas give sufficient consideration to the inescapable articulation of ethics and politics?

It has been argued by Simon Critchley that Levinas 'attempts to build a bridge from ethics understood as a responsible, non-totalizing relation with the other, to politics, conceived of as a relation to the third party . . ., to all the others, to the plurality of beings that make up the community' (1992: 220). It is a bridge which leads Levinas to develop a conception of an ethically informed politics, politics as 'mediated ethically' (ibid.: 221), perhaps politics as an ethics. As I have already noted above, there may appear to be scope here for potentially interesting parallels to be drawn with the work of Foucault, however the differences remain significant. For example, Foucault draws attention to the ways in which the modern Western state has employed both individualizing and totalizing political rationalities, and argues that it is necessary to attack 'political rationality's very roots' (1981a: 254), rather than simply its individualizing or totalitarian effects. Levinas in a broadly comparable manner outlines a critique of politics which, as Critchley comments, not only opposes 'the domination of politics enacted in totalizing or immanentist conceptions of society' but also takes issue with 'liberal politics, in so far as it has been dominated by the concepts of spontaneity, freedom, and autonomy' (1992: 222). Like Foucault, Levinas clearly considers that liberalism is not sufficient and, further, that it is inadvisable, if not dangerous, to assume that 'only political rationality can answer political questions' (ibid.: 222). For Foucault 'politics as an ethics' serves to describe an intellectual focus or interest, a way of operating as an intellectual which simultaneously rejects 'forms of totalization offered by politics' and attempts to open up problems by asking 'ethico-epistemologico-political' questions (1986a: 376). For Levinas politics as an ethics involves, if it does not necessitate, 'the possibility of sacrifice', it constitutes a different form of political life, one which is 'based on the irreducibility of ethical transcendence' (Critchley, 1992: 225).

The address of ethics and politics offered by Levinas involves more than a process of questioning, it simultaneously constitutes an attempt to recall and restore the ethical basis of politics. It serves to remind us not only that 'politics begins as ethics', but that ethics, the ethical relation to the other, 'is always already political', that it is not chronologically before politics, or a-political, but is always within a political context (ibid.: 225–6). When Levinas makes reference to the move from an ethical relation of responsibility for the other to 'the political world of the impersonal "third" – the world of government, institutions, tribunals, prisons, schools, committees, and so on' (Levinas and Kearney, 1986: 30), it is a phenomenological rather than a chronological or spatial move that is at issue. It is not a case of ethics, then politics, but rather of ethical discourse with the other being recognized from the beginning to be 'troubled and doubled into a political discourse with all the others . . . The immediacy of the ethical is always already mediated politically' (Critchley, 1992: 231). An understanding of the articulation of ethics and politics, of the respects in which ethical relations are always vulnerable to disturbance or interruption by politics, is argued to be a distinctive feature of Levinas's work. Indeed in the conclusion to his discussion of the ethics of deconstruction Critchley begins to outline a Levinasian *politics* of ethical difference which is described as 'the enactment of plurality, of multiplicity' (ibid.: 225). However, there are other interpretations of Levinas's work and other related perspectives on the subject of ethics.

A different view, at times a radically contrasting view, of both ethics in general and the work of Levinas in particular is provided by John Caputo. Caputo begins with a confession that he has misgivings about ethics:

> I have up to now always tried to strike a more respectable pose . . . I have always made it my business to defend ethics, a more originary ethics, an ethics of *Gelassenheit* and letting be, an ethics of dissemination, a veritable postmodern ethics . . . Who, after all, wants to be found wanting in the matter of ethics? Who wants to risk having no ethics, or questioning its good name? . . . That halcyon time is over now . . . My neighbours will soon know that I am registered in the opposing party. (1993: 1)

And having declared himself to be 'against ethics' Caputo proceeds to criticize Levinas for making 'ethics into a holy of holies' (ibid.: 125). Now, when he declares himself to be against ethics Caputo does not have in mind as an alternative something 'more primordial or originary', rather something more modest, namely that there is no firm and fixed ground available for judgement – 'to speak of being against ethics and of deconstructing ethics is to own up to the lack of safety by which judging is everywhere beset' (ibid.: 4). Of course we continue to take decisions, make judgements, and choose courses of action, but we have to do so, Caputo argues, without the benefit of secure foundations. Processes of decision-taking, judgement-making, and choosing between alternative courses of action are intrinsically risky. There are no safe paths to follow, 'one is rather more on one's own than one likes to think, than ethics would have us think' (ibid.: 4). Where Critchley outlines and argues for a Levinasian inspired ethics of deconstruction Caputo counters with references to the deconstruction of ethics, to ethics' undoing, to the anxiety of undecidability which accompanies decision-taking and judgement-making – 'Deconstruction issues a warning that the road ahead is still under construction, that there is blasting and the danger of falling rock. Ethics, on the other hand, hands out maps which lead us to believe that the road is finished' (ibid.: 4).

Ironically Caputo's criticism of Levinas's conception of ethics is predicated on a view of the relationship between ethics and politics which closely parallels the more positive interpretation offered by Critchley. 'Ethics is always already political' Caputo argues, and in this instance, by implication, Levinas is charged with 'maintaining an impossible duality between a (pure) ethics and a (dirty) *Realpolitik*' (ibid.: 124). Ethics and politics 'are not simply different essences or regions whose "relationships" are hard to work out; they always already bleed into each other' (ibid.: 125). It is in the light of the identified complex articulation of ethics and politics that Caputo finds problems with Levinas's conception of a relationship of responsibility for the other and takes issue with the implied obligation to be perpetually for the other. Caputo argues that obligation which does not include a vestige of self-enrichment is impossible and that when we act, even seemingly altruistically, we derive something, 'we get a return'. There is always 'a line that leads out from the agent to the action and then back again . . . a self-enriching hermeneutico-ontological link . . . Even the gift, the pure gift . . . belongs to this circle, because when I send a gift out, gratitude comes back, *whether I want it or not*' (ibid.: 124, emphasis added). From this standpoint Levinas's portrayal of the subject is found to be too self-effacing, if not potentially self-destructive. Caputo's contrasting view is that it is necessary to recognize that a sense of obligation is always paralleled by 'a certain self-love and self-interest' (ibid.: 124).

However, while Caputo is clearly critical of Levinas he simultaneously acknowledges that occasionally people do devote themselves entirely to the other, sacrifice themselves for the other, give themselves up 'for the good of the other'. But even here, even in these limit cases, even where life itself might be sacrificed, Caputo contends it is still, to a degree, 'what they want, their *bonum* . . . They are doing what they want, what something in them wants. That is their *bonum*' (ibid.: 128). Subjects who devote their lives to others, who serve others, who seem to exemplify in their conduct, a Levinasian ethical responsibility for the other, challenge our categories. We lack an idiom for such conduct, such 'foolishness' as Caputo terms it. Such exceptional and unlikely conduct is described as incomprehensible within the analytic parameters of 'Greco-onto-logic', and as literally belonging to another paradigm:

> Obligation is impossible, but that is not to say that it does not happen, here and there, now and then. Being impossible is not a conclusive objection, inasmuch as the most interesting things are often impossible. It is only to shift the scene from philosophy to poetics, from Greek reflection on what is possible and necessary . . . to a jewgreek poetics of what 'happens', or from Greek modal logic to jewgreek postmodal logic. (ibid.: 126)

As I have suggested, it is the self-effacing idea of being for others, articulated in (and with) the notion of ethics as first philosophy, with which Caputo takes issue. There is no denying that 'obligations happen', but while Caputo is clearly for obligation, by which I mean that there is both a recognition that obligations arise and that associated calls are to be heeded and demands met, he continues to be against ethics, arguing that 'the poetics of obligation must take its stand . . . "against ethics". "against originatory ethics", "against ethics of infinity"' (ibid.: 194).

Caputo admits to moving to and fro between Athens and Jerusalem and argues that the outcome is 'something that is otherwise than ethics', but which nevertheless remains 'very attached to its obligations' (ibid.: 220). The claim is that a different sense of the subject of obligation informs his discourse and distinguishes it from the ethics of Levinas. But how different is Caputo's notion of obligation? Obligations happen, but they do not, Caputo argues, derive their influence, their hold on or over us, from a cosmic source of power; they do not represent the 'trace of God', rather they are 'strictly local events, sublunary affairs, between us . . . matters of flesh

and blood' (ibid.: 227). In contrast to Levinas, for whom the figure of God
stands for 'the Good . . . beyond being' (1987b: 163), Caputo argues that
obligations simply arise from the vulnerability and fragility of life, from the
susceptibility of life to events bringing sorrow, loss, disaster and destruction
in their wake. There is no overarching rationale, no '*logos* or *telos*' at work,
no all-encompassing meaning to events. It is simply that things happen,
events occur, obligations arise. In contrast to Levinasian ethics, which finds
'the infinity of the personal at the core of events', Caputo contends that
there are no assurances, that we have to face the fact that we 'have to live
with the anonymity that insinuates itself into obligations (1993: 236). From
this standpoint obligation has no recourse to 'infinity', which in Levinas's
sense means perfection, 'a height and a nobility, a transcendence' (1969: 41),
rather obligations are said to occur 'with or without sacred names, with or
without the Infinite' (Caputo, 1993: 237).

Obligations happen, as Caputo acknowledges, but in the absence of any
'deep and reassuring ground'. We live with contingency, in the shadow of
what is described as 'the abyss', that is the continual occurrence of events
lacking intrinsic meaning, for which we perpetually construct meanings and
make sense, but increasingly with discomfort or anxiety about our lack of
security or certainty, and with a feeling of loss or omission, frequently
accompanied by a sense of ambivalence. Yet over the abyss, Caputo
suggests, a 'whole network of obligations takes root', 'a whole network of
interpersonal relations springs up'; obligations happen, a person 'makes
demands on me, . . . asks for a hand . . . the eyes of the other come over me,
overtake me, pulling me up short' (ibid.: 238). Is there implied within such
interpersonal relations, where demands arise in and from facing the other, a
responsibility to meet or honour obligations? Caputo's narrative suggests
that honouring obligations goes without saying; a person is a 'subject of
obligation', a person is 'a place where obligations happen' (ibid.: 238). But
if obligations happen, if they 'forge the links of "you" and "I" and "we"
and "he" and "she' . . . weaving a thin tissue of tender, fragile bonds and
multiple microcommunities' (ibid.: 246) – and it can be accepted that this is
the case in some respects at least, even if it seems at times that those
respects are too often infrequent and limited – it is also evident that
obligations may not be met, responsibilities may not be honoured, indeed
there may, too frequently, not even be a recognition or acceptance of
responsibility, or an acknowledgement of any obligation to be fulfilled. It is
precisely concern about the too frequent lack of a sense of responsibility for
the other, and the associated failure to identify let alone meet obligations,
which occurs as soon as proximity is replaced by distance, 'as soon as we
move into the political world of the "third"' (Levinas and Kearney, 1986:
30), which lends weight to Levinas's attempt to advance the critical idea of
ethics as first philosophy and to argue that the 'ethical relation' to the other
is prior to the 'ontological relation' to the self.

The problem identified is the displacement or diminishment of a sense of
responsibility for others within a culture of 'therapeutic contractualism', a

culture which in its preoccupation with the self has tended to marginalize, if not to denigrate 'solidarity with others', 'mutual responsibility', and so on, causing us to 'forget our obligations of solidarity and community, to harden our hearts and look out only for ourselves' (Bellah et al., 1996: xxxv). It is in this context, where obligations arise but are often avoided, where all too frequently making an obligation *does not* happen, that the discourse on the 'ethical exigency to be responsible for the other' (Levinas and Kearney, 1986: 23) has its resonance. It is because we are continually overly inclined to be for the self, first and last, that the wake-up call, the reminder, to watch over the other, to remember our ethical responsibility towards the other, achieves its critical analytical and political value.

But what of the self which bears responsibility for the other? How are ethical and moral concerns associated with the embodied self to be explored? What has become of the self with the 'developing "disenchantment" of modern culture' (Taylor, 1989: 26), with the weakening of modern culture and erosion of community belonging (Selznick, 1992)? It is to a consideration of such a range of ethical questions and concerns, expressed or implied in discussions of self, body and community, that the following chapter is directed.

Notes

1 See Philip Selznick's *The Moral Commonwealth – Social Theory and the Promise of Community* (1992) and personal correspondence with the author.

5

BODY, SELF, COMMUNITY: ETHICAL RELATIONS

Questions of ethics and morality are again analytically and politically prominent. Whether it is in respect of discussions of the self and modern identity, and associated matters of responsibility and integrity (Taylor, 1989: Selznick, 1992), or in relation to community and the requirements of commitment, value clarification and evaluation, and social responsibility (Etzioni, 1994), questions of ethics and morality have become an increasingly important focus of social analysis. However, in the case of social analyses of the body, conceptualized as 'an active, organic, organized, intentional, deed-doing agency' (Caputo, 1993: 206), ethical and moral matters are not always given the consideration they warrant.

The issue of the body has become a prominent feature of social and cultural analysis. However, rather than setting a new agenda analysts have been inclined to shadow or track popular practices, cultural representations, and longstanding everyday preoccupations. For the body conscious, now virtually all of us, including those committed to building or reducing their bodies through a combination of exercise and diet; those seduced by the wrappings of fashion and the transformative possibilities of cosmetic surgical procedure; and those others, most if not all of us, who have been subject to, if not subjects of, humour, tragedy, ridicule, discrimination, pain, pleasure, envy and a diverse range of other experiences, the importance of the body has never been in question, for our experiences are nearly always, to some degree, embodied. It is perhaps those of us who have tended to be excessively preoccupied with the world of the mind, the (over-) analytically inclined, for, and by whom the body has tended to be most neglected, only of late to become a topic of expanding interest. There are, of course, several notable exceptions, an early modern example being Nietzsche ([1930]1968) who was moved to comment on the way in which the body had been disregarded as a consequence of philosophical prejudice against the corporeal, and subsequently to counter that it is essential 'to start from the *body* and employ it as guide' (ibid.: 289). In Freud's therapeutic analysis a fragmented and over-sexualized body lies at the heart of a discourse on the difficult process of 'civilization' and its uneven consequences for self-identity and moral life. The '"*moral*"' demands of civilization' are identified by Freud ([1927]1985: 189–93) as making necessary a renunciation of instinctual bodily forces, for which modern subjects have continually to pay. Another obvious and prominent figure is Merleau-

Ponty for whom the Cartesian contrast between mind and body, to which I have alluded above, is the object of an existential-phenomenological critique. For Merleau-Ponty the subject is unavoidably embodied, in other words we are necessarily body-subjects (Crossley, 1995). In addition, there are a few contemporary analysts who have made a strong case for the body being accepted as a significant focus for social analysis (Turner, 1984; O'Neill, 1985; Irigaray, 1993; Shilling, 1993).

A number of important themes have been identified in respect of which the body is deemed to be of growing significance, and thus deserving of a prominent place on the analytic agenda, notably, in relation to questions of symbolic significance, agency, gender and sex differences, technological adaptation and/or reconstitution, health and illness, and sport and recreation (Featherstone and Turner, 1995). However, while the body can no longer be considered marginal to social and cultural analysis, a substantial amount of work clearly remains to be done. Four major parameters in particular have been identified along and around which analytic inquiries need to be developed. These concern:

(i)   the 'nature' or being of the body;
(ii) embodied human agency;
(iii) the embodied character of social processes of reciprocity and exchange; and
(iv) the historical constitution of bodily capacities and propensities (Featherstone and Turner, 1995).

Noticeably absent from the parameters identified above is any *direct* or *explicit* reference to the way(s) in which moral and ethical matters are, or might be, articulated with the body, or to put it another way, there appears to be a neglect of the embodied character of ethical and moral preoccupations.[1] Such a neglect of ethical and moral matters has been identified as a longstanding and 'astonishing' general feature of twentieth-century sociology and social anthropology; analytic reflection on ethics and morality being described as 'the great void in contemporary social science' (Lukes, 1988: 432).

In relation to the parameters noted above there are at least two possible appropriate locations for an address of ethical embodiment, notably within debates around questions of the being of the body and embodiment and the embodied character of human agency respectively, but both locations, both sources of potential inclusion, are ultimately less than satisfactory in that they serve to maintain the marginal status of, if they do not mask altogether, questions of ethics and morality articulated with the body. A fifth parameter, explicitly addressing ethical and moral concerns articulated with the body (but not only the body), is necessary to draw attention to the increasing importance of questions of ethics, following what has been variously termed 'the critique of metaphysics', 'the end of metaphysics' and the advent of 'a post-metaphysical age' (Cohen, 1992: 4).

While endorsing the importance of sociologically exploring the question 'what is the body', I will present a rather different response, one which acknowledges, and begins to explore, the significance of moral and ethical matters articulated with the body, but one which also moves on to give consideration to related moral matters associated with 'self' and 'community'. In effect I will be arguing that there is a need for something more than a sociology of the body which is content simply to explore the embodied character of 'processes of reciprocity and exchange between humans' (Featherstone and Turner, 1995: 8). While accepting the generally embodied character of relations between human beings, it is necessary to face the broader and more important matter of *ethical* relations between human beings, a matter which sociology has frequently tended to marginalize, if not to avoid addressing altogether. In brief, it might be argued that it is necessary to move beyond sociological reflections confined primarily to manifestations of 'face-work' in social interaction, as exemplified for example by the work of Erving Goffman, to engage analytically with the question of the ethical relation to the other embodied, for example, in what Emmanuel Levinas (1989) has called 'the face'. Indeed, it is precisely the *modern* preoccupation with the aesthetics of 'face-work' in everyday life, and modern sociological reflections largely confined to the same, which have served to obscure further the question of the ethical relation to the other. Certainly, as one analyst has belatedly acknowledged, 'insufficient attention' has been paid to questions of ethics in social and cultural inquiry (Lash, 1996).[2]

Face (As) Work

In a series of critical reflections on the modern metropolis and the money economy, Georg Simmel draws attention to the increasing prominence of intellectual functions over others (viz. emotional, ethical etc.). For Simmel (1990) the modern metropolitan subject is necessarily calculating, egoistic and blasé and it is precisely qualities such as these which are prominent in Erving Goffman's sociological explorations of the forms of conduct which are generally considered to be constitutive of modern social life. In an essay on ritual elements in social interaction, first published in 1955, Goffman places emphasis on the complex character of face-to-face contact and draws attention in particular to the significance of 'face-work'. Goffman's notion of 'face' is bound up with positive self-presentation, with the success of a 'line' taken in interaction, a 'performance' successfully accomplished, or a 'front' put on. Face involves work, it is 'put on'. Face is enhanced or maintained when the course of action, or line taken, is regarded by participants to be in accordance with socially approved attributes. Where this is not the case, or where it is in doubt, then loss of face is likely to follow, unless, that is, a face-saving move can be made, a move which attempts to create the impression that, after all, there has been no loss of face. In face-to-face interaction, where the necessity of maintaining and the prospect or possibility of losing or saving face continually arises, Goffman comments that 'the person's face clearly is something that is not lodged in or on his[/her] body' (1972: 7). But while 'face' is not equivalent to a corporeal form (the face), the maintenance (or saving) of face achieved through the taking of a particular line in an encounter or interaction necessarily involves, as Goffman recognizes, both 'verbal and nonverbal acts' (ibid.: 5). In short, face-work is not simply a question of talk, in most interaction settings bodies are also present and active as 'sign-vehicles'. While presentation of self may not always be embodied, it generally is, and bodily presence and expression – involving such matters as distance/ proximity, and forms of appearance, gesture, posture, poses struck, etc. – contribute significantly to the cultivation of a line.[3]

Face is bound up with the question of the way self is viewed by others party to an interaction, or to be more precise, it is 'defined as the positive social value a person effectively *claims for himself[/herself]* by the line *others assume he[/she] has taken* during a particular contact' (Goffman, 1972: 5, emphasis added). It is then not so much the line actually taken which matters as the line others identify or interpret, or are persuaded of. Face and face-work concern processes of self-projection and self-promotion, in which other participants are present to offer approval or 'judgemental support'. In brief, face is a perpetual preoccupation of the self. But if face is (in) the self's interest, Goffman also suggests that the presence of rules of 'self-respect' and 'considerateness' in social life, along with an 'emotional identification with others', means that conduct in encounters may be guided by a concern not simply to maintain one's own face, but in turn to help others maintain theirs. The clarification offered suggests that the reasons for helping others maintain their face are various, but with the possible exception of the briefly noted opinion that 'coparticipants have a *moral right* to [face-saving] protection' (ibid.: 12, emphasis added), the other reasons advanced appear to amount to little more than a question of the preservation or promotion of self-interest. For example, the reasons cited by Goffman for self being concerned with maintaining the face of the other(s) include (i) an 'emotional attachment' to a particular image of other(s); (ii) avoidance of the possibility of a hostile response from others which might follow from their loss of face; and (iii) preservation of self-image as 'the sort of person who shows compassion and sympathy to others . . . [in order] to retain his[/her] own face' (ibid.). In short, it seems as though it is the fragility of encounters that gives rise to concern, and that it is the way(s) in which successful maintenance of one's own face may depend upon consideration being shown to the lines taken by other participants which matters most. Face-work appears very much to be a matter of care of the self first, with consideration for others occupying a secondary and literally self-supporting position. Consideration for others, 'saving the[ir] show', becomes a matter of concern primarily where, and in so far as, it bears on the objective of maintaining/retaining one's own face.

The world inhabited by Goffman's face-savers is one in which concern with maintaining moral standards seems to take second place to 'the amoral issue of engineering a convincing impression'. As MacIntyre remarks, 'effectiveness and success in Goffman's social universe is nothing but what passes for success' (1987: 115), or, as Philip Selznick comments, the 'fragile self revealed by Goffman [is] defensive, cynical, [and] manipulative' (1992: 222). Although activity continues to be concerned, to a substantial degree, with moral matters, Goffman argues that 'as performers we do not have a moral concern with them. As performers we are merchants of morality' ([1959]1971: 243). Indeed, rather than morality and ethics Bovone (1993) reminds us that it is really etiquette with which Goffman is primarily concerned, that is with ceremonial rules and expressions which guide conduct. The problem of how to conduct oneself (in order to maintain or save face) is generally routinely resolved by 'testing the potentially symbolic meaning of his[her] acts against the self images that are being sustained [by the other(s) in the interaction/encounter]' (Goffman, 1972: 38–9). However, this does not necessarily mean, as Bovone suggests, that to 'save face . . . is to save the situation' (1993: 36). Such an interpretation is potentially misleading. Goffman clearly does accept congruence as one possibility when he observes that 'His[Her] aim is to save face; his[her] effect is to save the situation' (1972: 39), but later he also recognizes that face-saving may involve, if not require, other responses, namely 'quarrelling' or 'indignantly withdrawing', responses which effectively undermine the orders of interaction in which they are located. Far from saving the show, saving face may actually cost the show; it may require that the show is brought to an abrupt halt, or in circumstances where there is a perceived potential threat of loss of face individuals may withdraw, may abandon the show, seeking 'the safety of solitude rather than [face] the danger of social encounters' (ibid.: 39).

Impressions of Morality

While Goffman recognizes the person as a 'kind of construct' his analyses of the rituals of interaction, of the ceremonial rules and expressions which constitute the theatre of modern social life, place heavy emphasis on the ways in which a particularly self-interested individual calculatingly seeks to manage, promote, if not exploit, impressions. If impressions conveyed in dramatized interaction 'tend to be treated as claims and promises . . . [which] have a moral character' (Goffman, [1959]1971: 242), the moral lines of modern daily life identified involve 'a multitude of standards . . . pertaining both to social intercourse and task performance' (ibid.). Of course self-expression may occur without thought being given to the impression made, that is without, as Goffman suggests, 'guile or contrivance'. But frequently, if not virtually routinely, in modern social life individuals are preoccupied with influencing others (observers/audiences) through a manipulation of impressions, impressions which serve to maintain and/or promote a particular self (interest). In brief, calculating modern individuals, more '"in touch with *their* feelings" . . . and more able to seek what *they* want in relationships' (Bellah et al., 1996: 139, emphasis added), are primarily 'self'-serving, and in so far as this is the case they contribute, if inadvertently, to the further erosion of moral community. Being in touch with one's self, 'knowing how you are feeling', who you are, what you want and how to go about getting it, are core features of a hollowed out 'modern "civilised" morality' (Rieff, 1965: 307), a corollary of the pervasiveness of the modern culture of 'therapeutic contractualism' identified and explored by Bellah et al. (1996).

Processes of detraditionalization articulated with the emergence and development of modern forms of life, and in particular the undermining and devaluing of religious belief, fostered a moral irresoluteness which therapeutic forms of science such as psychoanalysis have sought to address and have attempted to resolve. However, the way in which the culture of 'therapeutic contractualism' has developed since Freud's ambivalent identification of an antagonism between 'the individual constitution and "the demands of civilization"' (Rieff, 1965: 308) has been predominantly in terms of a preoccupation with the self 'defined by its own wants and satisfactions, coordinated by cost-benefit calculation' (Bellah et al., 1996: 127). Can a preoccupation with such a self offer the prospect of any amelioration of moral uncertainty, or is the theoretic resolution to which therapeutic science has been oriented itself part of the problem, itself contributing to the fragmentation of moral responsibility? From an initial concern primarily with patients possessing 'tangible' or 'objective' symptoms of neurosis, therapeutic contractualism has been extended to cover virtually all forms of experience. As Rieff remarks, 'All experience is symptomatic now. People seek treatment because they sleep poorly, or have headaches, or feel apathetic toward loved ones, or because they are dissatisfied with their lives' (1965: 304). Alienated, anomic, and unhappy individuals, anxious about themselves and their lives, have increasingly turned to therapeutic discourses, as well as taking other measures, in pursuit of a remedy for the stresses arising from the pressures and uncertainties synonymous with modern metropolitan forms of life (Simmel, 1950).

Care of the self, taking care of one's self, has always been the central focus of therapeutic science, and is certainly fundamental to a culture of therapeutic contractualism grounded in the belief that 'each person's ultimate responsibility [is] to himself or herself alone' (Bellah et al., 1996: 129). However, while the focus of Freud's analytic concern falls on the figure of the dispirited modern individual, the objective being to redirect the energy wasted in neuroses of various kinds to a more positive and fulfilling expression in everyday life, effectively that is, in the terms Goffman might employ, to pull off a reconstitution and re-presentation of self in everyday life, it is clear that Freud was more ambivalent about the constraints and demands of 'civilized' morality, and that whilst critical of 'repressive culture' he was also a 'defender of its necessity' (Rieff, 1965: 323). Individuals were to be helped to come to terms with the demands and sacrifices of modern civilization, to achieve an 'accommodation to reality', through honest talk, through what has been described as an 'ethic of honesty' (ibid.: 300–28). In this context therapy serves as 'a moral pedagogy' (ibid.: 304), aiming both to facilitate an accommodation to the complex realities of modern everyday life and to cultivate an understanding of the uncomfortable consequences of choice opened up through reflexive analysis.

Conceiving the individual as a force field of unconscious instinctual impulses and drives, subject to the restraints and restrictions of 'civilization', Freud's primary concern was with the heavy costs borne by individuals, the costs to health and efficiency 'caused by the sacrifices imposed upon them' ([1908]1985: 33). The therapeutic aim was not an avoidance of the demands of sacrifice, or an unrealizable liberation from constraint, but rather the achievement, through ruthless, honest talk, of understanding and an associated subtle acceptance of the 'essentially contradictory character of reality' (Rieff, 1965: 327), which hopefully would facilitate a more healthy and beneficial self-regulation of conduct. In sum, an ethic of honesty is offered as a replacement for 'inefficient moral commitments'. In particular, for Freud the process of 'becoming conscious . . . of the limitations of . . . instinctual nature' (ibid.: 315, 322), through therapeutic discourse, promises to allow individuals to overcome crises and take better care of themselves, perhaps to achieve a 'new personal integrity'. However, as Rieff remarks, 'honesty has no content . . . Being honest, admitting one's nature, does not resolve specific issues of choice . . . Freud gives no reason why unblinking honesty with oneself should inhibit unblinking evil. Lucidity may render us exquisitely articulate and unapologetic about our aggressions' (ibid.: 321, 322). Indeed, given Freud's conception of the instinctual disposition of individuals, '[o]penness of character may well elicit more, not less, brutality' (ibid.: 322). Honesty guarantees nothing. Ruthless reflexivity focused on self-interest can offer no warrant that conduct will be(come) more humane, considerate and tolerant of others. An increase in self-understanding may allow individuals to take better care of themselves, but how that is expressed and what it might involve for others seems to lie beyond the scope of Freud's frame of reference.

Communal Life

Is honesty enough? Only, suggests Rieff, if it is assumed, 'as Freud did, that our real natures have been too much inhibited' (1965: 323). Our 'real nature' is for Freud a matter of primitive impulses which 'in themselves are neither good nor bad' ([1915]1985: 68). It is the character of the relationship between the form in which impulses are expressed and the particular values of the community in which judgement occurs, which determines the

classification of conduct as good or bad. However, notwithstanding the
implication of degrees of cultural and historical variability in the classification of conduct, the possibility of social life for Freud clearly requires a
form of socialization, a socio-cultural process of 'transformation of egoistic
trends into altruistic and social ones' (ibid.: 69). Implied here is a process of
'socio-political' regulation in which society constitutes 'the result of a
limitation of the principle that men are predators of one another'. An
'ethical' alternative, to which I will make reference below, asks whether
society might not result 'from the limitation of the principle that men are
for one another' (Levinas, 1992: 80).

   Freud's over-riding concern was with the way in which people, particularly the rising bourgeois, middle class, 'feel as a heavy burden the
sacrifices which civilization expects of them in order to make communal life
possible' ([1927]1985: 184). The implication being that the burden has been
too great and that even though 'every civilization must be built up on
coercion and renunciation of instinct' (ibid.: 185) there nevertheless
remained both a need and some scope to lighten the burdens of communal
life, particularly (but not exclusively) in regard to 'civilized' sexual morality.
Lightening the 'burdens' arising from modern civilization has been a central
objective of the culture of therapeutic contractualism, but the emphasis
placed on self-interest, on personal autonomy and an associated pursuit of
personal authenticity, and the employment of a reflexive calculus which
endlessly monitors (and prioritizes) one's own feelings over and above those
of others, has contributed further to the erosion of shared moral understandings and, along with that, a weakening of any positive sense of 'community'. Such a diagnosis leads Bellah et al. to argue that the processes of
differentiation and individuation synonymous with the advent of modernity
need to be 'balanced by a renewal of commitment and community if they
are not to end in self-destruction or turn into their opposites' (1996: 277).
The idea of community invoked in this context represents something more
than a collection of private individuals engaged in 'noncaring self-
actualization' (ibid.: 135). What is implied here is community as a repository of meaning, community as a shared and lived 'sense' which revolves
around the remnants of traditions (for example, perhaps biblical and
republican in the American context explored by Bellah et al.) which
modernity has yet to erode completely, vestiges that may 'help us to know
that it does make a difference who we are and how we treat one another'
(ibid.: 282).

   The central issue is whether 'communities of memory' can serve any
present purpose, other that is than a regeneration of nostalgia. Can such
communities be anything more than a memory? The conclusions towards
which Bellah et al. are drawn are indeterminate. There may be an expressed
yearning by individuals for a regeneration of community, but persuading
people to make an effective contribution is proving more difficult. For
example, there seems to be a reticence to ease back on the narrow pursuit of
private interest and advancement, a pursuit equated with the achievement

of ever-increasing levels of material wealth, and personal possessions and wellbeing. Elaborating on the growing tension already identified by Daniel Bell (1976) between continually increasing private interests and the problem of making appropriate provision for the public household, Bellah et al. comment that 'the solution to our problems remains opaque because of our profound ambivalence. When times are prosperous, we do not mind a modest increase in "welfare". When times are not so prosperous, we think that at least our own successful careers will save us and our families from failure and despair' (1996: 285). As I have noted above, in response to our profound ambivalence Bellah et al. propose a 'reappropriation of tradition' as a way to promote the revival of a 'moral ecology', and thereby a reconstitution of the social world. The hope expressed is that a 'new political atmosphere' can be cultivated around a 'conception of the common good', the problem being that what might genuinely and positively be held in common – as collective or shared values, interests and goals – has to date tended to represent little more than an endorsement of a cult(ure) of individualism. The cultivation of a meaningful conception of the *common* good, one with which individual interests can be reconciled, and where necessary and appropriate, subordinated, will require a raising of 'the level of public political discourse so that the fundamental problems are addressed rather than obscured' (ibid.: 287). However, while the pursuit of market-led seductive private vices continues to prevail, relatively unchallenged, over the promotion of more sober and necessary public virtues, the prospect of realizing the vision outlined seems, if not absurdly utopian, certainly very remote.

Bellah et al. argue that their vision of a preferable possible future 'does not seek to return to the harmony of a "traditional" society, though it is open to learning from the wisdom of such societies. It does not reject the modern criticism of all traditions, but it insists in turn on the [reflexive] criticism of criticism, that human life is lived in the balance between faith and doubt' (ibid.: 296). It is a vision in which community constitutes potentially the most significant source of meaning in life, a source of ethical commitment and security which somehow needs to be retrieved or reconstituted. A contrasting vision is provided by Zygmunt Bauman, who argues that the reality and meaning of community has been fundamentally transformed, that community has already been recast 'from the pledge of the individual's security it used to be, into the individual's burden and bane' (1995a: 271). From this perspective community appears not simply to have been undermined, fragmented or eroded, but to have become a problem, perhaps to be *the* problem, to have become closely associated with a series of needs (and associated tax-funded expenditures) to be met, difficulties to be addressed, and costs to be borne. If this is indeed the case, or it is widely felt to be the case, the objective of trying to retrieve a marginalized sense of 'community as belonging' is likely to encounter disinterest, if not resistance, and to attract little support. If we follow Bauman's line the prospects for a renewal of community, for a 'new community', are not good, for while the promise may be of 'togetherness, mutual understanding and love', the reality frequently portrayed (and recalled) is altogether different – '[p]ressure to keep the intended flock in the fold is unrelenting, the craved-for cosiness of belonging is offered as the price of unfreedom. The overall effect of all this is another case of the by-now familiar tendency to expropriate the individual's moral responsibility' (ibid.: 277). But this does not constitute the last word on the question of community, to the contrary, the process of erosion or undermining of community has consequences for the individual's expression and experience of 'freedoms'. The possibility of individuals being able to exercise moral responsibility requires the existence of, as well as an orientation or predisposition towards, *others*, towards that is some form of communal life. The corollary of which is that communal life needs must continually seek to embrace the conservation, reproduction, and/or cultivation of conditions conducive to the existence of moral selves and the nurturing of moral responsibility, or at the very least must attempt to counter contrary tendencies leading to an expropriation or dissolution of moral responsibility. Bauman's concern is that to date the promotion of community has been associated with promise of release from the 'torments of moral responsibility', but the price to be paid for a future merely portrayed as more secure has been 'the certainty of discipline and submission' (ibid.: 278). But what of the prospects for a new form of community, for the cultivation of a 'community fold' in which moral responsibilities are nurtured rather than abandoned?

The criticisms expressed by Bauman concerning the quest for community and its consequences do not represent an endorsement of liberalism, although that is certainly one of the ways in which they have been interpreted (Lash, 1996). The complex social, cultural and political realities addressed by Bauman do not lend themselves to conceptualization in terms which derive from a binary analytic distinction between, on the one hand, an allegedly favoured liberalism and, on the other, a supposedly denigrated communitarianism. On the contrary, both liberalism and communitarianism are portrayed as defective, as:

> projections of dreams born of the real contradiction inherent in the plight of autonomous individuals. Each one is but a one-sided projection, which for the sake of its own coherence tends to gloss over the fact that none of the virtues of the individual's plight may survive the elimination of its banes. Community without freedom is a project as horrifying as freedom without community. For better or worse, the life of the autonomous individual cannot but be navigated between the two equally unattractive extremes. (Bauman, 1996: 89)

The theme at the heart of Bauman's deliberations on contemporary conditions, and to which he has continually returned, is that the promotion and pursuit of community derives from our anxiety in the face of contingency. 'Community – ethnic, religious, political or otherwise – is thought of as the uncanny mixture of difference and company, as uniqueness that is not paid for with loneliness, as contingency with roots, as freedom with certainty; its image, its allurement are as incongruous as that world of universal ambivalence from which – one hopes – it would provide a shelter' (1991: 247). The civilized modern community has been found wanting in precisely this respect; it has been unable to provide shelter from ambivalence. Ambivalence appears to represent part of the price to be paid for modern civilization, if not civilization per se. As Freud ([1915]1985: 68) remarks, the 'ambivalence of feeling' which governs our emotional relations in particular arises from a complex process of inhibition-(re)direction-development-expression to which our 'instinctual impulses' are necessarily subject. To the extent that Freudian psychotherapy regards 'the struggle between the trends of love and death' as eternal, as synonymous with civilization, as 'set going as soon as men [and women] are faced with the task of living together' ([1930]1985: 326, 325), then it has as its objective 'the achievement of knowing one's ambivalence, accepting it, and working through it' (Segal, 1992: 96). Certainly a coming to terms, or an accommodation, with ambivalence would appear to be necessary, given, as Hanna Segal remarks, ambivalence constitutes 'part of the human condition' (ibid.: 92, 103), rather than a symptom of psychopathology. Although proceeding from assumptions which differ markedly from Freud's, and while not sharing the latter's essentialist conception of the human subject, Bauman's sociological analysis of modernity and its postmodern consequences nevertheless reaches broadly comparable conclusions. Through a sociological discourse which virtually assumes the form of a moral pedagogy, Bauman confirms that ambivalence is indeed a corollary of modernity, a part of the modern human condition rather than a sign of its incompletion or distortion; an associated condition with which we really have no alternative but to learn to live.

Those of us, most of us, subject to and subjects of a late modernity, a form of life in which social practices, relationships, even our sense of our self, our identity, are constantly open to reflection, (re-)examination and alteration in the light of changing ideas, forms of knowledge, and associated technologies – that complex process Giddens (1990) has termed 'wholesale reflexivity' – are all, to varying degrees, affected by Freud's legacy. Whether or not directly subjected to psychoanalysis, individuals now find themselves subject, in varying degrees, to a culture of therapeutic contractualism and its consequences. The discourse of psychoanalysis, as Bauman argues, has 'transformed the world, *the whole of it* . . . , into a text to be interpreted; it refused to accept the pinned-on labels as meanings, the filing-cabinet code-names as identities' (1991: 175). While it has contributed to the deconstruction of the world and simultaneously has 'sapped the *structure* whose substance was the prohibition of asking' (ibid.), psycho-analysis has also fuelled the obsession with self-scrutiny, an obsession which Bauman notes has deflected attention from 'the credentials of the world' and in turn has transformed the '[a]mbivalence of societal powers . . . into the nagging fear of own inadequacy' (ibid.: 176). The other side of which is the complacent assumption of own superiority on the part of accreditation agencies.

Moral(ity) Matters

Do we then, as Goffman suggests, 'dwell more than we might think in a moral world' ([1959]1971: 243)? Is it appropriate to regard the modern world dramatized in Goffman's discourse as 'moral'? And if so what kind of 'moral world' is invoked? Given Goffman's admission that his analytic focus falls on matters of etiquette governing 'ceremonial rules', rather than morality and ethics governing 'substantive rules and substantive expressions' (1972: 55), it is questionable whether the orders of modern social interaction he examines reflect moral values at all. One response to Goffman's admission is to suggest that while his analysis tends to reveal 'how, in the contemporary world, traditional moral problems are avoided' (Bovone, 1993: 37), his project nevertheless does simultaneously draw attention to the ways in which mundane, everyday activities involve 'moral matters'. One possible implication is that the modern subject is less concerned with the realization of moral standards, is less concerned with being moral than with appearing to be so, by virtue of the creation of convincing impressions, an implication which receives confirmation from Goffman's comment that 'the very obligation and profitability of appearing always in a steady moral light . . . forces one to be the sort of person who is practised in the ways of the stage' ([1959]1971: 244). Coolly calculating and cynically manipulating impressions, the modern subject appears to be an unencumbered, unburdened, virtually empty self, a self which appears to have become 'naturalized' albeit in a specific cultural setting, a setting with distinctive cultural and historical coordinates which are not themselves subjected to analysis by Goffman.

The context within which the modern self belongs is at the heart of the critical inquiry conducted by Bellah et al. (1996) into the moral dilemmas associated with too much emphasis being placed upon individualism and too little consideration being devoted to community and commitment to others, an inquiry to which I have already drawn attention above. Reflecting on the transformation of American culture, and in particular the loss of 'small town' America where social relationships were both more visible and amenable to moral understanding as 'parts of a larger common life', the authors note that now 'the individual can only rarely and with difficulty understand himself[herself] and his[her] activities as interrelated in morally meaningful ways with those of other, different Americans' (ibid.: 50). Rather than attempt to relate self to the larger context, it is suggested that the prevalence of a culture of therapeutic contractualism leads our energies to be directed towards making 'our particular segment of life a small world of its own' (ibid.). The difficulty of comprehending the abstract wider world, a world rendered increasingly complex by the articulation of global flows and local processes, is compounded by the epistemological preferences of the key players in therapeutic contractualist culture, namely managers and therapists, for whom the structure and organization of social life are taken for granted, as representing simply the backcloth against which the dramas of individual lives are enacted and (therapeutically) 'resolved'.

The culture of therapeutic contractualism constructs and promotes an unencumbered self, a self 'free of absolute values or "rigid" moral obligations', a self capable of altering its 'behavior to adapt to others and to various social roles', a self guided solely by the pursuit of its 'own personal wants and inner impulses' (ibid.: 77). The absence of shared moral meanings, of criteria of right and wrong, and the prominent presence of a tendency to regard normative commitments as effectively little more than 'alternative strategies of self-fulfillment' (ibid.: 48), lead Bellah et al. to an unwelcome conclusion, namely that 'the self and its feelings become our only moral guide' (ibid.: 76). But such an 'individualistic moral framework' can offer no effective guidance at all on the issues that really matter, on the issues that need to be addressed (even if they may not admit of resolution), for example 'the shape moral character should take, the limits it should respect, and the community it should serve . . . [or for that matter] which tasks and purposes are worth pursuing' (ibid.: 79). The prominence of a socially and morally 'de-centred' self, a self seemingly contrived from a 'series of social masks that change with each successive situation' (ibid.: 80), the modern self explored, if not implicitly promoted and endorsed, by Goffman, has increasingly overshadowed the critical social issue of responsibility for the other.

A similarly critical analysis, which in broad terms complements central aspects of the work of Bellah et al. on the cultural setting within which the modern self developed, is to be found in Alasdair MacIntyre's (1987) discussion of morality after virtue. MacIntyre makes reference to the bifurcation of the modern world into an organizational realm, a realm of markets, factories and bureaucracies, where ends tend to escape rational scrutiny, and a personal realm over which dominance is exercised, 'in which judgement and debate about values are central factors, but in which no rational social resolution is available, [a bifurcation which] finds its internalization, its inner representation in the relation of the individual self to the roles and *characters* of social life' (ibid.: 34). The key characters of modern social life, a way of life in which 'what once was morality has to some large degree disappeared' (ibid.: 22), or has been reduced simply to an expression of personal preference as emotivism 'has become embodied in our culture' (ibid.), are identified as the aesthete, the manager, the therapist and the bureaucratic expert. A character is generally held in high regard and 'morally legitimates a mode of social existence' (ibid.: 29), and in the case of the modern characters identified the mode of social existence legitimated is one in which the emphasis is placed firmly on issues of utility, on means for achieving largely unexamined objectives, one in which a possible distinction between manipulative and nonmanipulative social relations is largely obliterated. In such modern circumstances there is an intrinsic asymmetry to self–other relations – 'Others are always means, never ends' (ibid.: 24).

Outlining the distinctive features of what passes for moral experience in modern societies, MacIntyre argues that like the manager, the therapist 'treats ends as given, as outside his scope, his concern also is with technique, with effectiveness in transforming . . . maladjusted individuals into well-adjusted ones. Neither manager or therapist, in their roles as manager and therapist, do or are able to engage in moral debate' (ibid.: 30). Rather such modern characters present themselves as operating within realms where rational agreement already exists, or is at least a possibility, and to that end they attempt to be seen to be confining themselves to 'the realm of fact, the realm of means, the realm of measurable effectiveness' (ibid.), or 'performativity' in Lyotard's (1984a) terms. The emotivist self is a cultural corollary of such characters, a self which lacks agreed rational grounds or criteria for moral choices, but nevertheless has to choose, has to decide, has to judge. It is a self which has 'no necessary social content and no necessary social identity . . . [which] can be anything, can assume any role or take any point of view, because it *is* in and for itself nothing' (MacIntyre, 1987: 32). As I have already noted above, in the absence of agreed criteria for moral choices the self becomes its own 'source of moral guidance' (Bellah et al., 1996: 76–7). Such a consideration of the self would not be out of place in Goffman's narrative on the dramas of modern everyday social life, the difference being that whereas Bellah et al. and MacIntyre are largely critical of the consequences of modern individualism, Goffman appears to be more accepting.

Body as Face

Although Goffman may be credited with attempting to address what has been ignored by classical sociology, namely 'the encounter' (Bovone, 1993), as is too frequently true of contemporary sociology, he neglects to provide any sustained critical analysis of the largely self-interested character of modern morality. The 'moral' agenda identified by Goffman is associated with the way an individual 'projects a definition of the situation and thereby makes an implicit or explicit claim to be a person of a particular kind, [by so doing] he[/she] automatically *exerts a moral demand upon the others*, obliging them to value and treat him[/her] in the manner that persons of his[her] kind have a *right to expect*' ([1959]1971: 24, emphasis added). Predictably, from this perspective the demands in interaction tend to fall asymmetrically on others rather than on the self.

Goffman's account of the self-promoting 'merchants of morality', busily engaged in forms of face-work which create demands of others through a management of impressions, clarifies some of the problematic features of the modern moral condition. However, a preoccupation with the self and with an 'ethics of getting by' (Bovone, 1993: 25), or more appropriately an ethics of 'making out', simultaneously testifies to the occlusion of a disinterested concern with, or responsibility for, the other. Face-to-face interaction, documented by Goffman, revolves around self-interested forms of 'face-work' directed towards the successful management of impressions. Reality becomes a contrivance, a show, at best a display in which *moral concern* is merely simulated; more often the reality of social interaction is a performance in which a moral concern with moral matters appears to be almost entirely absent. For example, witness the growth in professional training where the demonstration of a caring concern for the other is increasingly a skill to be acquired, a discipline to be taught, learnt, examined, and later rehearsed and then deployed within a contractual relationship, perhaps best exemplified by the burgeoning field of social *work*.

In what may seem at first sight to be a direct contrast, Emmanuel Levinas argues that subjectivity is (to be) constituted differently, through a primary relationship of responsibility for the other, a relationship of proximity in which 'face' is not a status or property of self to be saved, maintained or enhanced through a performance, but rather constitutes 'the original site of the sensible' presence of the other, who 'summons me, calls for me, begs for me, and in so doing recalls my responsibility, and calls me into question' (1989: 82, 83). Once again a non-symmetrical relationship between self and other is implied, but in this instance it appears as the converse of the form found by Goffman in the interaction rituals of everyday modern social life. There may be dissymmetry, but this time it arises from the demand(s) of the other, from the way in which subjectivity is not for itself, but rather is constituted through a relationship of responsibility for the other. And it is the face which demands, the 'face, the expressive in the Other (*and the whole human body is in this sense more or less face)*' (Levinas, 1992: 97, emphasis added) which orders and ordains. In this instance face is not work performed in the interest of a self, rather it embodies the demand of the other which orders, ordains and constitutes the subjectivity of the self.

To appreciate the significance and distinctiveness of the notion of face introduced by Levinas it is necessary to comment briefly on the relationship of ethics to ontology outlined in his work. Levinas remarks that he is 'trying to show that man's ethical relation to the other is ultimately prior to his ontological relation to himself' (Levinas and Kearney, 1986: 21). In contrast to the philosophical tradition of the West, which makes a correlation between '*knowledge* . . . and *being* . . . the very site of intelligibility, the occurrence of meaning' (Levinas, 1989: 76), it is *ethics* which constitutes 'first philosophy' for Levinas. Rather than accede to the priority accorded to ontology in Western philosophical discourse, Levinas speaks of an 'ethical exigency to be responsible for the other' (Levinas and Kearney, 1986: 23) and of this ethical 'responsibility as the essential, primary and fundamental structure of subjectivity' (Levinas, 1992: 95). It is a responsibility which constitutes 'the very identity of the human' (ibid.: 101), a responsibility which follows from exposure to the face of the other, to what Derrida has termed the 'nonmetaphorical unity of body, glance, speech, and thought' (1978: 115). But it is also a responsibility which tends to become occluded at the point at which sociality is extended beyond face-to-face interaction. Here, in what Levinas terms 'the socio-political order of organizing and improving our human survival' (Levinas and Kearney, 1986: 29), is the province within which morality conventionally operates, albeit 'ultimately founded on an ethical responsibility towards the other'. The sensitivity and exposure of self to the call of the other, ethics for Levinas, becomes 'morality and hardens its skin as soon as we move into the political world of the impersonal "third" – the world of government, institutions, tribunals, prisons, schools, committees, and so on' (ibid.: 30). It is the critical task of ethics as 'first philosophy' to perpetually be seeking to unsettle this ontologically naturalized form of being-in-the-world, by continually recalling our responsibility for the other.

In a manner which closely parallels Derrida's (1982) understanding of critical engagement with the logocentricity of Western metaphysics, namely that such an engagement does not lead to a break, but rather remains, of necessity, with(in) the language of metaphysics, Levinas acknowledges that it is not possible to 'completely escape from the language of ontology and politics' (Levinas and Kearney, 1986: 22).[4] However, while there may be no escape from the language of metaphysics it remains possible to reflect upon – to question, interrogate and challenge – ontology, a possibility which Levinas suggests derives from 'the preontological interhuman relationship with the other' (ibid.: 22), a relationship of responsibility for the other embodied in the face. But, as I have noted above, this ethical relationship of responsibility for the other is problematized as the social network extends beyond the face-to-face relation, beyond the dyad. As Levinas remarks, '[a]s soon as there are three, the ethical relationship with the other becomes political and enters into the totalizing discourse of ontology' (ibid.: 21–2). The ethical relationship is diminished, concealed, if not at times dissolved altogether, by 'the fact of the multiplicity' (Levinas, 1992: 89) and the associated sclerotic consequences of what has been termed 'government', that is those modern techniques, practices and procedures which Michel Foucault (1982) identifies as having been introduced to facilitate the ruling, guiding and directing of conduct.

To govern, as Foucault remarks, is to 'structure the possible field of action of others' (1982: 221). But it is not only conduct that is formed or shaped with the development of modern governmental techniques and procedures, new forms of subjectivity and individualization which are primarily, if not entirely, 'self'-interested and 'self'-conscious also emerge. The modern moral experience, as MacIntyre notes, has a paradoxical character in so far as 'each of us is taught to see himself or herself as an autonomous moral agent; but each of us also becomes engaged by modes of practice, aesthetic or bureaucratic, which involve us in manipulative relationships with others' (1987: 68).

It is ironic that while Foucault was concerned to argue that the target for critical analysis nowadays is 'to refuse what we are [and] . . . to promote new forms of subjectivity' (1982: 216), the discussion of subjectivity he provides continues to accord priority to a notion of self over other(s). As I have argued in the previous chapter, the other may be acknowledged by Foucault to be a potential focus of responsibility, but it is always presented as secondary to a preoccupation with the self. An ethos of concern for the self continues to take precedence over an ethic of responsibility for the other, and as a consequence the modern cult of the self is affirmed and endorsed rather than challenged.

Facing the Body

It is indisputable that the modern project of the self is articulated with the project of the body. However, if the modern self is 'associated with the idea that the body can be fashioned in modern society to express the self through cosmetic surgery, body transplants, implants . . . diet, jogging, keep-fit regimes and so forth' (Featherstone and Turner, 1995: 7) it is necessary to remember that there are other, at least no less significant, examples of the way in which the projects of the self and the body may be articulated. It is important to bear in mind that *bodies*, those of *self* and *others*, may be 'fashioned' in other ways, for example through the diversity of sexual relations and their complex chains of possible consequences (pregnancy; abortion; AIDS), as well as through reproductive technologies and surrogate pregnancies. In brief, bodies may be fashioned through practices in which complex and potentially problematic relations of self to other(s) are integral.

In a series of comments on the late-modern self, Giddens draws attention to the 'repression of moral questions which day-to-day life poses', arguing that the 'reflexive project of the self generates programmes of actualization and mastery. But as long as these possibilities are understood largely as a matter of the extension of the control systems of modernity to the self, they lack moral meaning. "Authenticity" becomes both a pre-eminent value and a framework for self-actualization, but represents a morally stunted process' (1991: 9). It is the pervasiveness of a 'morally stunted' preoccupation with self-actualization which is raised, albeit inadvertently, by the examples of self-expression through body fashioning identified by Featherstone and Turner. Fashioning the body through cosmetic surgery, implants, diet or fitness regimes may be a necessity given injury, illness, or a risk of the same, but equally such practices may reflect nothing more than a cult of narcissism, a culture in which body obsession is widespread, and bodies are increasingly regarded as objects to be customized (Polhemus, 1996). Whether occasioned by injury, illness, or narcissism, with one notable exception, about which more below, the examples provided tend to lend themselves to, if not suggest, an affirmation of the modern cult of the self. Although, if the growing problem of a relative scarcity of qualified personnel, resources and services in health systems is taken into account, then some fashionings of the body, for example unwarranted cosmetic surgery practices – 'body cuts . . . for face, fat and skin which are to be brought under the aesthetic sign-form of the pleasure of seduction and the pain of desire' (Kroker et al., 1989: 186) – immediately become more controversial. It is in contexts such as this that repressed moral questions, here concerning the consequences of an increasingly market-regulated allocation of relatively scarce resources, may be retrieved, and moral dilemmas which arise from the difficulty of reconciling the pursuit of 'private' self-interest with some notion of 'public' or communal responsibility for others may be addressed rather than avoided.[5]

The notable exception to which I have alluded above, and to which I now wish to draw attention, is body transplants, a form of body fashioning which raises complex and difficult questions about sensitive relations to others, both the relation of the recipient to the donor *and* the donor to the recipient. If in respect of the former, the relation of recipient to donor, a narrative predicated on the idea of self-interest or self-preoccupation is understandable, in the case of the latter, the relation of a living human donor to a (potential) human recipient, another narrative is necessary, one which attends to the idea of responsibility for the other, one which gives recognition to 'the frailty of the one who needs you, who is counting on you' (Levinas, 1988a: 171). What is required is a narrative in which the question 'what is the body and what is embodiment' is approached by giving consideration to more than the project of the self. The practice of 'living donation' in America and continental Europe, and to a lesser extent in Britain, provides one example of an alternative narrative on the body, one in which responsibility for the wellbeing of another is paramount (Bolton, 1996). Another more modest example, but one with a longer history, is provided by the blood donor system in Britain, a system which relies upon the gifting of a replenishable bodily resource, blood, for others, generally unidentified and unknown others. The gifting of blood constitutes, in the majority of cases, an altruistic act, a moral transaction in which an ethical care and concern is paramount (Titmuss, 1970; Leonard, 1997).

The examples of body transplants and blood donation, and the others I have briefly noted above concerning reproductive technologies and surrogate pregnancies, as well as some of the consequences which may follow from sexual relationships, for example (unwanted) pregnancies, terminations, and sexually transmitted diseases including AIDS, underline the importance of analytic deliberations on the question of the body which encompass relations of self and other(s) and prioritize moral and ethical issues.[6] The requirement is for a concern with embodiment which extends beyond conventional sociological reflection, beyond that is simply 'an account of the representational or cultural notion of the body' (Featherstone and Turner, 1995: 8), to retrieve and embrace the concealed and neglected ethical relation equated by Levinas with 'the face to face of humans, in sociality, in its moral signification' (1992: 77). In short, it is necessary to 'face' the body, to be alert to the ways in which 'ethics is constitutively linked to corporeality' (Gardiner, 1996: 122), and corporeality is articulated with questions of ethics and morality.

The works of Goffman, and for that matter many other forms of sociological inquiry, are preoccupied with interhuman dramas, with what is of the world of everyday life 'qua *phenomenological intelligibility*' to the neglect of that axis to which Levinas is concerned to draw attention, namely 'what is "not of the world" qua *ethical responsibility*' (Levinas and Kearney, 1986: 20), effectively that which underpins the moral-political order of social life. It is precisely the prominence of 'face (as) work' in modern social life, and all that is implied in terms of self–other relations, notably a prioritizing of self over other, which exemplifies and contributes to that 'effacing' of ethicality as disinterested concern with the other (Bauman, 1990). Goffman's sociological exploration of verbal and non-verbal forms of face-work, in which the central preoccupation is with the employment of dramatic techniques of self-presentation conducive to the enhancement, maintenance, saving or salvage of face-as-status, unwittingly bears witness to the problems of a social order in which moral issues, and the significance of the inspiration and direction of 'the ethical norm of the interhuman' (Levinas and Kearney, 1986: 30), are too often marginalized, if not largely forgotten.[7]

Consideration has to be given not only to questions of the body and embodied agency and so on, but also to what kinds of analysis are necessary given the times in which we find ourselves living. An increasingly prominent feature of social analysis since the turn of the century has been a concern with the consequences of modern (Western) reason. Recall, for example, Max Weber's argument that rationalization, intellectualization and an associated 'disenchantment of the world' have brought about a retreat of 'the ultimate and most sublime values . . . from public life either into the transcendental realm of mystic life or into . . . direct and personal human relations' (1970: 155). It is evident, with the benefit of hindsight, that the processes identified by Weber have not ceased with personal human relations, that the retreat of ultimate values has continued and has contributed to the transformation of even the most intimate aspects of everyday life (Giddens, 1992). It is precisely the problems arising from the erosion of a 'generally internalized moral order' (Wolff, 1989: 327), problems which have become increasingly prominent in contemporary social and political discourse, which constitute the context for understanding Weber's critical reflections on the practice of science, in particular his recognition of the inability of science to answer 'the only question important for us: "What shall we do and how shall we live?"'(1970: 143).

Although the question 'how shall we live' cannot be answered by social and cultural analysis, the complex combination of moral, ethical and political issues implied by the question, *are* a legitimate, if not in the light of current concerns, a necessary focus of analytic reflection. If our analytic reflections on the complex articulations of 'body', 'self' and 'community' are to allow us to achieve an effective understanding of the ways in which we currently live, then a prominent place on the analytic agenda needs to be accorded to moral and ethical matters.

Notes

1 (i) Although an explicit address of both ethical and moral matters is missing from the agenda in question, Bryan Turner (1993) has sought to address the issue of human rights and ethics in relation to the body through a discussion of human frailty.

(ii) Following Levinas I will take morality to mean 'a series of rules relating to social behavior and civic duty . . . [which] is ultimately founded on an ethical responsibility towards the other' (Levinas and Kearney, 1986: 29).

2 Consider in turn Heller's remarks on the way in which philosophers and sociologists 'began to decentre morals in the process of sincere reckoning with the modern historical condition' (1994: 51) and Bauman's related comment that the 'tradition of the sociological analysis of morality must be, virtually, turned upside down' (1990: 22).

3 Time–space distanciation and/or disembeddedness etc., contribute to opportunities for presentations of self where bodies are not physically present, although they may remain at issue – being imagined, fantasized, provoked, virtualized, etc., through such media as telephone sex, internet communication, virtual reality systems.

4 If there are parallels between the positions adopted by Derrida and Levinas on the impossibility of writing/speaking philosophically outside of the language of metaphysics there is an important difference identified by Levinas, notably whereas Derrida 'tends to see the deconstruction of the Western metaphysics of presence as an irredeemable crisis, I see it as a golden opportunity for Western philosophy to open itself to the dimension of otherness and transcendence beyond being' (Levinas and Kearney, 1986: 28).

5 The problem of reconciling the pursuit of private self-interest with responsibility for other(s), with provision of an appropriate level and quality of resources and services for the public household or community, has been presented as a consequence of the 'destruction of the moral circle which engirds mankind' (Bell, 1976: 171).

6 Intimate and loving relationships provide a rich source of material for analytic reflection on moral aspects of some of the forms of embodiment which receive expression in self–other relations. See for example Irigaray's discussion of the 'mystery of relations between lovers' (1986: 235) and the issue of paternity addressed by Levinas (1992) which raises parallel questions about the body and relations of self and other.

7 The omission of any explicit address of moral and ethical matters articulated with the body from the agenda of 'deep theoretical and interpretative questions' (Featherstone and Turner, 1995: 6) designated for discussion in a leading inter-disciplinary international academic journal like *Body & Society* serves as an illustration of the way in which moral and ethical concerns have tended to be marginalized in the field of social and cultural analysis.

6

INDETERMINATE JUSTICE

What is justice in a world of difference(s)? Towards the close of his report on the condition of knowledge presented to the Conseil des Universités of the government of Quebec, a text which is perhaps best known for its introduction of a controversial notion of a 'postmodern condition' into contemporary social analysis, Lyotard remarks that '[c]onsensus has become an outmoded and suspect value. But justice as a value is neither outmoded nor suspect. We must thus arrive at an idea and practice of justice that is not linked to that of consensus' (1984a: 66), or for that matter, if we follow Lyotard, not linked to 'truth' either, since he also argues that prescriptions cannot be derived from descriptions, and that a politics of justice is not to be equated with a politics of truth (Readings, 1991). In a subsequent work, *Just Gaming* (1985), Lyotard engages in a dialogue which offers a series of philosophical reflections on the idea of justice, the problem, if not impossibility, of consensus, and the endlessness of politics and difference. Lyotard remarks that 'it is no longer a matter . . . of reflecting upon what is just or unjust against the horizon of a social totality, but, on the contrary, against the horizon of a multiplicity or of a diversity' (Lyotard and Thébaud, 1985: 87). In short, given the identi-fication of a politics of difference as a distinctive, if not defining feature of contemporary social life (Young, 1990; Taylor, 1992), a radical recon-sideration of the idea of justice has become inescapable.

The Transformation of Modernity

The context in which Lyotard reflects on the idea of justice is that of a modernity transformed by 'the predominance of technoscience . . . that is, the massive subordination of cognitive statements to the finality of the best possible performance' (1992: 18). The discrediting of legitimation through grand narratives, and the increasing predominance of a *de facto* process of legitimation through performativity, constitute signs of what is termed 'the defaillancy of modernity' and represent key features of a condition of knowledge designated postmodern. The aim of generating a single set of criteria which will hold in all times and all places seems, to say the least, a remote and far from desirable prospect, and the construction of a single language game, to which all others may be subordinated, is no more convincing. The loss of such hopes, such goals, simply shows 'that one of the less important sideshows of Western civilization – metaphysics – is in the process of closing down' (Rorty, 1991: 218; see also Vattimo, 1988, 1992 and the discussion of 'weak thought' in Chapter 2).

Lyotard is particularly concerned with the implications of the displacement of traditional forms of knowledge, based on revelation, by 'the pragmatics of scientific knowledge' requiring proof, and especially with the way in which the production of proof has fallen increasingly under the sway of performativity. The goal now, Lyotard argues, is 'no longer truth, but . . . the best possible input/output equation . . . the only credible goal is power' (1984a: 46). The funding of scientific and technological research has as its objective not the pursuit of truth, but the elaboration and enhancement of power. Scientific knowledge, as Marx (1973) anticipated, has become a force of production, 'a moment in the circulation of capital' (Lyotard, 1984a: 45). But whereas Marx's critical analysis may be read as mirroring capital, by according political hegemony to the economic genre, Lyotard's narrative, especially in *The Différend*, is directed towards an opening up of the question of the linkage between 'the multiplicity of genres' and 'the diversity of ends', that is, to an opening up of the question of the political, a question that has no finality.

Reflecting on his discussion of transformations in the condition of knowledge in *The Postmodern Condition*, Lyotard remarks that he was following 'the line of Kantian thought, and also, to a very large extent, that of Wittgensteinian thought' (1988b: 278). A Wittgensteinian notion of language games is particularly prominent throughout the text. Each language game has its own specific rules and there is said to be no common measure between different games. In brief, it is argued that there is an incommensurability between denotative, prescriptive and technical games. However, decision-makers attempt to order and manage the different language games constitutive of our sociality through performativity criteria and procedures which assume, claim, or attempt to impose commensurability on heterogeneous elements. And in so far as performativity 'increases the ability to produce proof, it also increases the ability to be right'; likewise 'the probability that an order would be pronounced just was said to increase with its chances of being implemented, which would in turn increase with the performance capability of the prescriber' (Lyotard, 1984a: 46). It is in this way, through 'context control' or appearing to master reality, that performativity effects a form of legitimation:

> since 'reality' is what provides the evidence used as proof in scientific argumentation, and also provides prescriptions and promises of a juridical, ethical, and political nature with results, one can master all of these games by mastering 'reality'. That is precisely what technology can do. By reinforcing technology, one 'reinforces' reality, and one's chances of being just and right increase accordingly. (ibid.: 47)

But if this assumption has become part of modern folklore, achieving mastery over reality has proven to be much more elusive; the consequences of modern attempts to master reality have proven to be unpredictable and uneven (Beck, 1992; Douglas, 1994). The modern quest to reinforce or redesign reality has continually been met by unintended consequences, by something less than a complete correspondence between programmes, practices and their effects.

Notwithstanding such qualifications to the modern project, it is efficiency or the optimization of system performance which has continued to be offered as legitimation in 'matters of social justice and scientific truth alike' (Lyotard, 1984a: xxiv). However, the logic of 'maximum performance' is not simply inconsistent with developments in social and economic life, as Lyotard readily acknowledges, it has also contributed to, if it is not primarily responsible for, the perception and experience of contradictions and inconsistencies, perhaps most dramatically exemplified by evidence of an increasing accumulation of risks and hazards (Lash et al., 1996). If an appreciation of the inconsistencies and contradictions which seem to be intrinsic to modern forms of knowledge has undermined the prospect of what Rorty (1989) refers to as a 'final vocabulary', or has led, in Lyotard's terms, to incredulity towards grand narratives and the associated prospect and/or promise of an increasing resolution of social and political diffi-culties, are we destined to exist in perpetual disenchantment? That does not seem to be Lyotard's view, for he argues that 'the postmodern condition is as much a stranger to disenchantment as it is to the blind positivity of delegitimation' (1984a: xxiv). But if the postmodern condition is not to be equated with perpetual disenchantment it clearly has contributed to a re-opening of the question of the social bond. In so far as postmodern knowledge has produced an 'incredulity toward metanarratives', refined 'our sensitivity to differences', and reinforced 'our ability to tolerate the incommensurable' (ibid.: xxiv, xxv), the grounds of the social bond, its legitimacy, have become more problematic. As Bauman remarks, 'It is not at all clear how the cause of morality, goodness, justice can be seriously promoted in a world which has seemingly come to terms with its own groundlessness' (1994: 16).

In such a 'groundless' world, a world of differences, what is to be made of justice?

The Problem of Justice

What is justice? In an age marked by the realization that the promised end of modernity, 'emancipation for humanity as a whole', is made unrealizable by the accelerating proliferation of modern forms of life and their costly consequences, how are we to think of justice and what does it mean to conduct ourselves justly? In an era of increasing political fragmentation and diversity in which new values and new social movements have emerged, can there be any place for theories of justice laying claim to universal validity (White, 1987/88)? Although ideas of justice, which 'serve as guiding principles for the norms and rules of a great number of institutions', may vary between different societies, Heller and Feher argue that justice remains bound up with moral virtue, with 'general principles of comparison and ranking' (1988: 121). Where rules and norms are considered to be beyond question, or unproblematic, then the conception of justice is identified as static, where rules and norms are held to be in question, or subject to challenge, Heller and Feher argue 'our conception of justice is a *dynamic one*' (ibid.: 123). While static justice is held to be universal, it being argued that no society can exist without it, precisely what constitutes the content of justice for different social communities may, and frequently does, vary considerably. Dynamic justice in contrast is not universal, although it is argued to be common in modern Western societies, where the norms and rules of justice are almost permanently in question.

But on what basis are the norms and rules of (dynamic) justice called into question and considered unjust, or less just, than alternatives? Is there any alternative to a nominalistic or relativistic stance? Heller and Feher appear to suggest that there might be, that there are 'ultimate yardsticks' for distinguishing between the just and the unjust in the modern world, for the emergence of the latter has 'been accompanied by the universalization of two values' (ibid.: 124), namely 'freedom' and 'life'. But this does not put an end to the problem of justice, on the contrary, for as the authors subsequently acknowledge, while the value of freedom may be universally invoked in relation to political justice and life-chances may frequently be invoked, particularly in the modern West, in relation to social justice, what is accepted as just may still vary between nations, cultures and ways of life. The value of freedom and to a lesser degree the value of life may appear to have been universalized, but appearances are deceptive, cultures and lifestyles remain different and 'the same norm which may be just in one country, in the context of a particular way of life, could still be unjust in another country with different traditions and cultures' (Heller and Feher, 1988: 126). And given the identification of cultural differences in relation to justice, not to mention evidence of the increasing incidence of value conflicts, it is necessary to ask whether it is appropriate to talk of the values of freedom and life as 'ultimate yardsticks'. Claims for political justice, in terms of freedom, and social justice, in terms of the distribution of life-chances, appear to be subject to disagreement and conflict precisely because there are no ultimate yardsticks to which a final appeal can be made. Ironically, Heller and Feher's concluding remark, that 'a completely just society is undesirable because "complete social and political justice" would only be possible where no one could any longer claim that "this norm or rule is unjust"' (1988: 131), effectively constitutes an acknowledgement of the absence of absolute or ultimate yardsticks for determining the nature of justice. Justice is always, indeed has always, to be in question, to be open to question.

It is precisely this problem of the contested character of justice which Lyotard begins to address in his dialogue with Jean-Loup Thébaud in *Just Gaming* (1985) and continues in his book *The Différend* (1988a). It is worth adding that in contrast to the attempt by Heller and Feher to articulate the principles of justice, Lyotard comments that '[n]o one can say what the being of justice is' (Lyotard and Thébaud, 1985: 66). However, before turning to a detailed discussion of Lyotard's sustained reflections on the question of justice, reflections which serve to clarify and develop the enigmatic reference at the end of *The Postmodern Condition* to 'a politics that would respect both the desire for justice and the desire for the unknown' (1984a: 67), I want to elaborate further on the notion, implied above, of an interpretive turn in philosophical reflections on justice, and the problems of interpretive conflict which are an unavoidable corollary. As one contributor has remarked, 'our society is not one of consensus, but of division and conflict, at least as far as the nature of justice is concerned' (MacIntyre, 1988: 1–2). The turn away from the idea that universally valid principles of justice might be established, and towards the notion that principles of justice are subject to cultural differences and interpretive conflicts, raises the question of how, if at all, in a complex, modern society or community, we are able to determine what is just (Warnke, 1992).

The question of justice, whether posed by philosophers or anyone else for that matter, frequently leads to disagreement. It is much easier, as Morris Ginsberg comments, 'to recognize injustice than to define justice' (1965: 73), easier, as Agnes Heller (1987) agrees, to denounce injustice than to determine what is justice. As the competing and conflicting conceptions and theories demonstrate, the debate over the question of justice is characterized by disagreement, at times fundamental disagreement, rather than consensus. In his study on moral theory, *After Virtue*, Alasdair MacIntyre outlines the dilemma confronting modern society in the following terms: 'we have all too many disparate and rival moral concepts, in this case rival and disparate concepts of justice, and . . . the moral resources of the culture allow us no way of settling the issue between them rationally' (1987: 252). Subsequently, in another text which addresses the question of justice in greater detail, MacIntyre re-emphasizes the point, arguing that we inhabit a culture (modern, Western, post-Enlightenment) in which 'an inability to arrive at agreed rationally justifiable conclusions on the nature of justice and practical rationality coexists with appeals by contending social groups to sets of rival and conflicting convictions unsupported by rational justification' (1988: 5–6). Note, it is not simply a matter of disagreement about the principles of rational justification, more is at stake, there is an awareness of the existence of a diversity of traditions, of 'rationalities rather than rationality . . . justices rather than justice' (ibid.: 9; see also Lyotard, 1988b; Lyotard and Thébaud, 1985).

Contemporary disputes over justice derive primarily from the limits and limitations of Enlightenment assumptions according to MacIntyre. In particular, it is a continuing inability to deliver on the promise of principles of rational justification, which can convincingly claim to be independent of 'social and cultural particularities', which is portrayed as the most significant limitation, and it is the exclusion of a conception of rational inquiry as embodied in a tradition, 'the conception of tradition-constituted and tradition-constitutive rational enquiry' as MacIntyre (1988: 6–10) terms it, which is presented as the most important limit. Acknowledging the existence of a diversity of traditions of inquiry and seeking to evade what he terms 'relativist' and 'perspectivist' challenges, MacIntyre argues that it does not necessarily follow that 'differences between rival and incompatible traditions cannot be rationally resolved' (ibid.: 352, 10). But precisely how disputes about criteria of rationality between different traditions are to be rationally conducted, let alone resolved, is not satisfactorily demonstrated.

At issue here are questions of understanding between or across traditions, and associated problems of (in)commensurability and (un)translatability between different tradition-informed, and/or tradition-constituted, communities. MacIntyre's position is simultaneously critical of both the idea of a globalizing modernity seeking to emancipate itself from 'social, cultural, and linguistic particularity and so from tradition' (ibid.: 388), and a relativist or perspectivist acceptance of differences between traditions as beyond rational resolution. The thesis outlined, reminiscent in some respects of Kuhn's (1970) reflections on the processes of transformation to which scientific paradigms are subject, is that some traditions may confront insoluble 'epistemological crises', or anomalies, and in such circumstances may 'encounter in a new way the claims of some particular rival tradition, perhaps one with which they have for some time coexisted, perhaps one which they are now encountering for the first time' (MacIntyre, 1988: 364).

Further, on achieving an understanding of a formerly alien tradition the adherents of a tradition-in-crisis may be 'compelled to recognize' that the other (alien) tradition is superior by virtue of the fact that it offers the necessary conceptual and theoretical resources to explain the problems and anomalies defeating the tradition-in-crisis. While reference is made to potential problems of translation between different tradition-informed communities, ultimately MacIntyre makes light of the difficulties of achieving an understanding of other traditions, and he has nothing to say on the subject of the politics of the complex process of recognition, interpretation and selection implicit in the movement from a tradition-in-crisis to an embrace of another, apparently alien tradition. Indeed MacIntyre is only able to make light of the difficulties of translation between and across ostensibly different tradition-informed communities because the traditions analysed – Aristotelian, Augustinian, 'the Scottish blend of Calvinist Augustinianism and renaissance Aristotelianism' (ibid.: 349), and liberalism – are in a relationship of resemblance, in so far as they already share assumptions about the character and conduct of rational inquiry. Despite an acknowledgement that there is 'no place for appeals to a practical-rationality-as-such or a justice-as-such' (ibid.: 346), in short that the social field is populated by rationalities and justices, MacIntyre finally (re)turns for inspiration to one particular tradition, the Aristotelian tradition, albeit re-cast, the assumption being that it alone offers the prospect of restoring 'intelligibility and rationality to our moral and social attitudes and commitments' (MacIntyre, 1987: 259). There may be an acknowledgement of 'contested justices and contested rationalities', but the Aristotelian tradition is ultimately presented as constituting, for the time being at least, and for reasons that are not always entirely clear or convincing, the best prospect of thinking through the problem of justice.

As I have noted, MacIntyre's argument is broadly informed by the Aristotelian idea of justice as a virtue, the 'first virtue of political life' (ibid.: 244). For Aristotle to be 'just is to give each person what each deserves; and the social presuppositions of the flourishing of the virtue of justice in a community are therefore twofold: that there are rational criteria of desert and that there is socially established agreement as to what those criteria are' (ibid.: 152). In particularly novel cases, where criteria may not yet be established or clear, virtue is to be found in pursuit of the mean: 'To judge *kata ton orthon logon* [according to right reason] is indeed to judge of more or less . . . justice [lies] between doing injustice and suffering injustice' (ibid.: 153–4). However, whereas Aristotle (1962) was able to proceed on the assumption that a communally shared conception of 'right reason', the good, and justice, was already present within the city-state, or at the very least was attainable, in a complex, pluralistic modern community such an assumption is much more problematic, for there are a variety of competing and conflicting conceptions of the good in play and associated criteria are frequently a matter of dispute. In short, in a highly individualistic modern moral culture agreed, socially established, 'rational criteria of desert' are for the most part absent, indeed such matters routinely constitute the fabric of political contestation. Given increasing social diversity, fragmentation and rootlessness are prominent tendencies within modernity, the identification of rival justices and competing rationalities as problematic features is hardly controversial, but MacIntyre's promotion of an Aristotelian 'resolution' remains contentious (Stout, 1990; Bernstein, 1991; Poole, 1991).

MacIntyre's Aristotle presents the good as a quest; 'the good life for man is the life spent in seeking for the good life for man, and the virtues necessary for the seeking are those which will enable us to understand what more and what else the good life for man is' (MacIntyre, 1987: 219). But this notion of virtue as a practice has been displaced within the modern context, as MacIntyre acknowledges when he discusses the marginalization of the tradition of the virtues following the development of a culture of bureaucratic individualism. The virtues, practices characteristic of a unitary life, have been undermined by the 'liquidation of the self into a set of demarcated areas of role-playing [which] allows no scope for the exercise of dispositions which could genuinely be accounted in any sense remotely Aristotelian' (ibid.: 205). Given the marginalization and transformation of the virtues – the fragmentation of the narrative unity of human life and an associated displacement of engagement in forms of practice 'with goods internal to itself' by forms of 'aesthetic consumption' (ibid.: 227, 228) – what is the point of promoting the Aristotelian tradition? Given a marginalization of the virtues in modern society, what is to be gained from a (re)turn to Aristotle? For MacIntyre, the attraction is the remote prospect of a retrieval of 'ethical life'; the possibility of sustaining 'civility' and 'intellectual and moral life . . . through the new dark ages which are already upon us' (ibid.: 242, 263). However, as one of his critics has commented, MacIntyre ultimately fails 'to clarify either his indictment of our society or the practical implications of his position. In fact it is hard to know where he locates himself in social and political space, despite his attempt to identify himself with Aristotle's legacy' (Stout, 1990: 223). Even if the indictment of modernity as a complete moral catastrophe is considered well-founded, MacIntyre's response is not, for it represents merely 'nostalgia for a past in which moral certainty was possible . . . [and constitutes] an evasion of the problems of modernity, not a solution to them' (Poole, 1991: 149, 150). In a comparably critical fashion Jeffrey Stout remarks, 'We can all dream of what life would be like in a world united in perfect rational consensus on the good, but this dream represents no accessible alternative to what we have now' (1990: 224). What we have now is not moral certainty, but moral ambivalence. Ironically, it is ambivalence of which we can be certain.

Like MacIntyre, Lyotard is concerned with the question of the relationship between traditions. However, unlike MacIntyre, Lyotard argues that traditions 'are mutually opaque' and further it is emphasized that 'a universal rule of judgement between heterogeneous genres is lacking in general' (1988a: 157, xi). Both analysts also share an indebtedness to Aristotle. But when Lyotard turns to Aristotle in his discourse on justice, it is not to finally resolve the problem of justice, to answer the question of justice, to the contrary, it is argued that if the quest for justice is to remain a possibility, then the question 'what is justice' must continually be (ex)posed. What Aristotle offers Lyotard is (i) the idea of the prudent (pagan) judge who, given the absence of true criteria, models, or universal grounds of validity to guide judgement in the ethico-political sphere, has to rely on the invention of rules; (ii) another perspective on the differentiation of language into types of enunciation, each of which has its own rules; and (iii) an example of the self-application of doubt, captured in the epigraph to *Just Gaming* drawn from *Nicomachean Ethics* – 'The rule of the undetermined is itself undetermined'.

Modernity and Justice – Without Criteria or Models

What are we to make of justice under conditions of modernity?[1] One of the defining features of modernity is 'an impulsion to exceed itself into a state other than itself' (Lyotard, 1991: 25); an impulsion which is not simply innovative, but experimental. In other words, modernity is not so much an historical period for Lyotard, rather it represents 'a way of shaping a sequence of moments in such a way that it accepts a high rate of contingency' (ibid.: 68). And in so far as it is experimental, modernity is necessarily without criteria, without models. As Lyotard remarks in *Just Gaming*, 'anytime that we lack criteria, we are in modernity' (Lyotard and

Thébaud, 1985: 15). But given the absence of criteria, how are we to differentiate between (political) opinions, to draw distinctions, or to determine whether a given thing is just or unjust? Lyotard's response to the question of how we make distinctions and reach judgements in the absence of universally agreed criteria is simply that we do it – 'It is decided, that is all that can be said. We are dealing with judgements that are not regulated by categories' (ibid.: 14). Such a situation, one in which judgements are made without criteria, is described as pagan. For Lyotard, 'modernity is pagan' (ibid.: 16).

Throughout Lyotard's discourse on justice there are two recurring themes, namely that 'one cannot derive prescriptions from descriptions' and that although one is 'without criteria, . . . one must decide' (ibid.: 59, 17). Implied here is the notion of language games, a notion which Lyotard employs to argue that there is no common measure between the multiplicity of language games, between, for example, a description of reality ('the game of scientific denotation') and an artistic, poetic, or prescriptive language game. In so far as language games are not commensurable, then it is not possible to translate across and between language games, and prescriptive statements can not be derived from statements that describe a state of affairs. From this standpoint a discourse of justice can not be derived from a discourse of truth. This view of Lyotard's stands in marked contrast to the Platonic determination of the essence of justice, its 'truth', to which practices or forms of conduct have to conform if they are to be judged 'just'. The latter constitutes a way of proceeding that is, as Lyotard remarks, characteristic of the West, it means that:

> we are dealing with discursive orderings whose operations are dual . . . on the one hand, a theoretical operation that seeks to define scientifically, in the sense of the Platonic *episteme*, or in the Marxist sense, or indeed in some other one, the object the society is lacking in order to be a good or a just society; on the other hand, plugged into this theoretical ordering, there are some implied discursive orderings that determine the measures to be taken in social reality to bring it into conformity with the representation of justice that was worked out in the theoretical discourse. So that there is, on one side, a theoretical ordering made up of denotative statements . . . On the other side, there is, paired to this ordering, a set of discourses that are implied by the previous one, at least in principle, but that differ nonetheless from it greatly, since their function is a prescriptive one with respect to social reality. (ibid.: 21)

But in so far as different classes of statements are incommensurable, as Lyotard contends, then it is not possible to find justification for a prescription in a denotative statement. In other words, in so far as justice is prescriptive it can not be derived from theorizing 'the true'.

Justice is a matter of politics and ethics, an open question, one which needs to be continually articulated. The question of justice can not be answered with models, rather it is to be met with 'statements about possibilities', 'statements of opinion'. It is a matter of case by case judgement, without the security of a meta-language, and, given the presence of justice lies only in just judgements, it is not possible to determine 'what the being of justice is' (ibid.: 66). There is no reality to which justice already corresponds, so it is not to be confused (or conflated) with 'conforming to laws', or accommodating to ontology. Justice is, of necessity, open to question, to debate, to suspicion, and to the future. Prohibition or obstruction of the possibility of debating the question of justice, of continuing to interrogate the question of 'the just and the unjust', is in consequence regarded by Lyotard as 'necessarily unjust'. In other words, the obligation which appears in the form of a prescriptive, the authority which prescribes/ commands, is not simply to be accepted and obeyed. Justice is not a matter of conformity, or 'unanimous convention', on the contrary, it is more a matter of (political) responsibility, of determining, in the absence of rules or criteria for conduct, what to do. What guides the pursuit of just judgement is imagining the effect of 'doing something else than what is' (ibid.: 23) in the absence of any knowledge guarantees as to the course events will take. In sum, justice is a matter of ethics and politics rather than knowledge.

The concept of rational politics is 'collapsing', if it is not already over for Lyotard. There is, as he puts it, 'no knowledge of practice. One cannot put oneself in a position of holding a discourse on the society . . . it is not true that a rational *knowledge* of social and political facts is possible, at least insofar as they imply judgements and decisions' (ibid.: 73, 75). In short, instead of a science of politics, a 'politics of judgement'; and rather than a politics of reason, a 'politics of opinions', which notwithstanding the absence of criteria offers the capability of deciding between opinions. Furthermore, rather than proceeding to develop an analysis of justice in terms of a notion of 'social totality', it is a matter of 'reflecting upon what is just or unjust . . . against the horizon of a multiplicity or of a diversity' (ibid.: 87). In brief, the problem of justice revolves around the politics of differences, the central issue being how to 'distinguish between what is just and what is not just' (ibid.: 88) in the absence of universal criteria and the presence of a 'multiplicity of small narratives'.

Given the idea of a totality, or a unity, has been eroded, if not entirely displaced, by the idea of a multiplicity or a diversity, how is a regulated politics, a politics able to continue to distinguish the just from the unjust, possible? The response offered is that it is necessary to countenance 'the idea of a justice that would at the same time be that of a plurality', to place justice not 'under a rule of convergence but rather a rule of divergence' (ibid.: 85), a rule appropriate to the presence of a multiplicity of 'minorities'. Where none of the minorities prevails, then 'we can say that the society is just' (ibid.: 95). But such a politics runs a risk of 'indifferentism', of simply reversing Kant's idea of totality, and this leads Lyotard to offer as a caution that 'one should be on one's guard . . . against the totalitarian character of an idea of justice, even a pluralistic one' (ibid.: 96). However, such a response continues to leave open the question of the basis on which the idea of a pluralistic justice associated with a 'rule of divergence' is to be upheld.

There is a predictable equation of minorities with 'territories of language', rather than 'social ensembles', in Lyotard's argument and this makes necessary an exploration of the question of the relation of justice to the implied multiplicity of language games. Given a purity of non-prescriptive language games (denotative, narrative, etc.) it is not appropriate or possible to 'judge from the point of view of justice' (ibid.: 96). But where language games are not pure, where prescription intrudes, then the idea of justice must play a regulatory role. Justice operates to keep different language games within their respective rules, regulates their 'excesses', maintains their differences and counters the idea that they may have 'the value of sources of universal obligation'. The corollary of the multiplicity of justices implied above, 'each one of them defined in relation to the rules specific to each game', is what Lyotard terms 'the justice of multiplicity . . . which prescribes the observance of the singular justice of each game' (ibid.: 100). But if the distinction between a 'multiplicity of justices' and a 'justice of multiplicity' clarifies matters it does not resolve the question of justice. For Lyotard, unlike Kant, the idea of justice has no finality. Quite simply what justice consists of 'remains to be seen in each case . . . one is never certain that one has been just, or that one can ever be just' (ibid.: 99). Certainty is not the objective, rather the strategy advocated is to work to the limit of 'what the rules permit, in order to invent new moves, perhaps new rules and therefore new games' (ibid.: 100). The desire for justice is very much a desire for the as-yet-unknown.

Lyotard's Limitations

Lyotard's view of justice is re-established in *The Différend*, but there is a shift from an anthropocentric Wittgensteinian notion of language game, with its implication of players making use of 'language like a toolbox', to an adoption instead of a notion of phrase regimens.[2] Lyotard argues that players are 'situated by phrases in the universes those phrases present "before" any intention' (1984b: 17) and that the phrase is the only object incapable of being doubted – 'it is immediately presupposed. (To doubt that one phrases is still to phrase, one's silence makes a phrase)' (1988a: xi). Although phrases from different regimens may be linked, it is argued that it is not possible to translate from one into the other. The decline of 'universalist discourses' means that the linking of phrases is a problem, a problem which is identified as the property of a 'philosophical politics', a discourse which, ironically, is presented as, if not exploring, certainly able to testify to the differences between phrases or narratives. In short, a philosophical politics seems to be able to mark the incommensurabilities between phrase regimens, illuminate différends, and thereby challenge the authority of discourses claiming to be able to resolve disputes by invoking criteria deemed appropriate for translating difference into 'the same'. Politics in this context becomes, as Lyotard remarks, 'the threat of the différend. It is not a genre, it is the multiplicity of genres, the diversity of ends, and par excellence the question of linkage' (ibid.: 138). But there is a

serious difficulty here, namely that a philosophical politics bearing witness
to différends and exploring the question of linkages itself begins to resemble
a *de facto* meta-language. Reading Lyotard's reflections on the politics of
difference and the problem of justice it is difficult to avoid the conclusion
that a form of philosophy is being repositioned, effectively as a meta-
discourse guaranteeing 'the inviolability of discursive boundaries' (Rasch,
1994: 61). Notwithstanding an acknowledgement that for 'the philosopher
to be at the governorship of phrases would be just as unjust as it would be
were it the jurist, the priest, the orator, the storyteller (the epic poet), or the
technician' (Lyotard, 1988a: 158), the philosophical discourse proposed
risks being identified as a meta-language. Following the paradoxical
presentation in *The Postmodern Condition*, of a grand narrative announcing
the end of grand narratives, a paradox which is acknowledged in *The
Différend* (1988a: 135–6), it seems as though Lyotard has proceeded to
assemble a meta-language charged with defending differends from the
injustice(s) of meta-languages.

Another way of stating the difficulty might be to ask how, or from where,
in which language game/phrase regimen, is it possible to know/argue that
there is 'no common measure . . . that we know of nothing in common with
these different language games' (Lyotard and Thébaud, 1985: 51), *other,
that is, than their differences*? Does Lyotard's discourse not depend upon
the possibility of a vantage point from which to identify the existence of
plurality/difference and the absence of a common measure? There is a brief
acknowledgement of the possibility of a problem in this regard in Lyotard's
comment that the 'fact that I myself speak of this plurality does not imply
that I am presenting myself as the occupant of a unitary vantage point
upon the whole set of these games' (ibid.: 51). However, given the differentiation of the various language games (phrase regimens) is based upon
identification of the different rules by which they are played (constituted),
the denial of a 'vantage point' is unconvincing. As Rasch argues, there is a
self-referential paradox in Lyotard's philosophical deliberations on the
problems of language. At the very moment Lyotard 'maintains the radical
incommensurability and radical, horizontally-structured autonomy of
discourses, he seems to remove one such discourse from the field of play'
(Rasch, 1994: 61).

In drawing a contrast between the role of 'the philosopher' and the role
which might be attributed to 'the intellectual' Lyotard argues that the
responsibility of the former lies in 'detecting différends and in finding the
(impossible) idiom for phrasing them', while the latter 'helps forget
différends, by advocating a given genre, whichever one it may be . . . for the
sake of political hegemony' (1988a: 142). The act of detecting différends
implies the possibility of identifying different phrase regimens, that is
reading and interpreting differences, effectively moving between, if not
translating differences in order to understand the specificities of, and
incommensurabilities between, phrase regimens, and this in turn suggests
the existence, or at the very least an assumption, of the *possible presence* of

an 'idiom' for phrasing both the regimens and their différends, effectively a meta-language. The possibility of detecting différends and finding an idiom for phrasing different phrase regimens is demonstrated by Lyotard's own narrative in *The Différend*, a text which privileges both the genre of philosophy and the faculty of judgement.

Now if what is at issue is justice, and Lyotard does after all argue that 'in *Le Différend*, what is specifically at stake is the re-establishment of justice under the form of the ethical' (1988b: 301), perhaps it might be possible to argue that there is no problem. Lyotard might be considered to be offering a form of prescription, a purely normative meta-language, rather than a description of what is the case. However, 'truth' also seems to be at stake, in the sense that statements about phrases and incommensurabilities between phrase regimens assume the form of descriptions. If reality 'entails the différend' (1988a: 55), différends certainly seem to constitute reality in Lyotard's discourse. In short, Lyotard appears to be playing two games simultaneously; description *and* prescription. But is he passing from one to the other, trying to 'figure out new moves', or even inventing new games, that is practising what he describes as 'paganism' (Lyotard and Thébaud, 1985: 61), or is he guilty of hesitating between, if not of conflating them?

In *The Différend* Lyotard continues to affirm that 'it is impossible to deduce a prescription from a description', illustrating his position at one point with an example – 'that two million people are unemployed in a country does not explain that the unemployment must be remedied' (1988a: 108). The example is very interesting for in another paper, 'A Svelte Appendix to the Postmodern Question' (Lyotard, 1993), written around the same time as *The Différend*, Lyotard argues that 'the penetration of capitalism into language', exemplified by the accelerating economic deployment of relatively inexpensive language machines, appears to be reducing the demand for wage labour, for 'working'. Lyotard proceeds to suggest that, in consequence, the emphasis in social policy will have to shift from work and employment to 'much more learning, knowing, inventing, circulating'. And further that '[j]ustice in politics lies in pushing in this direction. (It will indeed be necessary one day to reach an international accord on the concerted reduction of labour time without a loss of purchasing power)' (ibid.: 29). Does this not constitute a *svelte* deduction of a prescription from a description? And which figure is responsible for identifying the necessity of an international accord on the reduction of labour time? Given Lyotard's assertion that the only responsibility of the artist, writer or philosopher is to pose and explore the question 'What is painting, writing, thought?' (ibid.: 6), then the presence in his work of prescriptions concerning the virtues of free public access to data banks (*The Postmodern Condition*), and the necessity of responding imaginatively to the problem of unemployment ('A Svelte Appendix to the Postmodern Question'), suggests that the diagnosis he offers of the demise of 'the intellectual' is premature. Premature and misleading, for if there is no longer the possibility of intellectuals speaking 'in the name of an "unquestionable" universality' (Lyotard, 1988b: 301), a more 'local' role and responsibility remains, namely to respond to the problems which arise within specific sectors, 'at the precise points where their own conditions of life or work situate them' (Foucault, 1980: 126), which is precisely what Lyotard's reflections on transformations in the condition of knowledge and his more explicitly political writings (Lyotard, 1993) seem to exemplify. The task of the specific intellectual is not to claim competence and authority 'in matters where there isn't any . . . [for] example in matters of justice, in matters of beauty, of happiness, and perhaps even of truth' (ibid.: 98), rather it is, as Readings remarks, to question and challenge the assumption of a 'privileged access to the referent, [through which] discourse is legitimated' (Readings, 1993: xxii). In brief, it is to take on, to expose, what Foucault terms the regime of truth so essential to the operation of our society (Smart, 1986).

Activating Difference(s)

While it is not possible in Lyotard's view to determine the being of justice it is possible to say what is unjust, namely 'that which prohibits that the question of the just and the unjust be, and remain, raised. Thus, obviously, all terror, annihilation, massacre, etc., or their threat, are, by definition, unjust . . . moreover, any decision that takes away, or in which it happens that one takes away, from one's partner in a current pragmatics, the possibility of playing or replaying a pragmatics of obligation – a decision that has such an effect is necessarily unjust' (Lyotard and Thébaud, 1985: 67). It follows that Lyotard's preferred strategy is to try to counter forms of prohibition and exclusion, or their threat, by encouraging experimentation, which in practice means operating at the limits of what the rules permit, inventing new moves, or possibly new rules and games. It means activating differences and maximizing the 'multiplication of small narratives' (Lyotard, 1984a: 82; Lyotard and Thébaud, 1985: 59). But are there any limits to the differences to be activated, or any criteria for determining the (in)appropriateness of particular differences? Do there not have to be limiting criteria, or, at the very least, does there not have to be a regulative ideal? Experimentation and the pursuit of new rules and moves, if not new games, surely can not mean that all forms of difference are to be activated. The observation that it is the idea of a multiplicity, or a diversity, rather than the idea of a totality or unity, which is necessary today 'to make decisions in political matters' (Lyotard and Thébaud, 1985: 94), suggests as a corollary the unthematized presence of what Richard Bernstein calls a '*universal* regulative ideal', namely the need to 'learn to live in peace with incommensurable vocabularies and forms of life' (1991: 313), or rather, it should read, to learn to live in peace with incommensurable vocabularies and forms of life *which do not threaten the universal regulative ideal*.[3]

It is more than a matter of a tolerance of difference which is at issue here. On its own tolerance 'degenerates into estrangement', it fragments, and

with 'mutual links reduced to tolerance, difference means perpetual distance, non-cooperation, and hierarchy' (Bauman, 1991: 274, 275). For
tolerance to survive as something more than a silent partner of social
domination it needs to be 'reforged into solidarity: into the universal
recognition that difference is one universality that is not open to negotiation and that attack against the universal right to be different is the only
departure from universality that none of the solidary agents, however
different, may tolerate otherwise than at its own, and all other agents',
peril' (Bauman, 1991: 256). The solidarity identified is that within, or better
yet, of a community which is 'always keeping open the issue of whether or
not it actually exists' (Lyotard, 1988c: 38), a contingent, polycentric community, one constantly in a process of (re)constituting itself, one which is
perpetually in pursuit of the horizon of justice, but destined to remain 'not-
yet' just.

Class, Difference and Justice

A radically different response to the question of the fate of justice, but one
articulated in a comparable context, where the idea of universally agreed
norms and criteria is acknowledged to be a matter of increasing doubt and
suspicion, is to be found in David Harvey's (1993) deliberations on class,
justice and politics. Harvey's concern is that while it seems appropriate,
indeed necessary, to question the idea of a universally agreed conception of
social justice – 'too many colonial peoples have suffered at the hands of
Western imperialism's particular justice; too many African-Americans have
suffered at the hands of the white man's justice; too many women from
the justice imposed by a patriarchal order; and too many workers from the
justice imposed by capitalists, to make the concept anything other than
problematic' (ibid.: 48) – there is a risk that we may deprive ourselves of
the possibility of condemning forms of injustice. The implication is that to
condemn injustice we need first to be sure of what justice is, the problem,
as Harvey sees it, being that postmodern critiques of universalism threaten
to precipitate the 'death of justice'.

   In the course of a discussion of postmodern critical analyses Harvey
acknowledges a number of difficulties with the notion of justice. To begin
with there is a range of competing 'idealist and philosophical interpretations' of the notion of justice in Western thought, for example egalitarian
and utilitarian views, positive law theories, social contract and natural right
views, along with several other interpretations. The problem here is how to
differentiate between the respective theories, or as Harvey puts it, how to
determine 'which theory of social justice is the most socially just?' (ibid.:
48). Then there is the related difficulty of how to determine the respective
merits of the different interpretations and claims to justice held by
individuals and groups. Harvey argues that there have been two problematic responses to these problems of justice. One has been to accept that

'social justice has no universally agreed meaning' and to proceed instead to explore 'how the multiple concepts of justice are embedded in language' (ibid.: 49). The other has been to move from an admission of the 'relativism of discourses about justice' to place emphasis on the social and political context in which the different terms in and on which justice is articulated are constituted. Once again the possibility of a universal conception of justice, to which Harvey is committed, is displaced, if not denied, by the identification of local, 'competing, fragmented and heterogeneous conceptions of and discourses about justice' (ibid.: 50).

Harvey's critical response to the implications of postmodern reflections on justice takes the form of an acknowledgement of the possible risks and dangers of injustice arising from the application of universal principles of justice 'across heterogeneous situations', but this is subsequently heavily qualified by an expression of concern that unqualified respect for 'heterogeneity and openendedness about what justice might mean' (ibid.: 53) makes it difficult to argue against 'unacceptable' forms of otherness. The answer, for Harvey, involves trying to reconcile legitimate criticism of the possible risks associated with the application of universal principles of justice (viz. the marginalization of 'others') with the need to reconstitute some general principles of social justice. There are two main elements to the strategy proposed, namely the need to go beyond a focus on local, 'small-scale communities of resistance' and the importance of recognizing that while notions of justice may be situated in a 'heterogeneous world of difference' there may nevertheless be similarities which offer the possibility of communication and understanding across differences and, as a corollary, the prospect of alliances. For Harvey it is a matter of recognizing that in the final instance the most significant '[r]elationships between individuals get mediated through market functions and state powers' (ibid.: 56) and in consequence it becomes necessary to return to political economy, the question of contemporary capitalism and its transformation, and the importance of analytically identifying 'political and ethical solidarities and similarities across differences' (ibid.: 60–1). Implied throughout is the existence of a meta-discourse which is able to both reveal the basis of similarity between 'seemingly disparate groups' and, thereby, promote the possibility of, or legitimate a prescription advocating, the formation of a (working-class led) political alliance. As Harvey somewhat predictably concludes, '[o]nly through critical re-engagement with political economy . . . can we hope to re-establish a conception of social justice as something to be fought for as a key value within an ethics of political solidarity' (ibid.: 62).

The only *significant* difference for Harvey is class difference and, in consequence, to be effective the politics of difference has to be subordinated to class politics. Given Harvey's perspective, it follows that a descriptive statement, namely that 'the historical and geographical *process* of class war . . . has feminized poverty, accelerated racial oppression, and further degraded the ecological conditions of life', will in its turn be followed by, and will be deemed to authorize, a strategic recommendation, notably that 'a far more united politics can flow from a determination to check *that* process than will likely flow from an identity politics which largely reflects its fragmented results' (ibid.: 64). Such a conclusion assumes the continuing possibility, and relevance, not only of the constitution of an all-inclusive class-based form of political solidarity, but also that such a politics will protect 'rather than oppress and marginalize, interests based on gender and race' (ibid.: 59). In contrast to Harvey's assumption that it is either a question of fragmented and heterogeneous discourses about justice, and the implied corollary, a 'paralysis of progressive politics', or a return to a 'materialist' epistemology and a *de facto* modernist form of radical politics, which are deemed to authorize the right to speak for others and to guarantee a (*the*) progressive politics, there are other possibilities, other perspectives on the significance and radical potential of identity politics. For example, Soja and Hooper make reference to the emergence of a radical 'polyvocal postmodernism', the critical intent of which is to 'decon-struct . . . the ebbing tide of modernist radical politics . . . and to reconstitute an explicitly postmodernist radical politics, a new cultural politics of difference and identity that moves toward empowering a multi-plicity of resistances rather than searches for that one "great refusal"' (1993: 187). In this instance it is a matter of recognizing that the structural reality of social and cultural difference is not binary but multiple, and that political alliances are not analytically predetermined but contingent. In the terms employed by bell hooks (1990) it means recognizing the margins not so much as 'passive' places of exclusion, but as potentially 'active' sites of possible new polycentric interconnected communities of resistance capable of 'counter-hegemonic cultural practice'. It is a matter of simultaneously affirming 'marginal' identity while remaining 'open to combinations of radical subjectivities, to a multiplicity of communities of resistance' (Soja and Hooper, 1993: 194). And open to reflecting upon the question of (in)justice against, what Lyotard describes as, 'the horizon of a multiplicity or of a diversity' (Lyotard and Thébaud, 1985: 87).

Just Differences?

Does recognition of a multiplicity of justices lead to relativism, to 'anything goes', to an inability to make just judgements? For Lyotard the answer is clearly 'no', we continue to arrive at judgements, but we do so without criteria, without models, uneasily and insecurely. The question of justice is a matter of ethics and politics not truth, and recourse to criteria or models of universal justice is inappropriate and misleading. A universal model 'necessarily totalizes one narrative of the state of things and victimizes those excluded from political performativity' (Readings, 1992: 170), it does not offer a path to justice or a way around injustice, on the contrary, illegiti-mately invoked to provide a warrant for a prescriptive politics it exacer-bates injustice. The idea of justice is indeterminate, and necessarily so.

Representation of (the possibility of) justice in terms of correspondence to a model of the 'true being of society' (Lyotard and Thébaud, 1985: 23) simultaneously marginalizes and silences other narratives, and in consequence promotes injustice.

If universal models or criteria of justice are not available to us, then with what are we left? For Lyotard it seems that there is something like an obligation 'left hanging in midair', an obligation to conduct just judgements, an obligation to be guided by the idea of justice. An obligation which does not admit of derivation or deduction. Here judgement assumes the form of a process which is never finally concluded, it is always potentially open, or vulnerable, to the indeterminate idea of justice, to the obligation to keep open the 'question of the just and the unjust'. Given that 'we' (that problematic 'never stabilized' [non-]identity) are constituted through the politics of difference and are living amidst a 'diversity of cultures' (Lyotard, 1989a, 1989b), can there be any acceptable or appropriate alternative but to keep open the question of justice? Does the idea of justice permit any other conclusion? There can be no final word on justice, indeed that is a necessary condition of its possibility, as Derrida acknowledges when he cautions that 'one cannot speak *directly* about justice, thematize or objectivize justice, say "this is just" and even less "I am just", without immediately betraying justice' (1992: 10). However, while speaking of justice may be problematic, it is nevertheless necessary to do so. Again, as Derrida remarks, 'justice, however unpresentable it may be, doesn't wait. It is that which must not wait' (ibid.: 26). Just decisions are always required, and at the finite moment decisions have to be taken information and knowledge are always to some degree limited, and necessarily so. Justice is always in the balance. With justice there are always, as Levinas remarks, 'improvements to be made . . . justice is always a justice which desires a better justice' (1988a: 177–8). Once articulated it seems the question of justice is impossible to conclude and it will undoubtedly continue, as Bauman (1992a) has cautioned, to 'haunt and pester us'. We must hope so.

Notes

1 Although Lyotard has been identified as a key contributor to the discourse on what is sometimes termed 'postmodern justice' (White, 1987/88; Pavlich, 1996) there are very few direct references to the postmodern in the texts in which he addresses the question of justice. And the references which do exist emphasize the need to recognize that the 'postmodern is not to be taken in a periodizing sense' (Lyotard and Thébaud, 1985: 16n) and that thought, in any event, remains 'modern' (Lyotard, 1988a: 135–6). In a subsequent clarificatory essay Lyotard remarks that the term postmodern 'was a slightly provocative way of placing (or displacing) into the limelight the debate about knowledge. Postmodernity is not a new age, but the rewriting of some of the features claimed by modernity, and first of all modernity's claim to ground its legitimacy on the project of liberating humanity as a whole through science and technology. But as I have said, that rewriting has been at work, for a long time now, in modernity itself' (1991: 34).

2 In *The Différend* Lyotard makes a number of references to the limitations of the language game metaphor. For example, 'An I will be presumed to make "use" of language, to "play" it with "another" or "others". This is a success for anthropomorphism, a defeat for thought . . . The addressor must be understood as a situated instance in a phrase universe, on a par with the referent, the addressee, and the sense. "We" do not employ language' (1988a: 55); and later, 'You don't play around with language . . . And in this sense there are no language games. There are stakes tied to genres of discourse' (ibid.: 137).

3 In a similar vein Charles Taylor draws attention to a 'universal potential' at the basis of the politics of difference, namely 'the potential for forming and defining one's own identity, as an individual and also as a culture. This potentiality must be respected' (1992: 42).

7
MORALITY AFTER AMBIVALENCE

Modernity, that form of life associated with the constant pursuit of innovation and transformation, with the application of critical reason and
reflection to the conditions and circumstances of our being, has been
identified as a 'cultural project' and 'socially accomplished form of life'
which constitutes existence as in need of order(ing) and/or re-design
(Bauman, 1991: 4). But as the modern project has itself become a focus for
critical reflection, so 'ambiguity, confusion, undecidability [and] ambivalence' have come to be recognized as inescapable corollaries, if not
products, of the modern order's constitution (ibid.: 7). Notwithstanding the
promise of modernity and the rhetoric which has accompanied its course,
under modern conditions we find ourselves living more and more with
uncertainty. The flip side of the pursuit of order and control, and the
ostensibly greater freedom and wider range of choice generally equated
with modern forms of life, is a growing sense of uncertainty and an
increasing awareness of risk, if not direct experiences of the same.

The 'wholesale reflexivity' of modernity has been recognized to be
unavoidably 'unsettling' in so far as it undermines certainty and replaces it
with doubt. Such thoroughgoing reflexivity has been described as 'a
pervasive feature of modern critical reason [which] permeates into everyday
life as well as philosophical consciousness, and forms a general existential
dimension of the contemporary world' (Giddens, 1991: 3). In a broadly
comparable manner it has been suggested that it is possible to distinguish
between two kinds of doubt which have accompanied modernity from the
beginning. The first kind of doubt serviced the authority of science and
disarmed 'the uncertainty and ambiguity that ignorance brings in its wake'
by treating the latter as simply temporary, as an occasion 'to display the
potency of reason, and so it breeds . . . reassurance' (Bauman, 1991: 243),
for a time at least, until that is it is realized that knowledge and ignorance
are in tandem, such that where one advances the other surely follows. In
short, as Bauman remarks, 'the growth of knowledge expands the field of
ignorance' (ibid.: 244). The other, more potent doubt, implied above and
described as haunting the modern mentality, concerns the undermining of
the proclaimed superiority of scientific reason itself by the identification of
science as merely 'one story among many' (ibid.: 243). Similarly, the 'very
high degree of reflectiveness, deliberation and choice' associated with
modernity has been identified as bringing with it 'a high degree of deinsti-
tutionalization' and, in turn, social instability and uncertainty (Berger and

Kellner, 1982: 153). Likewise, it has been argued that the problems or costs of modernity are becoming increasingly evident, that 'many of the established ways of living together are not working well. Some of them are not working as they were intended to. Others are having alarming and unintended consequences' (Bellah et al., 1991: 4).

Uncertainty is a prominent feature of both science and everyday life, of analysis and social conduct. But while we may find ourselves living analytically and ethico-politically amidst uncertainty, and with ambivalence, it by no means follows that we must resign ourselves to continuing to *suffer* from uncertainty or ambivalence. To the contrary, there is no shortage of narratives outlining ways of responding positively to the predicaments associated with uncertainty, narratives offering suggestions for ways of living not simply *with* ambivalence, but in a sense *after* ambivalence, after coming to terms with ambivalence. For example, when Bauman offers a diagnosis of our condition as one of 'living with ambivalence', he makes reference to the necessary abandonment of a 'vocabulary parasitic on the hope of (or determination for) universality, certainty and transparency' (1991: 234) and proceeds to allude to the possible benefits of such a strategy, namely 'wider vistas' and 'new wisdom', as well as the chance to begin to build 'a human community resourceful and thoughtful enough to cope with the present challenges' (1995a: 287). Ironically, the diagnosis provided is delivered in such a manner as to suggest the continuing presence of precisely those qualities designated for abandonment. Delivered with certainty, and seemingly claiming universality, the analysis not only renders the consequences of modernity transparent, strongly implying that 'this is really how it is', but in a sense the analysis offered also constitutes a recommendation as to how to proceed, by providing an answer to the question 'what is to be done' in the face of the postmodern consequences of modernity. And just as Bauman has sought to outline the ways in which modernity has tended to diminish our sense of moral responsibility, insofar as it has 'emancipated purposeful action from moral constraints' (1991: 50), and has, in turn, attempted to construct an appropriate ethico-political response, so in a parallel manner, albeit with somewhat different, at times radically different ethico-political assumptions, a number of other analysts have drawn attention to the 'de-moralization' of modern society (Himmelfarb, 1995), the 'morally ambiguous' character of modern institutions (Bellah et al., 1991; Selznick, 1992), and 'the dire moral and social consequences' associated with modernity (Etzioni, 1994).

Moral Anxiety

An increasing concern with the moral consequences of modernity, or rather the impact of modernity on morality, is not confined to the intellectual fields of social analysis and philosophical inquiry, on the contrary the growing academic discourse on morality and ethics might be argued to be merely one sign of the wider prominence such matters now seem to assume in public reflections on contemporary social conditions and political processes. In Britain, politicians, religious leaders, educationalists and media commentators have joined debate over what has been described as our 'age of anxiety', an age of *moral* anxiety. In political pamphlets and policy statements, in debates in Parliament and the House of Lords, as well as in pronouncements from the pulpit and the screen, and in newspaper articles and editorials, the subject of morality, identified as in crisis, confusion, disorder, fragmentation or decay, has become, if not a commonplace, certainly a recurring theme to which analysts and commentators have been, and continue to be, irresistibly drawn.

A sequence of events in Britain during the 1990s have added to prevailing fears about the condition of the social and moral fabric, prompting concern to be expressed about the accelerating fragmentation and fragility of modern communities. These events include a number of widely reported tragedies affecting individual families and communities, for example the killing of Jamie Bulger, the West murders, the distressful deaths of school-children at Dunblane, and the murder of headmaster Philip Lawrence. Events such as these, coupled with longerstanding concerns about rising crime rates and other manifestations of social disorder and incivility; growing unease about the lack of availability of adequate resources necessary for effective treatment of sickness and ill-health; worries about provision for the poor, the homeless, the elderly, and others – those described by Bauman as 'flawed consumers' (1997: 14, 41–2) – worries compounded by an awareness that the economic and social policies of successive administrations between 1979 and 1998 have effected a further mal-distribution of wealth by taking resources from the unfortunate, the underprivileged, and the unemployed, only in order to bestow yet more riches on the already excessively privileged or over-endowed, have led a number of politicians, religious leaders, analysts and commentators to identify a moral crisis and to argue for the necessity of a moral reconstruction of community.

Acceptance of the importance of social morality to community life was a prominent feature of the political discourse of the British 'New Labour' Party in the period leading up to the 1997 General Election, and acknowledgement of the existence of a problem in this regard led to a series of calls for a regeneration of 'community', calls which effectively constituted an affirmation of the central concerns articulated in the American creed of 'communitarianism' (Etzioni, 1994). For example, in a series of policy statements and articles reference is made to the need to revive responsibility and the necessity of moving 'from dependency back towards mutual responsibility . . . to re-establish vibrant community life' (Straw, 1995); the importance of nurturing a 'new social morality' in which there is a recognition of a 'collective duty' to help the less fortunate, the goal being to 'create a society which acknowledges mutual rights and duties, not to hold back the individual, but as a necessary part of individual fulfilment' (Blair,

1996); and the existence of a growing body of evidence indicating that 'now people are asking what can be done to improve public goods, or . . . to help societies stick together' (Mulgan, 1997).

Such communitarian sentiments have received a degree of support from social analysts keen to speculate about the paths along which it might be possible to move in a context where the postwar social democratic consensus has been largely dismantled, now that we find ourselves living, in John Gray's (1996) terms, 'after social democracy'. However, support has not been unqualified. While emphasizing that there is no prospect of a return to policies of demand management and full employment, and no sense in turning the clock back on trade union rights and privileges in a context where there exists an over-supply of cheap labour in countries eager to attract international capital, Gray simultaneously pours scorn on what is described as the nostalgic rhetoric of a 'One Nation' variant of communitarianism as articulated by 'New Labour'. The alternative path outlined is for what is described as a 'liberal' variant of communitarianism, 'liberal communitarianism', which if it is not an oxymoron is certainly contentious in so far as it seems to assume that it is possible to reconcile the freedoms associated with liberalism with the responsibilities and constraints required to achieve the security and cohesiveness of community advocated within communitarianism. Gray is clearly critical of possessive individualism and he appears to distance himself from the idea of universal values, but it is difficult to understand how what is ultimately advocated, namely different communities upholding their own particular 'norms of fairness', will avoid a reproduction of the status quo, that is of conflicts within and between communities over the issue of precisely what constitutes 'fairness' and how it is to be achieved, or what policy measures and transformations will lead to 'fairness'. Contrary to Gray's assumption, it is questionable whether there is much *common* life or culture in which to have faith, beyond, that is, the culture industry's market-orchestrated range of 'popular' consumer commodities, services and media-relayed texts and narratives. Cultural norms, beliefs and practices are contested, they conflict and collide, and disagreements continually arise about interpretation and fulfilment. What is assumed by Gray, namely some shared notion of a common set of cultural values, is precisely what has been regarded as absent, problematic and increasingly a matter of dispute (Etzioni, 1994; Featherstone, 1995: Bellah et al., 1996).

Just as John Gray has responded to New Labour's embrace of communitarianism with criticisms which provide some intellectual substance to the political rhetoric on 'community', so Roger Scruton (1996a) has sought to do something broadly similar in relation to the Conservative Party, that is to serve up a critical interpretation of some of the features of communitarianism which, if they can be reconciled with a post-Thatcher rhetoric about 'social' issues and problems, a longerstanding Conservative endorsement of the necessity of affirming (but not necessarily upholding in conduct) particular 'traditional' values in respect of personal morality and sexual conduct, and the promotion of certain standards in relation to education and culture, might serve as the basis on which social (and political) cohesion can be (re)constituted. For Scruton, approaching communitarianism from a different, rather more critical point on the political spectrum, in so far as the objective is social order and cohesion, then enduring absolute values and respect for authority are to be regarded as non-negotiable prerequisites, a corollary of which is that the notion of a 'new social morality' is to be considered a contradiction in terms. Indeed, Scruton (1996b) caustically comments that the idea of a '"social" morality – as though morality could be constantly renegotiated to meet changing social realities – is pure humbug'. Moral values, as Scruton identifies them, are 'never new', they are timeless, the 'legacy of civilisation', which is of course an unacknowledged reference to a particularly 'local' form of civilization, for which even the adjective 'Western' may be too broad. The position occupied by Scruton is symptomatic of the difficulty Conservative thinkers and analysts have had in coming to terms with communitarianism, in particular with reconciling their commitment to a set of absolute values and parallel ambitions to reduce restrictions on individual choice and freedom, with the political reality of communitarianism, which requires a recognition of both the moral constitution of community and, as a corollary, the necessity of an unspecified degree of communal regulation of conduct. For Conservative thinkers the political consequences of communitarianism are frequently equated with a restriction of individual rights and an expansion of State regulation, the communitarian case for community being interpreted as simply a concealed call for coercion (Marenbom, 1996).

The debate about the moral reconstitution of community extends beyond the policy pronouncements of political parties and the reflections of their academic critics and acolytes to encompass religious leaders, educationalists and what has been described as a growing army of 'new moralists' (Harding, 1996). Religious leaders have argued that 'moral and spiritual values are a vital component of education, that there are important values which we share in common as a society . . . [and that we] should accord high importance to articulating them and trying to motivate our children to own and live by them for themselves' (Carey, 1996). A 'return to morality' has been identified as essential for the 'well-being of both individuals and society' (Harries, 1997). Such sentiments are in accord with calls for schools to return to teaching basic moral values and to contribute to civic renewal by playing a part in what has been described as a revival of 'communal virtues', objectives which have received expression in Britain in the School Curriculum and Assessment Authority's national statement on moral values (Tate, 1996).

If there seems to be a pervasive sense that we are indeed living in an age of 'deep moral anxiety' (*Guardian*, editorial, 1/1/97) and that some form of regeneration of morality is required, it is equally clear that there are substantial disagreements in public debate on the issue, in particular on the

question of the teaching of morals. For example, while it has been argued
that the identification of modern Western societies, and British society in
particular, as pluralistic and fragmented has been exaggerated, and a strong
pitch has been made for the existence of an unacknowledged common
moral code in opposition to an alternative construction of 'moral relativism' (Tate, 1996), there remain significant problems with both the diagnosis
and the remedy recommended. Although it is suggested that major
civilizations and faiths display 'a remarkable convergence when defining
those things in the human spirit worth valuing' (ibid.), and further, that
public response to the catalogue of tragic events identified earlier, coupled
with the high level of agreement reached within the School Curriculum and
Assessment Authority's national forum on values, constitute a challenge to
the idea that pluralism and fragmentation represent a dominant feature
of contemporary British social life, there is a simultaneous recognition of a
wide range of significant value differences which effectively call into
question the existence of a common moral code. The admission of dis-
ageements about the source or grounds of values, perhaps vested in
a particular divine being or a conception of human nature, along with a
recognition of marked differences over the application of any 'common'
values to such controversial matters as abortion and sexuality, coupled with
an acknowledgement that there exists a diversity of family forms and an
absence of consensus over the question of the value of any one particular
form of family life, suggests that the notion of an 'agreement on a range of
values to do with society, relationships, self and the environment' (ibid.), is
more apparent than real, rhetorical rather than lived, and that it conceals
significant differences of interpretation and meaning. An endorsement of
a notion of the 'good society', or an associated set of moral values, is a
hollow gesture unless there are adequate grounds for assuming that
a substantial level of agreement already exists about what might be meant
by 'good society' and how particular moral values are to be interpreted and
recognized to be realized, or realizable, in and through the cultivation or
nurturing of specific forms of conduct.

The idea that 'responsibilities' might need, for the time being at least, to
be put before 'rights' is one plank of the communitarian platform, although
it is qualified considerably in the communitarian narrative by a parallel
reference to the need to 'aim for a judicious mix of self-interest, self-
expression, and commitment to the commons – of rights *and* responsibilties' (Etzioni, 1994: 26). Likewise, the recommendation that it is time to
revive the sense that 'we belong to a civic society' and the recognition that
there exists 'a moral dimension to every aspect of our lives' (Tate, 1996)
constitute strong communitarian themes.

Communitarianism constitutes a programme directed towards a set of
social conditions in which the erosion of an effective common moral culture
is identified as a problem, if not *the* problem – the recommendation being
that it is necessary to move from an excessive preoccupation with '"I" to
"we" . . . that a strong commitment to the commons must now be *added* to

strong commitments to individual needs and interests that are already well ensconced' (Etzioni, 1994: 26). The reflections on morality offered within the SCAA national forum similarly take for granted that a common moral code already exists in some form and simply needs to be acknowledged and restored.

There is a further problem with the position outlined by the SCAA national forum on values and that is the assumption that introducing lessons on morals into the school curriculum will be conducive to a regeneration of civic morality. The call for schools to strengthen their teaching of morality is understandable in a context where it is being argued that there has been an erosion, if not a loss, of shared moral meanings. Given the significance assumed by the school, which along with the family is commonly regarded as a pivotal institution for the transmission of values from one generation to the next, it is hardly surprising that education and schooling should feature prominently in the debate over morality. But is it appropriate to treat morality as a subject for the curriculum? Can virtue be taught? To pose such questions is not to imply that morality and virtue have no place in the life of the school, on the contrary, but it is to raise doubts about the wisdom of loading the school curriculum with the subject 'moral values', particularly when such values, for the most part, remain confused and contentious, if they are not actually contradicted and undermined within the wider economy and polity.

What moral maxims are to be taught in a social context characterized by fluidity and flux rather than stasis? Nostalgia for a more traditional and morally ordered past (or perhaps it would be more appropriate to refer to a past which is fondly remembered as morally ordered) offers no substitute for an analysis of the present. The memory, or recalled experience, of shared moral maxims was, as Mary Midgley rightly comments, 'a consequence of more ordered [social] conditions, not the cause' (1996). The more ordered social conditions and shared moral maxims associated with traditional forms of life have been eroded, not because 'individuals have become morally feeble', but as a consequence of modernity, and in particular the increased mobility and flexibility which is a corollary of modern social and economic life. It is ironic that the very economic transformations and policies widely promoted and demanded by Conservative politicians and analysts between 1979 and 1997, transformations and policies which were re-affirmed by the following 'New Labour' administration, should require forms of labour mobility and flexibility which have proven to be so disruptive, if not seriously damaging, to the stability of family life – 'one spouse or other in a family may have to move elsewhere . . . people may have to move to places where they cannot have their children with them' (ibid.). Can campaigns for 'family values' and 'community' be anything other than hollow rhetoric in a context where 'market' economics increasingly holds sway? Where everything is reducible to a commodity, has a price, and is in principle exchangeable, what place, if any, can there be for morality? The calculating pursuit of self-interest and gain which is intrinsic

to the market-place and the associated culture of therapeutic contractualism sit uncomfortably with the idea of a regeneration of moral community.
What moral maxims are to be taught in a social context characterized by
(in)difference and diversity, rather than consensus and unity? What is to be
taught about morality in a society in which there seems to be little or no
moral consensus? Can we, Jonathan Sacks (1996) asks, 'teach anything
beyond the ability to make choices?' The positive response forthcoming is
that it is necessary to concentrate on inculcating virtues, that such necessary
civic habits of behaviour as patience and self-restraint, honesty and respect
for others may be acquired through example and practice. Morality, Sacks
adds, 'is learnt by practice long before it can be made the subject of
reflection . . . Morality is more than a subject on the curriculum. It is
integral to the character of a school. If a school's rules are clear, fair and
consistent, and if the teachers share and exemplify its aims, they will
naturally inculcate virtues. A school is a moral community and cannot help
but teach certain habits by what it rewards and punishes'. Such a process of
inculcation of virtue(s) implies good practices, that is practices considered
to exemplify, or to be compatible with, particular virtues. However, the
institution of the school is more complex and problematic than Sacks
appears to acknowledge or allow. If the school constitutes a 'moral
community' it is one with potential internal differences and divisions, an
institution which may be rejected and resisted by some of its members, an
institution within which sub-cultures may operate to resist and undermine
the inculcation of particular virtues. Good schools may, as Sacks suggests,
'inculcate discipline, responsibility and pride', but not all schools fit
the profile and, in any event, in many schools, if not the majority, the
inculcation of such virtues is a matter of continual struggle, for schools are
not islands, they exist in a social and economic context which has encour-
aged hedonism, promoted a competitiveness which too often has been
oblivious to the welfare and interest of others, stimulated acquisitiveness,
while disregarding associated social and environmental costs, and
celebrated the personal possession of material goods and riches as indices
of individual worth and signs of social value. In such a wider context the
demands and responsibilities placed upon schools to revive and nurture
virtue appear not simply unreasonable and impractical but virtually
Utopian. While Sacks recognizes that 'schools cannot be moral influences
on their own', the moral regeneration advocated requires not simply the
support of 'families and neighbourhoods' but a broader, more far-reaching
transformation of modern culture and economy. The optimistic note which
Sacks provides, namely that 'when it comes to the defence of a civilisation,
our fortresses are schools, our heroes are teachers, and our strongest
weapon is education', rings rather hollow and unconvincing, for the fortress
has long ago been breached, teachers have long since ceased to be regarded
as 'heroes', unsung or otherwise, or to be appropriately valued and
rewarded, revered or respected, and if education continues to be regarded
as a 'weapon' it is primarily, if not entirely, for its assumed ability to

improve the economic performance of the nation's workforce, rather than for its 'civilizing' or moral potential. In short, the acquisition of a range of skills and training, rather than reflection on, and the inculcation of, moral virtue has increasingly become the ordained target of education.

As one critic has remarked, the grander metaphysical narratives which once offered a rationale for education and schooling, narratives which gave guidance and inspiration and provided a 'sense of continuity and purpose', have been replaced by 'stories that are thin, crass, and certainly without transcendent meaning' (Postman, 1996). The narratives currently most likely to be promoted to justify schooling and legitimate the conflation of education with training include economic utility, consumership and technological change. Neil Postman argues that too often we hear that 'the main purpose of learning is to prepare . . . [the young] for entry into economic life', that the measure of a person's achievement is the level of their possessions, and/or that 'the main purpose of learning is to help the young to accommodate themselves to technological change'. However, rather than call for a 'deschooling of society' (Illich, 1973), Postman makes the case for a reorientation of education and schooling, effectively for a moral enrichment of schooling, by offering a series of alternative possible narratives. One possible alternative, 'human beings as stewards of the Earth', is argued to evoke an increased sense of responsibility towards others and the environment, as it promotes a greater understanding of our interdependence and of the need for increased global cooperation and solidarity. A second possible alternative narrative outlined is one which draws attention to the limits and limitations of both our knowledge and our ability to redesign and (re-)order our world, effectively a 'postmodern' narrative which accepts that fallibility is an intrinsic feature of existence, that human beings are perpetually vulnerable to making mistakes, and that living with, and responding to error and risk is an inescapable part of the human condition. If such a narrative were to find a prominent place within education then knowledge would be regarded more modestly, not as fixed or absolute, but as 'an on-going struggle to overcome human error' and, in turn, we would be more likely to appreciate that 'we are dangerous to ourselves and others when we aspire to the knowledge of gods' (Postman, 1996). One important consequence of such a narrative is its capacity to increase understanding of the ambivalence of modernity, of the respects in which the pursuit of advances in knowledge simultaneously produces error; the cultivation of order and certainty yielding further symptoms of disorder and contingency (Bauman, 1991).

The Cultural Contradictions of Modern Morality

At the heart of the current debate about morality lies a distinction between the 'private' and the 'public', one which has received expression in a series of studies and analyses. For example, a critical contrast has been drawn

between the pursuit of self or private interest and provision for the public
household (Bell, 1976); the quest for 'purely private satisfactions' and a
parallel neglect of the virtues of care and responsibility directed towards the
community (Bellah et al., 1991); and the promotion of 'self-interest' or
'individual interests' to the detriment of 'civic virtue' or 'the common good'
(Selznick, 1992). It has been argued that there is a need to counter 'the
unbridled pursuit of self-interest' and to 'shore up the moral foundations of
our society' (Etzioni, 1994: 248); that the material freedoms and rights of
the consumer subject have been emphasized at the expense of the moral
quality of communal life (Sacks, 1997); and that these 'great issues of
ethics', issues which include the balance between 'peaceful cooperation and
personal self-assertion, synchronization of individual conduct and collective
welfare' (Bauman, 1993: 4) now need to be dealt with in a different way.

Reflecting on the increasing influence of hedonism, 'the prevailing value
in our [Western] society', Daniel Bell (1976: xi–xii) draws attention to the
'unraveling of the threads' of Western capitalist modernity, and in
particular to the ways in which 'goodness morality' has been steadily
displaced by the pursuit of personal gratification. For Bell the initial focus
of discussion is the respect in which the production requirement of business
corporations for individuals to apply themselves diligently in the workplace, to become organization people, is at odds with, and has been
steadily undermined by, the widespread promotion of the pursuit of
'pleasure, instant joy, relaxing and letting go' (ibid.: 72) as a life-goal, a
promotion ironically in which business corporations must themselves, of
necessity, have a major interest, and to which they have contributed substantially as they have sought to increase the desire for and consumption of
a proliferating range of products and services. In short, the concern
expressed is that the respect for authority, discipline, restraint and delayed
gratification generally required in the workplace is in contradiction with,
and is being rapidly eroded by, the promotion of self-expression, spontaneity, pleasure and immediate gratification within modern culture. With
the 'abandonment of Puritanism and the Protestant ethic', synonymous
with the displacement of 'goodness morality' by what has been termed a
'fun morality', in other words a move from 'asceticism to hedonism' (ibid.:
71, 82), it is argued that there has been a simultaneous loss of the ability to
share and sacrifice, a devaluation and at times a denigration of the idea of
civic responsibility, and that the threads holding society together have
begun to unravel. The context in which Bell began to express such concerns, the late 1960s and early 1970s, was a period in which the assumption
of continuing economic expansiveness, and the associated prospect of
rapidly increasing 'material wealth as a solvent for social strains' (ibid.: 83)
began to be undermined by events and in consequence subject to increasing
doubt. It was a period in which the post-Second World War Fordist–
Keynesian economic boom was coming to an end; a period in which
international economic competition intensified and American economic
hegemony began to be challenged by reconstructed Western European

economies, the rapid economic development of Japan, and the emergence of a cluster of newly industrializing countries; a period in which, as David Harvey remarks, the 'inherent contradictions of capitalism became more and more apparent' (1989: 142). What living with those growing contradictions might involve is precisely the focus of Bell's analysis.

It is in this troubled economic and political context that the problem of the 'public household' is located, a problem which ultimately involves the 'legitimations of the society as expressed in the motivations of individuals and the moral purposes of the nation' (Bell, 1976: 83). The central concern articulated is that as traditional values have been eroded by the forces of modernity, so social life has lost its moral grounding, and lacking 'a culture that is a symbolic expression of any vitality or a moral impulse that is a motivational or binding force', Bell wonders what 'can hold . . . society together?' (ibid.: 84). What are the prospects for communal solutions, for a revitalized sense of public interest, in a context where individual or private interests continue to predominate? Bell's reflections have as their primary focus the prospects for the United States of America towards the close of the twentieth century, however as capitalism as a form of organization of economic life is now global in reach, and the complex consequences of an associated 'rampant individualism' and culture of modernism appear no less extensive, the related problematic issue of the public interest, or 'public household', has a broader relevance and in principle, if not increasingly in practice, it constitutes the major preoccupation for any democratic state.

A household, Bell remarks, 'consists in sharing things in common . . . and necessarily has to come to some common understanding of the common good' (ibid.: 222). As with the notion of the domestic household, the primary concern of the public household, Bell suggests, has been 'needs'. In the case of the domestic household, as conventionally understood, it is the wellbeing of the members of the household which is central, to be achieved through the provision of basic needs (food, shelter, clothing, care and companionship, etc.); with the notion of the public household the focus falls upon needs identified as common, that is a range of goods and services which it has been assumed 'individuals cannot purchase for themselves' (ibid.: 224). Above and beyond the forms of economic activity to be found in the domestic and public households there is the modern capitalist market economy, characterized by production for profit, the pursuit of increasing levels of capital accumulation, where 'the ends of production are not common but individual; and . . . the motives for the acquisition of goods are not needs but *wants*' (ibid.: 223). Both the domestic and the public household have been (and continue to be) transformed by the expansion of the capitalist market economy, in particular by a complex process of constant cultivation of seemingly inexhaustible levels of private want. However, it is not simply that 'wants' have replaced 'needs', which is all that Bell appears to allow at this stage, but that former 'wants' may become, and in some cases have become present 'needs', become defined, experienced and accepted within communities as necessities.[1] For example, within many if not all late-modern communities easy access to, if not household ownership of, a range of appliances – telephone, television, video-recorder, stereo system, etc. – has come to be recognized as virtually a necessity. And as the scale and range of 'want' generation has accelerated, so the disposable income requirements of most domestic households have increased and, in an economic context characterized by problems of inflation, unemployment and slow or no growth, the financing of forms of public consumption associated with an extended public household has encountered resistance and in consequence has become increasingly problematic.

Although attempts have subsequently been made to reset the parameters of the public household, the general observations offered by Bell on the predicaments confronting the democratic polity remain pertinent. Notwithstanding the neo-liberal free-market orientations of successive American and British administrations throughout the 1980s and 1990s, the provision of a substantial range of common goods and services continues to remain the primary responsibility of the public household. However, while there continue to be goods and services which individuals cannot purchase for themselves, Bell mentions in this context 'military defense, roads, [and] railways' (ibid.: 224), and at the time he might have added to the list a justice system and penal institutions, as well as law enforcement agencies, throughout the 1980s and 1990s in Britain a process of privatization of public utilities and services, introduced, in part, as a response to the very range of economic and political difficulties Bell has identified, has transferred the provision of a range of goods and services from the overt and contestable context of the public household to the 'hidden hand' of the market economy.

In his discussion of the public household Bell emphasizes the significance of commitments (made in the 1960s in America and in the immediate post-Second World War period in Britain) to a normative social policy, in particular a commitment to a welfare state. Such commitments are described as 'largely irreversible' and in turn as responsible for the creation of 'new and deep dilemmas'. As questions concerning economic direction, 'costs, redress, priorities, and goals have all become matters of conscious and debated social policy' (ibid.: 226), so potentially contentious issues have become explicit, have been identified as matters about which something may be done, and in respect of which demands may be made of government. Bell adds that the public household has increasingly become the 'arena for the expression not only of public needs *but also of private wants*' (ibid.: 226), and that successive governments have found it increasingly difficult to honour the responsibility, inappropriately attributed to them, to deliver levels of economic growth required to satisfy public needs and fulfil private wants. Increasing claims and/or rising demands for public goods and services, for example in health, welfare and education, have not been 'matched by the mechanisms to pay for them, either a rising debt, or rising taxes' (ibid.: 227). And as what Bell terms 'rising expectations' have been transformed into 'rising entitlements', that is increasing claims for social rights in respect of 'economic security, social services, educational access, and the like' (ibid.: 233 n16), so the problem has been exacerbated, leading one analyst to argue, in a subsequent 'communitarian' agenda on rights and responsibilities, for a 'moratorium on the minting of most, if not all, new rights; [re-establishment of] the link between rights and responsibilities; [and recognition] that some responsibilties do not entail rights' (Etzioni, 1994: 4).

The problems currently facing the public household, and those anticipated, are argued to be directly, or indirectly, a reflection of the difficulty of reconciling private wants with public interests, the difficulty of managing the competing claims and demands made for private and public forms of consumption in a context in which the continuing sustainability of economic growth – its very possibility as well as desirability given the damaging costs and consequences increasingly recognized to be a corollary – has been called into question. In so far as it is no longer possible to assume that the recurring 'dilemmas of private vices and public interests' (ibid.: 236) can be resolved by ever-increasing levels of economic growth, something has to give. In exploring the policy options available to the polity to manage the dilemmas arising from a complex and contradictory combination of 'bourgeois appetites which resist curbs on acquisitiveness, either morally or by taxation', a rising demand for 'social' entitlements, and 'an individualist ethos which at best defends the idea of personal liberty, and at worst evades the necessary social responsibilities and social sacrifices which a communal society demands' (ibid.: 249), measures which might restrain or reduce demand by raising unemployment and/or cutting government expenditure are identified as 'politically unacceptable', as measures which Western governments would not countenance. Such observations underline the perils of intellectual punditry, for within a few years administrations in both America and Britain introduced 'deflationary' economic measures which not only served to deny, for substantial numbers of people, the very expectations of 'a job and a rising standard of living' which Bell had argued 'no government can deny' (ibid.: 239), but in addition reduced social provision for a range of beneficiaries. Subsequently other Western governments, for example in New Zealand, Australia, France, Italy and Germany, have proceeded to introduce their own variants of the 'economic restructuring' (read austerity) policy packages implemented by successive American and British administrations. Contrary to Bell's expectations, governments have not been reticent about attempting to reduce the scale and/or rate of increase of public expenditure, even though levels of unemployment have been rising.

If in Bell's analysis of the problems confronting the public household there is a serious underestimation of the political willingness of Western governments to introduce deflationary economic measures which inflict selective damage on the interests of already vulnerable and relatively impoverished sections of the community, 'the loss of *civitas*' identified as a corollary, that is the 'spontaneous willingness to obey the law, to respect the rights of others, to forgo the temptations of private enrichment at the expense of the public weal' (ibid.: 245), remains a prominent feature of both analytic reflection and political debate on contemporary social life. How appropriate and effective provision to meet the requirements of the public domain can be reconciled, if at all, with the continuing cultural and economic emphasis which tends to be placed upon the pursuit of self-interest remains a key question.

In his attempt to explore the parameters of a potential 'public philosophy' which might allow the question of the relationship between self-interest and public interest to be more effectively addressed and perhaps agreeably resolved, Bell argues that the classical Aristotelian notion of the *polis* is of limited value for it offers a view of social life modelled on the family. Not only are the associated assumptions of the natural fitness of those in authority and the need to curb acquisition and restrain desire 'uncongenial to a democratic ethos and to the modern temper', but in addition, as Bell remarks, the scale is inappropriate, for it signifies a form of social life where individuals 'know one another well and can express their concern for each other' (ibid.: 252). Bell adds that such a 'communitarian ethic', in which it is assumed that individuals share common principles and are predisposed to help one another, can only prevail on a small scale, and that the late-modern public household is 'not a community but an arena in which there are no normative rules' (ibid.: 256). Given the existence of a pluralistic society, a society of differences, Bell argues that it is necessary 'to establish which differences are relevant and legitimate for the normative functioning of the public household' (ibid.: 256), and to that end he identifies a number of key issues, central to which, predictably, is the fundamental matter of the articulation of public and private.[2]

The picture drawn is of a virtually unregulated individualism, which is deemed responsible, in America and other modern Western societies, for environmental degradation and an increasing 'neglect of social services and other community needs' (ibid.: 258), and for which the diversity of interest groups can offer no remedy, no consolation, for there is no common denominator between the plurality of groups, no all-encompassing 'overriding interest', no universally endorsed civic morality to which a broad appeal can be made. In consequence, the type of remedy for the forms of social disorganization and anomie arising from the fragmentary effects of increasing modernization outlined by Durkheim (1964), that is smaller community groups, not necessarily restricted to professional and occupational communities, 'standing between the unchecked egoism of the individual and the enormous and threatening power of the state' (Bell, 1976: 258), is regarded as, at best, of doubtful relevance. The egoism of the modern individual has been subject to only a relatively limited degree of regulation and this has tended to be justified in terms of a notion of respect for liberty – rhetoric promoting the 'freedom of the individual' – the cost of such freedom being increasing inequality of outcomes, or increasing disparities between individuals and groups of individuals, which in turn has consequences for the practice of liberty. At what point disparities between individuals, arising from differential advantage having been taken of available opportunities, begin to undermine the principle of equality of opportunity is not made clear. Likewise, the level such disparities might have to reach for them to be *recognized* to be contributing to the under-mining of equality of opportunity, and thereby to require redress through social measures, which needs must qualify and regulate 'the liberty of *some* . . . in order to make *others* more equal to them' (ibid.: 264), is similarly not addressed.

The response offered by Bell is ambivalent in the extreme. While there is an acknowledgement that using achieved outcomes, such as wealth to obtain additional privileges, creates the problem of unacceptable disparities – for example, he comments that 'we need to find some way of equalizing health services, of insuring everyone's access to adequate medical care' – he subsequently proceeds to argue that the rights of individuals to spend their money as they see fit should not be restricted, rather the aim should be 'to upgrade the services for all' (ibid.: 266). Appropriate universally available provision, if indeed that is what is meant by upgrading the services for all, is a commendable aim. However, the problem left unaddressed is how to get from here to there, how to move from a social and economic context in which there exist significant and increasing disparities between individuals and social groups in respect of access to key resources, as well as significant variations in the quality of resources available, by virtue of differences of wealth, income level, occupational benefits and privileges, status, and region, to a social order in which such differences do not determine, to anything like the current extent, the degree, level, or quality of access to resources. To simply assert the need for an upgrade of services to all, without addressing the critical issue of how the political will required to achieve an introduction of the social and economic measures necessary to improve public provision, by upgrading services to all, will be mobilized in the face of the continuing promotion and defence of vested self-interest, leaves more questions unanswered than it resolves. Whether it is in respect of health, education, welfare, or any other sphere of everyday life in which there is currently a pronounced tension between public and private interests, for example transport, a policy which effectively continues to encourage individuals to spend their money to purchase private provision as they see fit, not only serves to undermine the resource base and demand for existing (and potential) levels of public provision, making the idea of any future upgrade at best fanciful, but also ends up being self-defeating, for '[i]ndividual frustration and collective distraction are the contradictory outcomes of the unlimited pursuit of individual purposes' (Bellah et al., 1991: 270).

While expressing criticism of 'bourgeois hedonism, with its utilitarian emphasis on economic appetite', Bell wishes to affirm and promote 'political liberalism, with its concern for individual differences and liberty' (Bell, 1976: 277). Briefly acknowledging that bourgeois hedonism has been damaging for social need provision, that it can not provide a 'moral foundation for society' and needs to be rejected, Bell confidently asserts that it 'can be sundered' from political liberalism and that 'We can . . . insist on the necessity of public goods' (ibid.: 277), while still protecting the individual from coercion, and simultaneously assuring personal effort and merit is rewarded, 'within appropriate spheres' (ibid.: 277). Once again a number of key matters are quickly glossed over, notably the question of how a disarticulation of bourgeois hedonism and political liberalism is to be achieved, and how an insistence on the necessity of public goods, if it is to be more than rhetorical, will be operationalized (which goods will qualify?) and reconciled with a persisting commitment to reward personal effort and merit in 'appropriate spheres' (how is personal performance to be rewarded and which spheres are to be regarded as 'appropriate'?). Moreover, continuing to reward personal effort is itself likely to constitute a continuing source of the very difficulty already identified, namely that additional achieved outcomes may be deployed to obtain further privileges. One of the risks arising from the latter possibility is that public goods and services become undermined and eroded, save that is for 'private accumulation and private pleasures', which in a cultural setting 'focused relentlessly on the idea that individuals are self-interest maximizers' are paradoxically often the only 'measurable public goods' (Bellah et al., 1991: 50). As to what spheres might qualify as appropriate and, given an acknowledgement of the pluralistic character of contemporary society, how social processes of negotiation or decision-making might be expected to reach an accord, is not made clear, and in consequence it is difficult to avoid the conclusion that Bell's concern with achieving a re-affirmation of liberalism has merely led to a restatement of the problem of the public household.

Bell perceptively identifies the issue of the balance between public and private as a problem, one which is increasingly central to modern Western societies, and offers clarification of many of the issues involved. However, while noting the importance of finding 'a social cement' or 'common purposes', the significance of recognizing 'the limits of resources and the priority of *needs*, individual and social, over unlimited appetite and wants', and the associated necessity of trying to achieve 'agreement upon a conception of equity which gives all persons a sense of fairness and inclusion in the society' (Bell, 1976: 278–82), little if any consideration is given to the scale and the extent of the moral and cultural transformations required to counter hedonism, to diminish the pursuit of self-interest and promote the virtues of what Bell, briefly and enigmatically, refers to as a 'social compact'. Given the continuing existence of a well-entrenched culture of individualism, which is strongly implied in Bell's reaffirmation of liberalism, the question of how a moral concern with social needs and the 'good condition of human beings' is to be regenerated warrants consideration, but it is left unaddressed and unexplored. It is to a consideration of these issues, as they are articulated in the communitarian doctrine, to which I will now turn my attention.

The Moral Community

The terms in which the debate on the relationship between public and private interest is now being conducted have been transformed markedly and the sharp policy contrast drawn by Bell (ibid.: 275) between, on the one hand, preserving economic freedom and enforcing moral regulation and, on the other, enforcing economic regulation while upholding moral freedom, does not offer an effective purchase on the conditions currently encountered. The agenda now being constituted calls for the exercise of greater civic responsibility, for attention to be directed to a regeneration of moral community, to counter the neglect of the consequences of increasing social inequality and the frequent indifference displayed towards 'human misery and environmental degradation' (Bellah et al., 1991: 268), which has been associated with a capitalist, market-orchestrated, pursuit of self-interest, expressed in terms of the achievement of ever-increasing levels of consumption of goods and services. As one key communitarian figure has argued, 'in recent decades we have been tilting too far in the direction of letting everybody do their own thing or pursue their own interests and have concerned ourselves too little with our social responsibilities and moral commitments. It is time to set things right' (Etzioni, 1994: 38). But what does setting things right involve from a communitarian perspective?

The communitarian claim is that it is possible to balance the pursuit of self-interest with an effective 'commitment to the community', a commitment that does not necessitate 'a life of austerity, altruism, or self-sacrifice' (ibid.: 2). A moral (re-)ordering of social life is presented as being achievable 'without puritanical excesses', without a 'charge into a dark tunnel of moralism and authoritarianism' (ibid.: 1, 2). At the core of the communitarian campaign lie a number of virtues which are presented as being in need of regeneration or revival. Specifically, it is argued that there is a need to promote a resumption of social responsibilities, a need to recognize that a period of 'reconstruction' is required following the late-modern deconstruction of social institutions and values, and that this will necessitate 'shoring up the social foundations of morality' (ibid.: 14). In particular, Etzioni expresses concern about some of the consequences of processes of deconstruction to which the institution of the family, education, and moral traditions and values have been subject, but such concern is not articulated as a lament for the passing of traditional forms, on the contrary, it is acknowledged that longstanding practices and assumptions deserved 'a critical going over'. The difficulty is that associated dramatic increases in individual rights, and related claims, have been paralleled by a fragmentation of moral foundations, a rapid decline in social responsibility, and an undermining and discrediting of the notion of the public interest. It is argued that communities now lack a moral voice and in consequence that 'we live in a state of increasing moral confusion' (ibid.: 12). And in so far as individuals and a multiplicity of special interest groups compete to achieve self-serving goals by lobbying for, and frequently successfully claiming, large shares of the public budget, through 'subsidies, tax concessions, special credits' and the like, the prospect of underwriting a shared community or public interest becomes increasingly problematic.

The recovery of morality is argued to be articulated with a reconstitution of community, a renewal of both the idea and the experience of communal belonging. But where to begin? Etzioni's starting point is that there is a requirement for 'basic settled values', values that 'we as a community [can] endorse and actively affirm' (ibid.: 25). To whom 'we as a community' refers is not entirely clear – all citizens of the USA, WASPs, an enlightened middle class? – the context suggests that it is a conflated reference to the nation-state as a community, but rather than resolve matters this simply raises further questions about the meaning of 'community' for Etzioni, concerns about what the concept of 'community' represents. In contrast to a conception of morality as a property of individual conduct or action, exemplified, for example, by Bauman's concentration on the 'moral person', description of the 'moral call . . . [as] thoroughly personal', and comment that 'moral *responsibility* exists solely in interpellating the individual and being carried individually' (1993: 60, 54), communitarianism presents morality as a community matter, and regards communities as 'the most important sustaining source of moral voices' (Etzioni, 1994: 31). In short communitarians are concerned about the wellbeing of 'community' because it is identified as underpinning and sustaining morality by calling members to account, by making claims on them. It is community which constitutes the source of morality and which reinforces moral commitments and inclinations. But there are many different communities, a multiplicity of communities in fact, and the late-modern or *postmodern* predicament, is that the claims made by different communities on their members seem to vary considerably, and their respective 'moral' voices are rarely, if ever, in unison, on the contrary cacophony and conflict are as likely to characterize moral conversations.

Etzioni goes some way towards acknowledging the existence of a multiplicity of communities, however the very terms in which the acknowledgement is couched diminish the significance of existing community differences, as well as the substantial potential for disagreement and conflict over values, which is a prominent feature of contemporary community life:

> Communitarians . . . are often asked which community they mean. The local community? The national community? The sociologically correct answer is that communities are best viewed as if they were Chinese nesting boxes, in which less encompassing communities (families, neighbourhoods) are nested within more encompassing ones (local villages and towns), which in turn are situated within still more encompassing communities, the national and cross-national ones (such as the budding European Community). (ibid.: 32)

How Etzioni arrives at the answer given, and why it is considered to be 'the sociologically correct answer' is difficult to understand, for while it may be the case that some communities do indeed stand in a relationship for which the spatial and territorial configuration deployed might be appropriate, there are many other types of community (and inter-community relations) for which such a spatial configuration is inappropriate and very misleading. To be fair Etzioni does proceed to make brief reference to 'nongeographic communities that criss-cross the others' and does also acknowledge, in passing, that there is a possibility, given multiple communities, that people may 'choose at will which moral voice to heed', but this does not lead to a satisfactory consideration of the range of different possible manifestations of 'community', or of the problem of community differences and the potential for disagreement and conflict between communities.

Transformation of the relationship between place and identity, arising in part from increasing population migration and personal mobility (Keith and Pile, 1993), as well as the existence of various nongeographic and 'virtual' forms of relating and belonging (Featherstone and Lash, 1995), have major implications for our understanding and experience of community, but these do not seem to feature significantly on the communitarian analytic agenda, neither do the difficulties of relating across and/or achieving reconciliation between communities, nor the problems of living with the tensions and conflicts between communities with contrasting, if not incompatible, sets of values. Where Etzioni acknowledges the existence of different communities, multiple communities, the acknowledgement seems to serve merely as a pretext for a legislative exhortation to recognize that 'our society is neither without community nor sufficiently Communitarian' and that what is now required are 'communities that balance both diversity and unity . . . In short we need new communities in which people have choices and readily accommodate divergent *sub*communities but still maintain common bonds' (1994: 122). Precisely what bonds might be considered 'common' and capable of providing the basis of such a meaningful (comm)unity is another matter.

What kind of meaningful moral unity can be constituted amidst increasing social diversity is open to debate. How appropriate criteria are to be arrived at and agreed upon for deciding where the balance between diversity and unity might or should be set, which forms of diversity are to be tolerated and/or accommodated, and which choices are to be considered acceptable, are no less difficult matters to resolve. Etzioni argues that resolution of such matters is urgently required, for 'societies in which different communities pull in incompatible directions on basic matters are societies that experience moral confusion' (ibid.: 32). Increasingly, this is precisely the state in which many members of modern Western societies currently find themselves living. Given the existence of a pervasive sense of moral confusion, it is likely that the related general proposition advanced by Etzioni, notably that there is a 'need – on all levels, local, national – to agree on some basics' (ibid.: 32), will receive considerable support. How-ever, in so far as 'the moral community, one that sets norms and monitors conformity, is increasingly fragmented and pluralized' (Bauman, 1995a: 152), then precisely what is to count as basic, which values are to be considered fundamental, and how agreement is to be achieved, become far more contentious matters than Etzioni appears willing to allow.

Moral Voices – Paying Attention to Differences

Where consideration is given in Etzioni's narrative to the question of how to proceed to achieve what is described as 'a sense of we-ness' (1994: 124), how to restore and nourish an all-encompassing sense of moral community in the face of a multiplicity of different cultures and values, literally how to cultivate a 'community of communities', a distinction is invoked between unacceptable ('unbounded and unwholesome') and acceptable ('pluralism-within-unity') manifestations of difference and diversity. Cultural differ-ences are considered positive only in so far as they are able to be accom-modated within 'a framework of unity . . . that provides a set of overarching and nestling values and bonds' (ibid.: 155–6). The problems arising from cultural differences which effectively challenge, or conflict with, the com-munitarian advocated 'pluralism-within-unity', are briefly acknowledged, but only to be dismissed as threatening the break up of society. The communitarian preference outlined is quite clearly for a specific form of cultural and historical unity, the existence and assumed all-embracing quality of which, in the American cultural setting invoked by Etzioni, must be regarded as contentious. The debatable 'unity' invoked is one which, in any event, is itself being rapidly unsettled and transformed, if not dissolved. If there remains something approaching a unity it is predicated on an unacknowledged and on-going process of cultural hegemony, which in turn is being exposed and challenged by various forms of identity politics invoking as alternatives 'a black nation, a Hispanic hemisphere, a Native American country' (ibid.: 156). The latter represent more than ideas, they reflect existing forms of social and cultural life, which have been marginalized within, if not in important respects excluded from the cultural mainstream. Such alternatives, rendered peripheral if not excluded from the hegemonically constituted unity described as 'a supracommunity, a community of communities – *the* American society', the virtues of which Etzioni (ibid.: 160) is concerned to promote, simultaneously represent and constitute cultural dis-unity through their resistance to 'supracommunity' incorporation.

A surprising feature of Etzioni's narrative is that while a claim to be concerned about morality is made in a number of ways, for example through references to the importance of the 'moral voice' of the community, the current lack of 'firmly established moral positions', and the significant role 'communities play in sustaining moral commitments' (ibid.: 23–53), the issue of morality itself is not directly addressed or clarified; it is not a subject of analytic reflection. Rather, morality is simply presented as an ordering of behaviour and conduct which 'rests on intricate interactions among three factors: individual conscience, the moral voice of the community, and the state. Each one helps to sustain the others' (ibid.: 48). Once again we encounter a statement which is ultimately misleading in so far as it represents an oversimplification of the complex relationships between the factors identified. If there are historical moments and cultural contexts where each factor does indeed help to sustain the others, an assumption which is open to dispute (Bauman, 1995a), there are also many examples, possibly many more examples, where individual conscience may not accept the morality articulated by a dominant community, and may consequently engage in conduct which constitutes dissent from the perspective of the state. Likewise, the moral voice of a marginalized or minority community may be in a different and/or incompatible register to that of the dominant community and/or the state. In asserting that 'each one sustains the others' Etzioni is guilty of substituting communitarian prescription for analysis. If each factor was indeed always helping to sustain the others there would be no cause for communitarianism to promote, no community in need of reconstitution, and no morality in need of being shored up.

What morality actually involves, what counts as morality for communitarianism, has ultimately to be gleaned from examples given of relevant behaviour and conduct. On that score Etzioni makes reference to a variety of social situations and forms of conduct, ranging from the seemingly mundane, yet culturally revealing 'disapproval of those who flush their engine oil down the drain, refuse to sort their garbage, or wash their cars and water their lawns when the town's water reservoir is low' (1994: 24), to the expression of more profound concerns about what is required to reconstitute morality. In relation to the latter Etzioni emphasizes the importance of the family in moral education and calls for a 'higher valuation of children'; acknowledges the requirement placed on schools to transmit knowledge and skills, but adds that education should also include the reinforcement, and where necessary, the introduction of moral values; draws attention to neighbourhood, work and ethnic communities 'that bind individuals, who would otherwise be on their own, into groups of people who care for one another and who help maintain a civic, social, and moral order', but argues that such communities themselves need to be shored up; and finally emphasizes that 'the national society' must watch over local communities to ensure that they 'will not lock in values that *we*, as a more encompassing and overriding community, abhor' (ibid.: 248, emphasis added). For good measure Etzioni also calls for 'a new political energy' to counter political corruption, special interests, and the subversion of 'shared, community wide interests' (ibid.: 209–10). A consistent feature of the narrative is the assumption of a higher-level community, a pre-existing (comm)unity of communities, whose values constitute a seemingly sacrosanct measure or standard to which all other (sub)communities must accommodate themselves. There is no sign of ambivalence, no trace of doubt in Etzioni's narrative, but then there is no serious engagement with the question of moral differences, or with the complex social and political consequences of moral differences. There is no consideration of the different moral voices which contribute to the multiplicity of communities, which summon individuals and make demands of them in different ways, moral voices which may be raised in resistance to the claims a particular (supra)community may make to be hegemonic.

In contrast, in their related discussion of *The Good Society* Robert Bellah and his colleagues, while covering broadly similar ground to Etzioni, offer a more sober view of both prevailing conditions and future prospects. Like Etzioni, Bellah et al. identify the family and education as pivotal community institutions in the quest for 'a good society', but the family is described as 'no longer certain', not just in a state of 'flux' but in 'trouble' and education, in turn, is held to be overly focused on the achievement of individualistic economic and occupational advancement to the detriment of alternative social and moral objectives. Signs of trouble with the family identified by Bellah et al. include factors like an increasing turnover associated with a continuing growth in divorce rates, the diversity of relations and forms of organization of domestic life, which make the 'very meaning of the family . . . problematic', and the disarticulation of functions which have conventionally been regarded as synonymous with the 'nuclear family', for example 'emotional intimacy . . . , sexual life, and the nurture and socialization of children' (Bellah et al., 1991: 45). The 'decomposition of the family' is closely identified with an increased cultural emphasis placed upon the pursuit of individual fulfilment and an associated tendency to shirk responsibility. But if the diagnosis is unequivocal, the response is more ambivalent. While recognizing the diversity of family forms and distancing themselves from a categorical endorsement of the modern nuclear family as 'the only morally respectable form of the family', they nevertheless argue for the latter's centrality and value for the raising of children and for teaching an 'unselfish concern for others', and proceed to call for a reinvigoration of the family (ibid.: 47, 49).

Given the way in which the modern family has been fragmented by a series of social and economic transformations, what are the prospects of achieving a 'reinvigorated family'? And what would a reinvigorated 'post-traditional' late-modern family look like? In addition to proposing 'an extended national discussion' on the subject of what might be expected and desired from the family, Bellah and his colleagues call for more 'attentive' families. By the latter they seem to mean families that offer appropriate 'attention', particularly as far as the care of children is concerned; 'an intense family life' which is deemed necessary 'for the raising of responsible children who can nurture themselves and the world they live in' (ibid.: 258).[3] But in circumstances where family life is increasingly subject to diverse processes of de-construction and re-construction, and where concerns are being expressed about the possible 'de-institutionalization' of the family, what are the prospects for 'giving and receiving attention'? Ultimately not good according to Bellah and his colleagues, for as 'a "job culture" has expanded at the expense of a "family culture"' (ibid.: 260) not only is there not enough time to cope with the growing pressures of employment, domesticity and nurturing, but in addition there has been a widespread dislocation of the relationship of 'generational rootedness' between family life and community.

It is 'the pressures generated by our current form of political economy' that is identified as responsible for undermining long-term commitment to a particular 'public' place and/or community, and in so far as this continues to be the case security is likely to be sought in, if not equated with, 'private' wealth and personal possessions, and the prospect of restoring or reconstituting 'stable and attentive' forms of family life, families attentive to civic and other 'public' involvements, will remain relatively poor (ibid.: 261–2). The measures proposed to counter the dislocating tendencies identified are, for the most part, rather vague yet relatively familiar. Reference is made to the need to 'halt the decline of the family' and to do something to restore the identity and value of schools as 'learning communities for the creation of citizens', in contrast to the tendency to treat them as principally 'machines for the production of competitive, skilled workers' (ibid.: 262, 264). In respect of the family, and the objective of achieving more stability and 'attentiveness', it is the potential benefits of a decentralization of economic life, or 'localism', made possible by 'new developments in high technology', which is the focus of discussion. While the prospect of jobs and training being re-located, rather than people, may represent a precondition for preserving or nurturing a greater degree of generational community rootedness, a focus on such predominantly 'economic' measures offers little purchase on the wider range of 'cultural' factors which have had such a significant impact upon community and family life.

The movement or flows of personal relations associated with cultural transformations in sexual conduct and gender roles and identity have had significant consequences for family life (Giddens, 1992), but Bellah and his colleagues do not attend to such matters, indeed the closest they come to acknowledging that there might be an issue to address is in a few brief comments on the current diversity of family forms, comments which simply emphasize the importance of 'the quality of family life' without offering any clarification of the criteria for determining 'quality'. However, given the critical comments offered by Bellah and his colleagues on the subject of a shift from a 'child-centred family to an adult-centred family', following the marginalization of 'family culture' by 'job culture', and other related comments on the centrality and value of 'the modern nuclear family . . . in bringing children into the world and raising them' (1991: 46, 260, 47), the clear implication is the necessity of some kind of return to a child-centred family. The importance of such a return is made more explicit in Etzioni's communitarian call to rebuild moral foundations starting with the family. Emphasizing the responsibility of families to provide 'moral education and character formation', as well as material necessities, Etzioni moves on to criticize parents 'consumed by "making it" and consumerism, or pre-occupied with personal advancement', and argues that the task of moral education can not be left to child-minders 'or even professional child care centers' (1994: 256–7). Elaborating on the moral responsibilities of the family Etzioni calls for greater flexibility in the workplace to allow parents to fulfil their 'educational-moral duties', as well as increased social recognition of the value of childcare work. Warming to his theme Etzioni proceeds to make explicit the importance he attaches to two-parent families (preferably supported by relatives), by arguing that because of the nature of childcare, particularly its labour-intensive character, they are 'better able to discharge their child-raising duties' than single or lone parent families. Etzioni's assessment of family life begs a number of questions, particularly in respect of the contribution each parent in a two-parent family might make to the care of their children. Given a conventional modern nuclear family, no longer the most common form of family life, labour-intensive childcare has tended to be disproportionately, if not in some respects exclusively, the province of the mother figure, the figure of the father being relatively, if not in many cases absolutely, marginal to the process. But leaving to one side the question of whether in a two-parent family each parent pulls their weight, or whether, as the question is more frequently formulated, fathers feature sufficiently in the parenting frame, what is striking is the disparity between the expectations raised as to what 'communitarian' family life might be able to achieve and the current reality of an increasingly de-centred, individualizing and primarily adult-orientated family life experienced by a substantial, if not a growing, number of children.

Bellah and his colleagues make reference to the importance of tasks and activities which it is assumed have served in the past to bring families together. They identify the common family meal as a potential focus for regularly reconstituting the family, as a forum for celebrating family, as well as raising and hopefully resolving difficulties. What happens in the dual career family, they ask, 'when no one has time to prepare a meal, when for days on end the family has no common meal?' (Bellah et al., 1991: 260).[4] The short answer offered is that the opportunity to build a 'warmer family' and to enhance 'everyone's capacity for attention' is being lost. More broadly, in a cultural context powerfully influenced by therapeutic contractualism, where every commitment is potentially subject to a process of critical reflection which undercuts 'the possibility of other than self-interested relationships' (ibid.: 139), what are the prospects for a moral reconstitution of the family and of the community?

The very process of reflexivity intrinsic to modernity, exemplified in one form by social analysis but increasingly practised in mundane forms by modern subjects as they go about their everyday lives, relativizes and/or calls into question the moral content of social relationships. The life-world of the Goffmanesque modern subject characterized by 'the relentless insistence on consciousness and the endless scanning of one's own and other's feelings while making moment-by-moment calculations of the shifting cost/benefit balances' (ibid.: 139) is not one which is conducive to the re-establishment of common moral commitments and understandings. Notwithstanding the presentation of a long wish-list of desirable trans-formations regarded as conducive to the rebuilding of the moral foundations of social life, involving the family, school, community, and the polity, there is really relatively little of substance within the communitarian doctrine to indicate precisely how a radical shift from an increasingly de-moralized common culture, which is fundamentally individualist in character – 'expressive and utilitarian' in the words of Bellah et al. – might be achieved. However, the 'search for common moral understandings continues even in the face of the assertion that they are impossible' (ibid.: 141). If nothing else, communitarianism has restored questions of morality and ethics to the forefront of social analysis.

Communitarianism and the Question of Responsibility

The idea of assuming more responsibility is integral to the communitarian line, and to persuade self-interested modern subjects to do so appeal is made to the very self-interest identified as problematic. For example, Etzioni makes reference to those who are 'under the spell of modernity' (1994: 123) choosing to invest more and more of themselves 'in the pursuit of "making it"' and then goes on to caution that such efforts are not only ultimately 'unsatisfying' but also 'self-defeating'. Likening the endless pursuit of 'making it' to an addiction or obsession, or a 'distraction' from the virtues of 'attention' to use the terms employed by Bellah and his colleagues, Etzioni proceeds to argue that the 'communitarian nexus' offers the prospect for individuals of 'genuine inner satisfaction'. To enhance communitarian connections Etzioni proposes measures which involve (i) a re-orientation of personal life; (ii) a reduction in the emphasis placed upon 'career needs' and a greater recognition of and reconciliation with 'community bonds'; (iii) a fostering of effective (in contrast to symbolic) voluntary community endeavours; and (iv) architecturally redesigning the environment to facilitate increased community interaction, literally to create less austere or alienating and more community-friendly spatial terrains. Each of the first three measures proposed entails a marked shift of emphasis from a defensive preoccupation with a narrow sense of private interest to a positive embrace of the virtues of the public domain, a move away from solitary self-interest to a recognition of the virtues (and responsibility) of being for (and with) others. How such a radical transformation of attitude and orientation is to be achieved is another matter, once again one which is not adequately addressed. Perhaps there is no realistic potentially persuasive alternative, given the increasingly individualistic cultural context which we inhabit, but to proceed in terms of the cultivation of a critical appreciation of the respects in which the self might benefit, or be better served, by a regeneration of the public domain and the constitution of a communitarian nexus. In short, the call for exercise of greater responsibility, for some 'measure of caring, sharing, and *being our brother's and sister's keeper*' (ibid.: 260), is couched in terms of the problems which appear to follow from a failure to do so, notably that 'our brothers and sisters' – the unemployed, lone parents, disabled etc., etc. – become dependent on 'ever more expansive government, bureaucratized welfare agencies, and swollen regulations, police, courts, and jails' (ibid.: 260), the identified risk of which is erosion of the very social order conducive to the continued enhancement and fulfilment of individual self-interest. A similar diagnosis of the potentially self-defeating consequences to which the pursuit of *purely* individual or 'private' fulfilment is held to be vulnerable is outlined by Bellah and his colleagues. Like Etzioni, they argue that the 'quest for purely private fulfilment is illusory' and leads only to emptiness, and that what is required is some articulation of 'private fulfilment and public involvement' (Bellah et al., 1996: 163).

The communitarian call is for 'partnerships' between private and public, a reconciliation or articulation of 'own interests' with those of others, but it is almost entirely a prescriptive rather than an analytic narrative, one which carefully steers clear of any critical consideration of the socio-cultural and economic forces which arguably are responsible for the undermining and fragmentation of social cohesion, and diminution of a related collective sense of belonging which has been regarded as constitutive of community. It is a narrative which neglects to offer any clues as to how appropriate radical transformations in personal orientation might be achievable in the face of the continuation of powerful market-driven forces which promote, if they do not actually constitute, the self-preoccupied consumer subject as sovereign, as they simultaneously largely ignore, and thereby effectively diminish, the notion of moral responsibility for others. Offering a list which identifies the virtue of 'duties to the polity', including the need to pay rather than avoid taxes, to participate in voluntary activities and discharge 'community responsibilities', is all very well but the path from fine sentiments to appropriate other-directed forms of conduct remains largely uncharted territory. The observation that 'individuals have a responsibility for the material and moral well-being of others' (Etzioni, 1994: 264) may be timely and commendable, but unfortunately it is generally not borne out in practice, it is not realized in conduct.

One of the virtues of Bellah et al.'s *The Good Society* is that there is an attempt, albeit too brief, to account for the failure to honour or meet responsibilities. The authors argue that it is the erosion and/or relative weakness of 'sustaining institutions' that explains the moral indifference which has become a characteristic feature of too much of modern life – 'without sustaining institutions that make interdependence morally significant, individual attention becomes fragmented in focus and delimited in scope' (Bellah et al., 1991: 268). The disruption and/or break up of communities, following processes of geographical dispersion and isolation of populations which have been features of the dynamic development of modern city life, has led to increasingly segregated and fragmented lives and rendered meaningful expression of concern for others far more difficult. Others are, for the most part, made more anonymous and social inequality and human misery, if not rendered totally invisible through geographical dispersion and isolation, have increasingly become matters of communal indifference (Tester, 1997). From time to time such indifference may receive a token response, and possibly a measure of brief redress, for example through the mobilization of people in and around campaigns to restore 'traditional values', nurture personal morality, and combat expressions of violence considered to be symptomatic of the erosion of community wellbeing, as well as through the spectacle of media-orchestrated charity events which proffer a combination of humour and hysteria in the guise of entertainment, in exchange for a demonstration of compassion, or a simulation of such, which itself is generally expressed in the form of consumption.[5] If the former constitute transitory communal responses to the erosion of moral responsibility, responses which subside with the memory of the tragic events which are frequently their catalyst, the latter appear to be more about enjoyment and private fulfilment, and if they meet the communitarian call for more 'partnership' and 'public involvement', they do so merely tangentially, for they simultaneously continue to reinforce the very pecuniary preoccupations of an increasingly market-orientated modernity identified as responsible for a deterioration in the moral quality of social life.

To turn things around it is suggested that more 'attention' and less 'distraction' is required, that we have a responsibility 'to concern ourselves with the larger meaning of things in the longer run, rather than with short-term payoffs' (ibid.: 273). The argument outlined is that the 'distractions' of money, power, possessions and the pursuit of self-interest have too often taken precedence over 'attending' to or 'caring for' what is genuinely of importance. The possibility of identifying what is genuinely of importance in the midst of all the noise and interference accompanying the accelerating proliferation of expertise, opinion and information which tends to be associated with the preservation of vested interests, depends upon the cultivation of critically reflexive analytic skills and moral sensibilities within the educational process, which in turn requires a renewed commitment to the idea of the school as a learning community for the creation of responsible citizens. As Bellah and his colleagues argue, 'democracy is not the rule of experts. It is basic to the education of citizens that they learn how to evaluate expert opinion . . . Weighing the moral implications of different options is what is fundamental' (ibid.: 272). Such a recommendation calling for the 'repair or drastic reform' of modern institutions is reminiscent, in some respects at least, both of Ivan Illich's (1985) identification of the 'disabling' character of modern professionalism and parallel promotion of the 'convivial society' as the good society, and to a lesser extent Ulrich Beck's argument that increasing evidence of the fallibility of expert opinion is a manifestation of the emergence of a 'Risk Society'. The 'politics of generativity' outlined by Bellah and his colleagues occupies a position somewhere between Illich's more radical libertarian 'politics of conviviality' and Beck's more conservative politics of a reconstituted, albeit reflexive, modernity in which emphasis is placed upon the 'right to criticism *within* professions and organizations' (1992: 234), in contrast to the cultivation of a broader more democratic ability and right to be critical *of* professions and organizations promoted by Bellah et al. and Illich respectively.

In the cause of promoting the virtues of paying attention to what is of genuine importance, that is to 'the larger meaning of things in the longer run', Bellah et al. elaborate on the necessity of a 'politics of generativity'. At the heart of a politics of generativity lies a concern with the consequences of present practices for future generations, a concern about the wellbeing of our children, society's children, 'our children's children', and the need to overcome the obsessive pursuit of ever-rising levels of material wellbeing, paradoxically equated with the goal of increasing economic growth. The politics of generativity constitutes a moral discourse which simultaneously draws attention to the necessity of 'effective democratic intervention and institution building' to prevent the global economy accelerating 'in ways that will tear our lives apart and destroy the environment' (Bellah et al., 1991: 276). In so far as it takes issue with the cult of the individual and the distractions of modern mass culture and politics it is a counter-modern discourse. In so far as it has as a central objective a (re)constitution of 'responsible attention' and 'social trust' it represents a reflexively modern response to the limitations of modernity, a response which promotes 'the moral life as the responsible life', where the latter is exemplified by the care and concern shown by the 'good' parent for the child, which in turn constitutes a necessary precondition for the development of a 'basic trust' towards others and the world in which the child finds itself placed (ibid.: 276, 283–4). But such a moral life requires more than a narrow concern with one's own 'other' – child, family, community – for trusting only in 'this person or this occupation or this ethnic group or this religion or this nation, but not in others . . . impairs the possibility of responsible action' (ibid.: 284). In order to attend to the wider world of 'others' it is argued that appropriate effective forms of social organization are necessary, but as Bellah and his colleagues caution, there is always a risk with institutionalization that organized ways of paying attention will 'become socially organized ways of distraction' (ibid.: 285). The issues identified of nurturing attentiveness towards others, of countering ambivalence and indifference towards 'impersonal' others, might be argued to be precisely what is at stake in the idea of ethics as first philosophy outlined by Emmanuel Levinas.

Facing Up To Morality

In a dialogue on his philosophical thought Levinas is questioned about the practicality of his views on ethical responsibility. What is the status of the idea of ethical obligation or responsibility towards the other in 'a concrete historical world governed by ontological drives and practices, be they political and institutional totalities or technological systems of mastery, organization and control'? (Levinas and Kearney, 1986: 28). In reply Levinas offers a carefully drawn distinction between a 'series of rules relating to social behavior and civic duty', which he calls 'morality', and a form of 'responsibility towards the other' which is termed 'ethical' and described, in turn, as foundational. There is no denial by Levinas of the fact that we live in the 'political world of the "impersonal" third – the world of government, institutions, tribunals, prisons, committees, and so on' (ibid.: 30) – (how could there be) but what is identified as vital is the need to preserve, if not to continually (re)generate, a sense that the moral-political order is, and needs to be, predicated on an ethical foundation. In Levinas's terms, terms which in some respects appear to parallel, to a degree, those offered by Bellah et al. in their discussion of the necessity of cultivating attention if the prospects for an enhancement of 'moral life' are not to be dissipated by the proliferating distractions of an increasingly prominent form of sociality which promotes the self-interested consumer subject as sovereign, ethical responsibility is equated with 'wakefulness', with being alert or with watching over the other. Where Levinas contrasts the 'insomnia or wakefulness' of ethical responsibility to the slumber and complacency of the 'totalizing discourse of ontology' (ibid.: 30, 21–2), Bellah et al. call on us to pay greater 'attention' and warn of the dangers which derive from 'distraction'. There seems to be a mutual concern to respond to moral ambivalence and 'self-seeking indifference' by nurturing ethical responsibility (Levinas) or 'responsible attention' (Bellah et al.), and in both instances care for children is invoked to illustrate the kind of relationship to the other that is to be considered exemplary.[6]

The care of children, their prospects, and the kind of world with which they will be endowed are matters intrinsic to the articulation of a 'politics of generativity'. And where Bellah et al. invoke the virtues of 'generativity', a concern or care which extends beyond the relationship between parents and children to encompass 'care for all persons and things we have been entrusted with' (1991: 274), Levinas makes reference to 'filiation and fraternity', as involving something more than a relationship of responsibility arising from biological kinship, as 'current metaphors of our everyday life' (1992: 71). A relationship of filiality, free of its 'biological limitation', stands for Levinas for the descent or derivation of related others, others related by virtue of their sharing the historical endowment of a particular set of social conditions and/or forms of organization of social life, over which they have had no jurisdiction and for the constitution of which they bear no immediate or direct responsibility. Likewise, fraternity is not reducible to biology, but rather represents for Levinas a prototype of the ethical relation to the other.

But what status or significance do the narratives on the 'politics of generativity' and the responsibilities of 'filiation and fraternity' have in a context where production remains subject to the calculus of the capitalist marketplace, and a consumer culture of waste and excess, and an associated cult of the individual, still predominate? Where a politics of accumulation and gratification prevails and 'the modern individual' remains preoccupied with a calculatingly hedonistic project of life-stylization, with 'customizing a life-style', then other-directed virtues and responsibilities tend to be marginalized (Featherstone, 1991: 86). While it would obviously be unwise and inappropriate to follow the 'so-called experts, untroubled by caution or scholarly nuance', who have been criticized by Maffesoli for presenting a caricature of contemporary conditions by placing unwarranted emphasis on 'the withdrawal into the self, the end of collective ideals or, . . . the public sphere' (1996: 9), it remains necessary to draw attention to the extent to which modern individual subjects, possessing if not possessed by a 'stylistic self-consciousness' (Featherstone, 1991: 86), continue to be constituted as decision-making subjects within a political economy and culture of consumption which valorizes the pursuit of private or self-interest over concern for the public sphere.

As a modest counter to analyses of individualism which are deemed to place too great an emphasis on a process of withdrawal into the self and a related erosion of the public sphere, Maffesoli suggests that there are accumulating signs of new forms of social life – 'the undefined mass, the faceless crowd and the tribalism consisting of a patchwork of small local entities' (1996: 9). The existence of such manifestations of sociality is not in dispute here, however the idea that such social forms are 'new' is contentious, and the related observation that micro-groups or tribes are 'founded . . . on the transcendence of the individual' (ibid.: 67) is potentially misleading, because the very forms identified are necessarily dependent upon the selective 'aesthetic' practices of individuals. Indeed, the social forms identified are simultaneously the emergent manifestations of complex patterns of conduct chosen or followed by individuals, sometimes calculatingly, sometimes under the sway of feelings and emotion, and in turn they represent the conditions in and through which patterns of conduct are (re-)constituted and experienced as 'individual(s)'.

The affectual and empathetic forms in which groups of people come together are multiple and transient in character, as Maffesoli implicitly acknowledges when he remarks that 'the persons of which these tribes are constituted are *free to move* from one to the other' (ibid.: 6, emphasis added). However, what Maffesoli overlooks is that the 'micro-groups' or tribes identified as new are 'formed . . . by the multitude of individual acts of self-identification' (Bauman, 1991: 249). In short, if it is the 'time of the tribes' it remains simultaneously the 'time of the individual', for (post)modern tribes, as Bauman remarks, 'exist' solely by *individual* decisions to sport the symbolic traits of tribal allegiance. They vanish once the decisions are revoked or their determination fades out. They persevere thanks only to their continuing seductive capacity. They cannot outlive their power of attraction. Neo-tribes are . . . the vehicles (and imaginary sediments) of *individual self-definition*. The self-construction efforts generate them; the inevitable inconclusiveness and frustration of such efforts leads to their dismantling and replacement. (ibid.: 249, emphases added)

In short the 'new' forms of social life identified are not 'beyond the individual'.

The (comm)unities which the identified forms of 'post-modern sociality' (Maffesoli, 1990) represent are argued to be characterized by ephemerality, lack of definition and organization, changing composition or membership, and a 'local' orientation. Maffesoli comments that such 'emotional' communities represent manifestations of 'those who think and feel as we do' and he adds that it is precisely such 'commonly held feelings or emotions', rather than the reflexive powers of reason, which 'constitute the solidarity of the community's existence' and which, in turn, promote 'a common ethos' or 'ethical experience' (1996: 13, 18). Ethical experience is held by Maffesoli to be 'communal' and is said to involve a 'crystallization of shared feelings'. This 'communal' ethic is deemed to be a product of proximity, and the 'sharing of the same *territory* (real or symbolic)' is described as arising through 'force of circumstance' (ibid.: 16). In so far as the communal ethic has its foundations in 'warmth, companionship [and] physical contact with one another' (ibid.: 16), and is in turn considered to be bound up with locality, with the proximity of 'neighbourhood', then it might seem that there is an implication of the ethical significance of something like face-to-face relations. But if there is an ethical corollary to the communal sociality of the neighbourhood for Maffesoli it is of a quite different order to the asymmetrical face-to-face ethical relation accorded significance by Levinas. Ethical experience for Maffesoli is a matter of being *with* the other; it arises from a *symmetrical* relation of shared sentiment, from 'communal being-together', in contrast for Levinas ethics is all about being *for* the other, the relationship between self and other is one of *dissymmetry*, self and other are 'not on the same level' (1988a: 179), the (ethical) relation to the other is prior to the (ontological) relation to self.

Ethical experience for Maffesoli is necessarily communal; it is 'the collective bond' (1996: 20). This communal form of ethics is situated between, on the one hand, an atomized individuality, which it is held to supersede, and on the other a totalizing rationalization of existence. Throughout, Maffesoli places emphasis on what is close or local, but without devoting any sustained consideration to the respects in which spatial and emotional correlates (and associated experiences) of closeness and locality may be subject to transformation, as a consequence of developments in forms of communication and changes in lifestyle and patterns of personal mobility. Given the argument advanced by Pieterse that with 'hybridization' we are witnessing a process of transition taking place from the provenance of 'territorial' culture to 'translocal' culture, that is a transition from culture with an 'inward-looking' sense of place to one with an 'outward-looking sense of place' (1994: 177, 179), the assumption made by Maffesoli that 'collective imagination' and 'collective sensibility' are necessarily locally grounded becomes highly problematic. Furthermore, while in the course of his discussion of collective sensibility and its 'ethical corollary' Maffesoli makes reference to the 'ideal' of the neighbourhood and the village, little if any consideration is given to the radical respects in which neighbourhood and village communities have been, and continue to be, transformed and in some cases fragmented and undermined, by processes of social and economic restructuring. And although there are references to the contribution new means of communication may make to 'the feeling of tribal belonging' (Maffesoli, 1996: 139), the possibility that the meaning and experience of belonging (and of community) may have been significantly altered, rather than simply 'reinforced' by technological developments is not adequately addressed.

The ethical experience emphasized by Maffesoli and deemed to be '*emotionally common to all* (sentimentally and organically)', is one which he remarks 'had been abandoned by the rationalization of existence' but is now the object of a 'renewed moral order' which tries inappropriately to 'rationalize and universalize *ad hoc* reactions or situations and present them as new *a priori*' (ibid.: 18). The strength of such reactions derives not from any universal rationale, but from being 'grounded in a local sensibility'. However, the other unaddressed side of a local 'collective sensibility', of a capacity to respond with *moral feeling* to those identified as 'like us', is a possible expression of *insensibility* or *moral indifference* to those deemed different, those regarded as 'not like us'. The constitution of community around commonly held feelings and emotions simultaneously brings into being excluded communities of others for whom 'we' may feel little or no responsibility, the darker consequences of which continue to cast a shadow over 'civilization' (Tester, 1997). The emphasis placed upon the importance of proximity to the constitution of a communal ethic fails to take into consideration the respects in which proximity may instead bring into play not solidarity but (in)difference between 'us' and 'them'. If there is something approaching an acknowledgement of such important concerns in Maffesoli's narrative it is to be found in a brief remark on the way in which the community or group 'by highlighting what is close (persons and places) . . . has a tendency to be closed in on itself' (1996: 141). However, the potential ethico-political implications for others, for those excluded, are not considered and the associated risks and 'dangers of tribalism and fundamentalism' (Castells, 1989: 351) are not addressed.

It is precisely the problems that arise with the emergence of a plurality of 'micro-' or 'self-interested' groups, 'multiple communities' with contrasting and perhaps conflicting affiliation requirements, and in particular 'neo-tribes' engaging in practices of inclusion–exclusion through which they constitute a sense of their belonging, while simultaneously distancing themselves from others in the course of their 'obsessive search for community', which cause concern and lead Bauman (1991) to argue for 'solidarity', that is for each 'difference' not simply to tolerate other differences, but to be ready to struggle for them. The promotion of solidarity with others in response to the potential problems of exclusion and intolerance associated with difference raises a number of issues germane to the question of self–other-community relations. In particular, what are we to understand by 'solidarity', and what relationships of solidarity are implied between self and other(s), and with the increasingly indeterminate figure of community? Solidarity is presented as a relationship in which self recognizes that,

> there are other places and other times that may be with equal justification (or equal absence of good reason) preferred by members of other societies, and that however different they are, the choices cannot be disputed by reference to anything more solid and binding than preference and the determination to stick to the preferred. The preference for one's own, *communally shared* form of life must therefore be immune to the temptation of cultural crusade. Emancipation means acceptance of one's own contingency as is grounded in recognition of contingency as sufficient reason to live and to be allowed to live. It signals the end to the horror of alterity and to the abhorrence of ambivalence. (Bauman, 1991: 234–5, emphasis added)

What is required for solidarity is to support and/or fight for the differences of others; if necessary struggle is to be joined 'for the sake of the other's difference, *not one's own*' (ibid.: 256, emphasis added). Solidarity, in short, is a relationship in which self is to be held responsible for upholding the difference of the other, difference being described as 'one universality that is not open to negotiation' (ibid.).

But is difference beyond negotiation? Is it not necessary for differences, or perhaps particular expressions of difference, to be open to question, negotiation, and even challenge? What is the status of manifestations of difference receiving expression in values, beliefs and forms of conduct of communities, tribes, groups and individuals which threaten, challenge or attack the differences of others; what about expressions of difference which directly or indirectly 'attack . . . the universal right to be different' (ibid.: 256)? Bauman argues that such an attack 'is the only departure from universality that none of the solidary agents, however different, may tolerate' (ibid.), but consistent as this might seem to be with the idea of a right to be different, it follows by implication that some manifestations and expressions of difference are (or need) to be regarded as unacceptable and are (or need) to be opposed and curbed. To cite an obvious example, collectivities and communities whose 'difference' receives expression in forms of political totalitarianism or fascism will be open to the charge that they directly or indirectly represent an attack on the rights of others to be different. In short, there can be no right to differences which interfere with the 'legitimate' rights of others, but beyond the extremities of political totalitarianism and fascism the precise status of a claimed right to be different may be more difficult to resolve, more difficult to reach agreement on. It is not necessarily the case that survival 'in the world of contingency and diversity is possible *only* if each difference recognizes another difference as the necessary condition of the preservation of its own' (ibid.: 256). Particular manifestations of difference may prove to be damaging to the preservation of other differences and may threaten their very survival. Survival may require recognition of the potential threat posed by particular manifestations of difference and appropriate action to counter any anticipated or actual threat, one obvious difficulty here being how to differentiate between xenophobic fears and associated misrepresentations of the 'threat' posed by difference and 'genuine' threats posed to the right to be (solidaristically) different. Another related issue which may arise in connection with the claimed right to be different is how to reconcile differences which stand in opposition to one another, differences which appear unable to accommodate, let alone support, each other's right to be, conflicting differences which may give rise to acts of terrorism, genocide, and other forms of barbarism.[7]

Implicit in my reflections on difference and solidarity is the indistinct figure of community. When Bauman makes reference in his discussion of solidarity to the importance of 'solidary agents' countering attacks on the 'universal right to be different' there is a strong implication of community, of the constitution of a community of solidary agents moved to affirm the right to be different. The identification of communications, particular forms of conduct, or practices, as constituting an attack on the 'universal right to be different' is an interpretive matter which implies the existence, or constitution, of an interpretive community which is able to reach agreement. In identifying and responding supportively to any attacks on the rights of their neighbours to remain different 'solidary agents' are going to be constituted in some form as a community, and they are going to recognize themselves as such – as the community of those who agree on the legitimacy of their neighbour's right to be different, who find a particular course of action or conduct threatens such a right, and in turn give their support to an appropriate form of response. Where the issue of community is directly addressed in Bauman's narrative it tends to be in the context of a critical response to the objectives associated with the notion of communitarianism. The pursuit of community is considered to have a paradoxical consequence, to 'result in more dissipation and fragmentation, more heterogeneity', rather than increasing communal agreement, and only the most minimal consensus – 'acceptance of the heterogeneity of dissensions' – is considered to have any chance of succeeding (ibid.: 251). The communitarian vision is roundly criticized in so far as its 'postulated' communities serve to 'expropriate the individual's right to moral choice' or 'curtail . . . individual moral discretion' (Bauman, 1993: 45, 46).

Bauman's argument tends to counter-pose community, critically conceived as 'limiting and streamlining . . . individual choices' in the cause of its own conservation or renewal of what is claimed to be common to all (the public interest), to the existence of the 'moral person', credited with the ability to exercise 'moral choice' and 'moral judgement', but regarded, in turn, as vulnerable to community suppression (ibid.: 44–7). If communitarians are vulnerable to the charge that their idea of 'moral community' tends to be more *postulated* than real, Bauman's notion of the 'moral person' may be open to a comparable criticism. It is precisely the relative infrequency of examples of individuals being morally responsible subjects – and a felt sense that the currently inadequate frequency is still declining – which causes concern to communitarians and leads emphasis to be placed on the necessity of (re)constituting a moral community (Bellah et al., 1991; Etzioni, 1994). The communitarian line is that modern society has been characterized by too many rights and too few responsibilities, and that a shift of emphasis is now required *from* individual right *to* responsibility for the other, conceived in terms of 'social responsibility'. Moral responsibility is in this context regarded as a necessary means to the achievement of an improved social and political environment (Etzioni, 1994); as a vital element in the associated pursuit of that continually elusive goal of the 'good society' (Bellah et al., 1991). The emphasis placed on social responsibility and the moral community leads Bauman to argue that rather than 'shoring up morality' there is within communitarianism an implication of a subversion of moral individuality, or a suppression of moral autonomy. Such a criticism assumes 'the *impossibility* of not being responsible' for the other (Bauman, 1993: 53), treats the 'moral person' as effectively a given, and in addition postulates 'community' as necessarily a threat to moral responsibility. However, the criticism may be overstated, for moral responsibility can and does express itself in a communal form in solidary action, as Bauman subsequently implicitly acknowledges when he remarks on the way in which '[t]ime and again we hear of people gathering to promote or defend a cause they seem to consider to be shared by them all' (1995a: 274). The possibly temporary communities so constituted do not inevitably serve to erode or, as Bauman puts it, 'expropriate the individuals' moral responsibility' (ibid.: 277), on the contrary, such manifestations of shared concern for the other might be regarded as an exemplification of 'communal' moral responsibility, as evidence that the journey along 'the long road from . . . tolerance to solidarity' (1991: 238) can be sustained.

There are many different manifestations of community and the 'community of belonging' criticized by Bauman, because it is deemed to undermine freedom and independence, represents merely one possibility. Another 'communal' possibility, to which brief reference is subsequently made, might be argued to represent the horizon of moral life towards and by which vision and conduct can be, and to a degree already are, guided. Reflecting on the impoverished character of human existence when it is simply equated with material accumulation, or the consumption of commodities and services, and its potential fulfilment is reduced to the art of 'practising one-upmanship', Bauman remarks that:

> [l]ife has not got to be like this. The space we co-habit may be well – consensually – structured; in such a space, in which many things vital to the life of each of us (transport, schools, surgeries, media of communication) are *shared*, we may see

each other as conditions, rather than obstacles, to our collective, as well as individual well-being. Much as the fragmented and discontinuous life promotes *the waning of moral impulses*, a shared life of continuous and multi-faceted relationships would *re-invigorate moral responsibilities* and awaken the urge to shoulder the task of managing – now truly common – affairs. (1995a: 284, emphases added)

Ironically such a diagnosis of prevailing moral conditions, and possible future prospects for reconciling collective and individual existence, might be argued to be compatible with some elements of a communitarian analysis. Consider, for example the following remarks made by Etzioni in the course of a discussion of moral conduct – '"making it" becomes a self-defeating endeavour because it is inherently Sisyphean in nature . . . People are better off when they combine their self-advancement with investment in their community'; and 'we find reinforcement for our moral inclinations and provide reinforcement to our fellow human beings, through the community. We are each other's keepers' (1994: 123–4, 31). However, if there appear to be some similarities in the diagnoses offered, critical differences between the two positions outlined remain, particularly in the way in which morality is regarded.

For the communitarians morality is presented as the 'voice' of community, as a 'claim' made on errant individuals, as a social ordering of conduct, which ultimately seems to require more than a degree of subordination of individual autonomy or independence to 'community'. In contrast, for Bauman, following the traces left by Levinas, the very possibility of morality derives from the primal ethical responsibility of the self for the other, a responsibility which is continually vulnerable to a form of political life that is 'fragmentary, episodic and inconsequential' (Bauman, 1995a: 282). What is promoted as a potential remedy within communitarianism, notably the regeneration or reconstitution of community, necessarily raises the question of the criteria and practices of inclusion and exclusion required to constitute a particular form of 'unity' – common causes, concerns, values and forms of life – as more worthy, appropriate and/or inclusive than other possible forms of communal life which are devalued, subordinated, marginalized, and/or excluded. The communitarian emphasis on community regeneration raises another question concerning the costs borne by individuals, costs which Bauman suggests include the curtailment of 'individual moral discretion'. In so far as a particular form of unifying 'interest' is promoted as worthy and appropriate, indeed is recognized to be constitutive, in part or whole, of 'community', then it is likely that there will be an expropriation of the individual's right to moral choice, or judgement, 'in such areas of life as are considered relevant to the "common weal"' (Bauman, 1993: 46). In short, the price to be paid for the constitution of a 'communitarian' moral community is, in Bauman's view, the suppression of the very resource which is necessary if life is to become more moral, namely individual moral autonomy or responsibility.

Concluding Remarks on the Horizon of Moral Life

The ethical relation of responsibility for the other invoked by Levinas has provided a key philosophical resource for the development of what has been termed a 'politics of ethical difference' (Critchley, 1992), or a 'post-modern ethics' (Bauman, 1993). However, while making an influential contribution to analytic reflection on the postmodern predicaments which have been identified with the ambivalence of modernity, the ethical philosophy outlined by Levinas has been criticized for being too demanding, impractical, or unrealistic. Levinas has responded to such charges by articulating a distinction between 'the way the world functions concretely' (1988a: 177) and something else, that of which he often speaks, namely 'ethical responsibility towards the other', or a 'concern for the other', which is described as a 'perpetual duty' (Levinas and Kearney, 1986: 29, 32). Elaborating on the distinction provided, Levinas comments that there is something like a 'utopian moment' in his argument, by which he does not mean a modern blueprint for the 'good society', but rather 'the recognition of something . . . which, ultimately, guides all moral action' (1988a: 178).

Reference to a utopian moment does not mean that the ethical relationship Levinas describes is to be regarded as one which is never practised, to the contrary, as he remarks:

> its being utopian does not prevent it from investing our everyday actions of generosity or goodwill towards the other: even the smallest and most common-place gestures . . . bear witness to the ethical. This concern for the other remains utopian in the sense that it is always 'out of place' (*u-topos*) in this world, always other than the 'ways of the world'; but there are many examples of it in the world. (Levinas and Kearney, 1986: 32)

But if, as Levinas suggests, there are many small and commonplace expressions of a 'utopian' ethical concern for the other being displayed 'in this world', it is also the case, as the statement implies, that there are many instances, for the communitarians – but not only the communitarians – too many instances, where such an ethical concern is absent, where responsibility for the other is not evident. Indeed, the very promotion of ethics as first philosophy derives its critical relevance from the evidently all too frequent 'out-of-placeness' of an ethical concern for the other. Far from being a given, 'moral personhood' too often does seem like a distant, if not devalued, potential to which individuals might aspire, at best a 'utopian moment' which serves to disturb conscience and inspire hope in everyday life. Far from being an impossibility, *not* in practice being responsible for the other continues to be too prominent a feature of modern subjectivity, of 'the way the world functions concretely', which is why communitarians have called for a shift of emphasis from self-interest to a concern for the other, and Levinas has promoted the idea of ethics as first philosophy to affirm the necessity of our being for the other, to remind us of the ultimate inescapability of our being for the other.

Both positions offer a critical purchase on the way the modern world currently functions, on the ways in which self-interest and self-fulfilment have effectively marginalized notions of responsibility, or concern for the other. However, the two accounts appear to proceed from somewhat contrasting assumptions about the relationship between 'society' and 'individual'. The communitarian agenda seems to cleave to something like a Freudian and Durkheimian notion of 'human nature' as it depicts modern social life as 'suffering from a severe case of deficient we-ness', a deficiency requiring a 'move from "I" to "we"' (Etzioni, 1994: 26), that is a 'moral' limitation or regulation of the expression of self-interest. When the question of responsibility is broached the emphasis ultimately tends to be placed upon the importance of 'community' rather than the 'individual'. In contrast, Levinas seems to depict society itself – 'the political world of the impersonal "third"' – as the source of the occlusion of our ethical responsibility for the other, and argues that it is necessary to continually recall that the 'ethical norm of the interhuman' (Levinas and Kearney, 1986: 29–30) constitutes the very foundation of the moral-political order. In this instance, emphasis falls on the 'ethical' respect in which the self is synonymous with responsibility for the other. Responsibility may (have) be(come) occluded, but it is inalienable. The difference identified between the two accounts is important, but contrary to Levinas's suggestion it is not possible '*to know* if society . . . is the result of a limitation of the principle that men are predators of one another, or if to the contrary it results from the limitation of the principle that men are *for* one another' (1992: 80, first emphasis added). The contrast identified between the two positions has constituted one of the basic dichotomies in the field of social and philosophical thought, one which has been intrinsic to ethico-political debate and seems impervious to resolution through knowledge. The contrast has a long history and remains a significant point of difference between social analysts, but is it one to which it is necessary to remain resigned?

Ambivalence is now recognized to be a corollary of modern life. The process of accommodating or coming to terms with the possible 'permanence and omnipresence of ambivalence' (Bauman, 1991: 230), or with a 'postmodern' reconditioning of modernity which the idea of living with ambivalence implies, has not only prompted a (re)turn to questions of ethics and morality, but also has stimulated thought about more appropriate, or better forms of communal living, towards the achievement of which we might work, and in terms of which a critical evaluation of the prevailing morality of modern social life can be conducted. This is clearly exemplified by the narratives discussed above on the prospects for a 'social compact' (Bell), 'good society' (Bellah et al.), and 'moral community' (Etzioni), and is implied in less programmatic references to the social virtues of 'tolerance' coupled with 'solidarity' (Bauman). Notwithstanding differences in analytic approach and ethico-political assumptions, each of these analysts have responded critically and constructively to the difficulties identified with the form of life we know as modernity by cultivating ideas about alternatives which might serve to promote the prospects of morality *after* ambivalence. But where within the communitarian agenda the prospect of a regeneration of moral community appears to be synonymous with a *resolution* of the ambivalence of modernity, it being argued that 'responsibilities are anchored in community' and that there is an associated 'urgent need for communities to articulate the responsibilities they expect their members to discharge' (Etzioni, 1994: 264), for a critic such as Bauman it is the *continuing uncertainty* of ambivalence, regarded as a 'permanent condition of life', which is considered to constitute 'the very soil in which the moral self takes root and grows' (1995a: 287). From Bauman's Levinasian standpoint the corollary of community-determined responsibility is likely to be disciplined and submissive forms of subjectivity, and an associated abdication of the moral self, rather than a restoration of moral life. While the communitarian 'modern' legislative programme tends to counter-pose individual self-interest to the potential moral virtue of the community, and argues for a regeneration of moral life through the promotion and reconstitution of community, Bauman provides a critical 'postmodern' response which calls into question the very distinction drawn between community and individual, and concludes that the prospect for moral renewal depends upon a recognition of the close connection between 'more vigorous sharing of *collective* responsibilties' and 'more autonomy for *individual* moral selves' (ibid.: 286).

In the face of the ambivalence which is a corollary of the radical reflexivity of late modernity, Levinas has cautioned that there can be 'no moral life without utopianism' (1988a: 178), no moral life, that is, without something which guides all moral action. There can be no moral life without the idea(l) of improvement, hence for Levinas 'justice is always a justice which desires a better justice . . . [and] there are always improvements to be made in human rights' (ibid.: 177–8). However, there is no implication here of models of the 'just', 'moral' or 'good' society. In the broadly comparable terms employed by Lyotard, it might be argued that ethico-political existence, moral life, is to be reflected upon and guided by an idea without finality (unity or totality), by an idea postulated 'as a horizon', a regulatory idea without a given content (Lyotard and Thébaud, 1985: 77, 87–92). The problem we face now is that of reflecting on matters like morality and justice 'against the horizon of a multiplicity or of a diversity' (ibid.: 69, 87); of reflecting on existing institutions, questioning them, considering how to improve them, 'of doing something else than what is' (ibid.: 23), but in the absence of unity and totality and in the presence of multiplicity, diversity and continuous uncertainty.

There can be no moral life without the choices, responsibilities and risks which are an inescapable corollary of ambivalence. No moral life without the uncertainty of ambivalence, but equally no moral life without the prospect of what Levinas refers to as 'something which cannot be realized but which, ultimately, guides all moral action' (1988a: 178), and Lyotard describes as a 'horizon' to regulate our prescriptives and to guide us. Moral

life is destined to remain uncertain, for there are 'no indubitable and
universally agreed codes and rules' (Bauman, 1995a: 287) to which it is
possible to turn, and while the reflexive critical capacity of reason offers the
prospect of an enhanced understanding of the current conditions in which
moral responsibility is expressed, compromised, or expropriated, it is
unable to resolve the problem of morality, or to determine moral choice.
Moral problems and dilemmas are an inescapable part of the human
condition and it is necessary to face up to the inescapable uncertainty of
moral life. Facing up to the moral ambivalence of modernity seems
increasingly unavoidable, but it is also a necessary precondition for the
exercise of moral responsibility.

Notes

1 Bell subsequently acknowledges that needs are redefined 'so that former wants become
necessities' (1976: 254).
2 The four issues singled out are:

(i)   arbitrating between the competing claims of individuals, intermediate interest groups,
       the community, and the state;
(ii)   managing disparities between persons in terms of the core values of liberty and
       equality;
(iii) balancing 'efficiency' and 'equity' – operationalized as a question of reconciling
       economic and non-economic modes of social organization, as well as considering the
       need to regulate present production-consumption, and associated consequences, to
       conserve and protect future prospects; and
(iv)   the core issue which is implied in the above, notably 'the balance between the public
       and the private and the definition of their appropriate spheres' (Bell, 1976: 274).

3 Attention for Bellah et al. involves 'an openness to experience, a willingness to widen the
lens of apperception' (1991: 256). Paying attention involves bringing resources of 'intelligence,
feeling and moral sensitivity' to bear on matters in a self-controlled, self-disciplined, and by
implication, particularly given their critical references to the predominance within Western
modernity of an individualizing culture of therapeutic contractualism, self-effacing manner.
4 Perhaps a parallel example might be found in the fragmentation of family television
viewing with the advent of multiple-set homes, a proliferation of terrestrial and satellite
channels, and segmented audience programming policies.
5 Consider for example the moving responses and public campaigns which followed the
tragic events associated with the names of Jamie Bulger, Dunblane, and Philip Lawrence. The
central difficulty such campaigns have faced is how to conserve, if not increase, the momentum
behind public concern expressed in the immediate aftermath of a particularly tragic event so
that relevant policy initiatives might be introduced, appropriate action taken, and a measure of
improvement eventually achieved.
   How to retain wider public concern and interest as personal, family, or local community
tragedies, themselves a symptom of larger social processes and problems, become old news,
perhaps recalled annually if they find a place on the media's diary of newsworthy anniversary
events, remains a problem.
6 There are in addition significant differences in their respective approaches and
formulations. For example, Levinas identifies an ethical relationship of responsibility for the
other as synonymous with human fraternity, or as constitutive of human subjectivity itself, and
then proceeds to argue that ethical relations are generally occluded and rendered problematic
by the fact that we exist in 'the political world of the impersonal "third"' (Levinas and

Kearney, 1986: 30). In contrast Bellah et al. present a communitarian argument which places emphasis on the inadequacy of existing social institutions for sustaining 'moral ecology' and call for more 'democratic intervention and institution-building' to regenerate 'organizations of the "third sector"' to give substance to 'the collective purposes of justice, mutual aid, enlightenment, worship, [and] fellowship' (1991: 5–6, 276, 269).

7 I am alluding here to a number of concerns raised by Emmanuel Levinas in a dialogue with Alan Finkielkraut on 'Ethics and Politics', in particular that alongside responsibility for the other, respect and support for the difference of the other, there is 'certainly a place for a defence' against those who attack us or our neighbours. Levinas adds that 'Its necessity is ethical – indeed, it's an old ethical idea which commands us precisely to defend our neighbours' (1989: 292). But what if conflict arises between local differences, if one 'neighbour attacks another neighbour or treats him/[her] unjustly . . .?' Then, Levinas argues, 'alterity takes on another character, in alterity we can find an enemy, or at least then we are faced with the problem of knowing who is right and who is wrong, who is just and who is unjust. There are people who are wrong' (ibid.: 294). The context for the dialogue in 1982 was massacres at camps in the Lebanon, but the questions raised are no less applicable to other disputes over differences, for example in the late 1990s in the Balkans, Northern Ireland and many parts of the African continent.

REFERENCES

Ahmed, A. (1992) *Postmodernism and Islam: Predicament and Promise*. London: Routledge.

Albrow, M. (1987) 'Editorial: Sociology for One World', *International Sociology*, vol. 2, no. 1.

Albrow, M. (1990) 'Introduction', in M. Albrow and E. King (eds), *Globalization, Knowledge and Society*. London: Sage.

Appadurai, A. (1990) 'Disjuncture and Difference in the Global Cultural Economy', *Theory, Culture and Society*, vol. 7, nos. 2–3.

Archer, M. (1990) 'Foreword', in M. Albrow and E. King (eds), *Globalization, Knowledge and Society*. London: Sage.

Archer, M. (1991) 'Sociology for One World: Unity and Diversity', *International Sociology*, vol. 6, no. 2.

Aristotle (1962) *The Politics*. Translated by J.A. Sinclair. Harmondsworth: Penguin.

Asad, T. (1986) 'The Concept of Cultural Translation in British Social Anthropology', in J. Clifford and G.E. Marcus (eds), *Writing Culture: The Poetics and Politics of Ethnography*. Berkeley, CA: University of California Press.

Atkinson, D. (1971) *Orthodox Consensus and Radical Alternative*. London: Heinemann.

Bahro, R. (1978) *The Alternative in Eastern Europe*. London: New Left Books.

Bates, S., Brown P. and White, M. (1996) 'New Scare Wrecks Beef Truce', *Guardian*, 2 August.

Baudrillard, J. (1975) *The Mirror of Production*. St Louis: Telos Press.

Baudrillard, J. (1983a) *Simulations*. New York: Semiotext(e).

Baudrillard, J. (1983b) *In the Shadow of the Silent Majorities . . . Or the End of the Social*. New York: Semiotext(e).

Baudrillard, J. (1984a) 'Game With Vestiges', *On The Beach*, no. 5: 19–25.

Baudrillard, J. (1984b) 'On Nihilism', *On The Beach*, no. 6: 38–9.

Baudrillard, J. (1987) *Forget Foucault*. New York: Semiotext(e).

Baudrillard, J. (1988a) *The Ecstasy of Communication*. New York: Semiotext(e).

Baudrillard, J. (1988b) *America*. London: Verso.

Baudrillard, J. (1989a) 'Politics of Seduction', interview in *Marxism Today*, January: 54–5.

Baudrillard, J. (1989b) 'The Anorexic Ruins', in D. Kamper and C. Wulf (eds), *Looking Back on the End of the World*. New York: Semiotext(e).

Baudrillard, J. (1990a) *Fatal Strategies*. New York: Semiotext(e).

Baudrillard, J. (1990b) *Cool Memories*. London: Verso.

Baudrillard, J. (1992a) 'Transpolitics, Transsexuality, Transaesthetics', in W. Stearns and W. Chaloupka (eds), *Jean Baudrillard: The Disappearance of Art and Politics*. London: Macmillan.

Baudrillard, J. (1992b) 'Revolution and the End of Utopia', in W. Stearns and W. Chaloupka (eds), *Jean Baudrillard: The Disappearance of Art and Politics*. London: Macmillan.

Baudrillard, J. (1993) *The Transparency of Evil – Essays on Extreme Phenomena*. London: Verso.

Bauman, Z. (1987) *Legislators and Interpreters: On Modernity, Post-modernity and Intellectuals*. Cambridge: Polity Press.

Bauman, Z. (1988) 'Is there a Postmodern Sociology?', *Theory, Culture & Society*, vol. 5, nos 2–3: 217.

Bauman, Z. (1990) 'Effacing the Face: On the Social Management of Moral Proximity', *Theory, Culture & Society*, vol. 7, no. 1: 5–38.

Bauman, Z. (1991) *Modernity and Ambivalence*. Cambridge: Polity.

Bauman, Z. (1992a) *Intimations of Postmodernity*. London: Routledge.
Bauman, Z. (1992b) 'The Solution as Problem', *The Times Higher*, 13 November.
Bauman, Z. (1993) *Postmodern Ethics*. Oxford: Blackwell.
Bauman, Z. (1994) 'Morality Without Ethics', *Theory, Culture & Society*, vol. 11, no. 4.
Bauman, Z. (1995a) *Life in Fragments – Essays in Postmodern Morality*. Oxford: Blackwell.
Bauman, Z. (1995b) 'Searching for a Centre that Holds', in M. Featherstone, S. Lash and R. Robertson (eds), *Global Modernities*. London: Sage.
Bauman, Z. (1996) 'On Communitarians and Human Freedom, Or, How to Square the Circle', *Theory, Culture & Society*, vol. 13, no. 2: 79–90.
Bauman, Z. (1997) *Postmodernity and its Discontents*. New York: New York University Press.
Beck, U. (1992) *Risk Society – Towards a New Modernity*. London: Sage.
Beck, U. (1994) 'The Reinvention of Politics: Towards a Theory of Reflexive Modernization', in U. Beck, A. Giddens and S. Lash (eds), *Reflexive Modernization – Politics, Tradition and Aesthetics in the Modern Social Order*. Cambridge: Polity Press.
Beck, U. (1996) 'Risk Society and the Provident State', in S. Lash, B. Szerszynski and B. Wynne (eds), *Risk, Environment and Modernity*. London: Sage.
Bell, D. (1973) *The Coming of Post-Industrial Society: A Venture in Social Forecasting*. New York: Basic Books.
Bell, D. (1976) *The Cultural Contradictions of Capitalism*. New York: Basic Books.
Bellah, R.N., Haan, N., Rabinow, P. and Sullivan, W.M. (eds) (1983) *Social Science as Moral Inquiry*. New York: Columbia University Press.
Bellah, R.N., Madsen, R., Sullivan, W.M., Swidler, A. and Tipton, S.M. (1991) *The Good Society*. New York: Alfred A Knopf.
Bellah, R.N., Madsen, R., Sullivan, W.M., Swidler, A. and Tipton, S.M. (1996) *Habits of the Heart – Individualism and Commitment in American Life*. New York: University of California Press.
Benjamin, A. (ed.) (1989) *The Lyotard Reader*. Oxford: Blackwell.
Benjamin, A. (ed.) (1992) *Judging Lyotard*. London: Routledge.
Benjamin, W. (1973) *Illuminations*. London: Fontana.
Berger, P. and Kellner, H. (1982) *Sociology Reinterpreted – An Essay on Method and Vocation*. Harmondsworth: Penguin.
Berman, M. (1992) 'Why Modernism Still Matters', in S. Lash and J. Friedman (eds), *Modernity and Identity*. Oxford: Blackwell.
Bernauer, J. (1992) 'Beyond Life and Death: On Foucault's post-Auschwitz Ethic', in T.J. Armstrong (ed.), *Michel Foucault Philosopher*. London: Harvester Wheatsheaf.
Bernstein, R.J. (1991) *The New Constellation: The Ethical-Political Horizons of Modernity/Postmodernity*. Cambridge: Polity Press.
Best, S. and Kellner, D. (1991) *Postmodern Theory – Critical Interrogations*. London: Macmillan.
Blair, T. (1996) 'Towards a Decent, Responsible Society', *The Times*, 4 November.
Bloom, H. (1996) *The Western Cannon*. London: Papermac.
Bolton, A. (1996) 'The Gift of Life', *Guardian*, 4 June.
Bourdieu, P. and Wacquant, L.J.D. (1992) *An Invitation to Reflexive Sociology*. Chicago: University of Chicago Press.
Bovone, L. (1993) 'Ethics as Etiquette: The Emblematic Contribution of Erving Goffman', *Theory, Culture & Society*, vol. 10, no. 4: 25–39.
Boyne, R. and Rattansi, A. (1990) 'The Theory and Politics of Postmodernism', in R. Boyne and A. Rattansi (eds), *Postmodernism and Society*. London: Macmillan.
Brown, P., Smithers, R. and Boseley, S. (1996) 'Beef Warning Sparks Panic', *Guardian*, 21 March.
Callinicos, A. (1989) *Against Postmodernism*. Cambridge: Polity Press.
Caputo, J.D. (1989) 'Disseminating Originary Ethics and the Ethics of Dissemination', in A.B. Daltery and C.E. Scott (eds), *The Question of the Other: Essays in Contemporary Continental Philosophy*. Albany: State University of New York Press.

Caputo, J.D. (1993) *Against Ethics – Contributions to a Poetics of Obligation with Constant Reference to Deconstruction*. Indianapolis: Indiana University Press.

Cardoso, F. (1986) 'Foreword', *International Sociology*, vol. 1, no. 1.

Carey, G. (1996) 'Morality is More Than a Matter of Opinion', *Daily Telegraph*, 5 July.

Castells, M. (1989) *The Informational City*. Oxford: Blackwell.

Castells, M. (1992) 'The Beginning of History', *Socialism of the Future*, vol. 1, no. 1: 86–96.

Cohen, R.A. (1992) 'Translator's Introduction', in E. Levinas *Ethics and Infinity*. Pittsburgh: Duquesne University Press.

Connor, S. (1996) 'Poison Risk that Lurks in "Healthy" Eating', *Sunday Times*, 2 June.

Critchley, S. (1992) *The Ethics of Deconstruction: Derrida and Levinas*. Oxford: Blackwell.

Crossley, N. (1995) 'Merleau-Ponty, the Elusive Body and Carnal Sociology', *Body & Society*, vol. 1, no. 1: 43–63.

Denzin, N.K. (1986) 'Postmodern Social Theory', *Sociological Theory*, vol. 4, no. 2: 194–204.

Derian, J.D. and Shapiro, M.J. (eds) (1989) *International/Intertextual Relations – Postmodern Readings of World Politics*. Massachusetts: Lexington Books.

Derrida, J. (1967) *De la grammatologie*. Paris: Editions de Minuit.

Derrida, J. (1978) *Writing and Difference*. London: Routledge.

Derrida, J. (1982) *Positions*. Chicago: University of Chicago Press.

Derrida, J. (1984) 'MOCHLOS ou le conflit des facultes', *Philosophie*, 2: 21–53.

Derrida, J. (1986) 'But beyond . . . (Open Letter to Anne McClintock and Rob Nixon)', *Critical Inquiry*, no. 13: 155–70.

Derrida, J. (1992) 'Force of Law: The "Mystical Foundation of Authority"', in D. Cornell, M. Rosenfeld and D.G. Carlson (eds), *Deconstruction and the Possibility of Justice*. London: Routledge.

Dews, P. (1989) 'The Return of the Subject in Late Foucault', *Radical Philosophy*, no. 51, Spring.

Douglas, M. (1994) *Risk and Blame – Essays in Cultural Theory*. London: Routledge.

Durkheim, E. (1964) *The Division of Labour in Society*. New York: Free Press.

Durkheim, E. (1974) *Sociology and Philosophy*. New York: Free Press.

Etzioni, A. (1994) *The Spirit of Community – The Reinvention of American Society*. London: Simon & Schuster.

Featherstone, M. (1991) *Consumer Culture and Postmodernism*. London: Sage.

Featherstone, M. (1995) *Undoing Culture – Globalization, Postmodernism and Identity*. London: Sage.

Featherstone, M. and Lash, S. (1995) 'Globalization, Modernity and the Spatialization of Social Theory: An Introduction', in M. Featherstone, S. Lash and R. Robertson (eds), *Global Modernities*. London: Sage.

Featherstone, M. and Turner, B. (1995) 'Body & Society: An Introduction', *Body & Society*, vol. 1, no. 1: 1–12.

Filmer, P., Phillipson, M., Silverman, D. and Walsh, D. (1972) *New Directions in Sociological Theory*. London: Collier-Macmillan.

Foucault, M. (1973) *The Order of Things – An Archaeology of the Human Sciences*. New York: Vintage Books.

Foucault, M. (1976) *Mental Illness and Psychology*. New York: Harper & Row.

Foucault, M. (1977) 'What is an Author?', in D.F. Bouchard (ed.), *Language, Counter-Memory, Practice – Selected Essays and Interviews*. Oxford: Blackwell.

Foucault, M. (1979) 'Governmentality', *I & C*, no. 6.

Foucault, M. (1980) 'Truth and Power', in C. Gordon (ed.), *Power/Knowledge – Selected Interviews and Other Writings 1972–1977 by Michel Foucault*. Brighton: The Harvester Press.

Foucault, M. (1981a) 'Omnes et Singulatim', in S.M. McMurrin (ed.), *The Tanner Lectures on Human Values, Vol II*. Cambridge: Cambridge University Press.

Foucault, M. (1981b) 'Foucault at the College de France I: A Course Summary', translated with an introduction by James Bernauer, *Philosophy and Social Criticism*, vol. 8, no. 2: 235–42.

Foucault, M. (1982) 'The Subject and Power', Afterword to H.L. Dreyfus and P. Rabinow (eds), *Michel Foucault – Beyond Structuralism and Hermeneutics*. Brighton: The Harvester Press.
Foucault, M. (1983) 'Structuralism and Post-Structuralism: An Interview', *Telos*, no. 55: 195–211.
Foucault, M. (1986a) *The Foucault Reader*. Edited by P. Rabinow. Harmondsworth: Penguin.
Foucault, M. (1986b) 'Kant on Enlightenment and Revolution', *Economy and Society*, vol. 15, no. 1: 88–94.
Foucault, M. (1986c) 'On the Genealogy of Ethics: An Overview of Work in Progress', in P. Rabinow (ed.), *The Foucault Reader*. Harmondsworth: Penguin.
Foucault, M. (1986d) 'What is Enlightenment?', in P. Rabinow (ed.), *The Foucault Reader*. Harmondsworth: Penguin.
Foucault, M. (1987a) 'The Ethic of Care for the Self as a Practice of Freedom – an Interview', *Philosophy and Social Criticism*, vol. 12, nos 2–3.
Foucault, M. (1987b) *The Use of Pleasure, The History of Sexuality, Volume 2*. Harmondsworth: Penguin.
Foucault, M. (1987c) 'Questions of Method: An Interview', in K. Baynes, J. Bohman and T. McCarthy (eds), *After Philosophy – End or Transformation?* London: MIT Press.
Foucault, M. (1988a) *Technologies of the Self – a Seminar with Michel Foucault*. Edited by L.H. Martin, H.Gutman and P.H. Hutton. London: Tavistock.
Foucault, M. (1988b) *The Care of the Self, The History of Sexuality, Volume 3*. London: Allen Lane, The Penguin Press.
Foucault, M. (1988c) 'The Concern for Truth', in L.D. Kritzman (ed.), *Michel Foucault – Politics, Philosophy, Culture*. London: Routledge.
Foucault, M. (1989) *Foucault Live*. Edited by S. Lotringer. New York: Semiotext(e).
Freud, S. ([1908]1985) '"Civilized" Sexual Morality and Modern Nervous Illness', in *Civilization, Society and Religion: Group Psychology, Civilization and Its Discontents and Other Works*, vol. 12, The Pelican Freud Library, general editor Albert Dickson. Harmondsworth: Penguin.
Freud, S. ([1915]1985) 'Thoughts for the Times on War and Death', in *Civilization, Society and Religion: Group Psychology, Civilization and Its Discontents and Other Works*, vol. 12, The Pelican Freud Library, general editor Albert Dickson. Harmondsworth: Penguin.
Freud, S. ([1927]1985) 'The Future of an Illusion', in *Civilization, Society and Religion: Group Psychology, Civilization and Its Discontents and Other Works*, vol. 12, The Pelican Freud Library, general editor Albert Dickson. Harmondsworth: Penguin.
Freud, S. ([1930]1985) 'Civilization and Its Discontents', in *Civilization, Society and Religion: Group Psychology, Civilization and Its Discontents and Other Works*, vol. 12, The Pelican Freud Library, general editor Albert Dickson. Harmondsworth: Penguin.
Friedman, J. (1990) 'Being in the World: Globalization and Localization', *Theory, Culture and Society*, vol. 7, nos 2–3.
Friedrichs, R.W. (1972) *A Sociology of Sociology*. London: Free Press.
Gane, M. (1991a) *Baudrillard – Critical and Fatal Theory*. London: Routledge.
Gane, M. (1991b) *Baudrillard's Bestiary – Baudrillard and Culture*. London: Routledge.
Gane, M. (ed.) (1993) *Baudrillard Live: Selected Interviews*. London: Routledge.
Gardiner, M. (1996) 'Alterity and Ethics: A Dialogical Perspective', *Theory, Culture & Society*, vol. 13, no. 2: 121–43.
Geertz, C. (1988) *Works and Lives: The Anthropologist as Author*. Stanford: Stanford University Press.
Giddens, A. (1987) *Social Theory and Modern Sociology*. Cambridge: Polity Press.
Giddens, A. (1990) *The Consequences of Modernity*. Cambridge: Polity Press.
Giddens, A. (1991) *Modernity and Self-Identity – Self and Society in the Late Modern Age*. Cambridge: Polity Press.
Giddens, A. (1992) *The Transformation of Intimacy – Sexuality, Love and Eroticism in Modern Societies*. Cambridge: Polity.
Ginsberg, M. (1965) *On Justice in Society*. Harmondsworth: Penguin.

Goffman, E. ([1959]1971) *The Presentation of Self in Everyday Life*. Harmondsworth: Penguin.

Goffman, E. (1972) *Interaction Ritual – Essays on Face-to-Face Behaviour*. Harmondsworth: Penguin.

Gorz, A. (1989) *Critique of Economic Reason*. London: Verso.

Gouldner, A. (1972) *The Coming Crisis of Western Sociology*. London: Heinemann.

Gray, J. (1996) *After Social Democracy*. London: Demos.

Green, D. (1996) *Communities in the Countryside*. London: Social Market Foundation.

Grove-White, R. (1996) 'Environmental Knowledge and Public Policy Needs: on Humanising the Research Agenda', in S. Lash, B. Szerszynski and B. Wynne (eds), *Risk, Environment and Modernity – Towards a New Ecology*. London: Sage.

Habermas, J. (1984) *The Theory of Communicative Action: Volume One – Reason and the Rationalization of Society*. London: Heinemann.

Habermas, J. (1987a) *The Theory of Communicative Action: Volume Two – Lifeworld and System: A Critique of Functionalist Reason*. Oxford: Polity Press.

Habermas, J. (1987b) *The Philosophical Discourse of Modernity*. Cambridge: Polity Press.

Hall, S. and Jacques, M. (eds) (1989) *New Times: The Changing Face of Politics in the 1990s*. London: Lawrence & Wishart.

Harding, L. (1996) 'Charge of the Right and Proper Brigade', *Guardian*, 23 December.

Harries, R. (1997) 'Why it is Time to Return to Morality', *Guardian*, 1 January.

Harvey, D. (1989) *The Condition of Postmodernity*. London: Blackwell.

Harvey, D. (1993) 'Class Relations, Social Justice and the Politics of Difference', in M. Keith and S. Pile (eds), *Place and the Politics of Identity*. London: Routledge.

Hassan, I. (1987) 'Pluralism in Postmodern Perspective', in M. Calinescu and D. Fokkema (eds), *Exploring Postmodernism*. Amsterdam: John Benjamins Publishing Company.

Heidegger, M. (1971) *On the Way to Language*. London: Harper & Row.

Hekman, S. (1990) *Gender and Knowledge: Elements of a Postmodern Feminism*. Cambridge: Polity Press.

Heller, A. (1987) *Beyond Justice*. Oxford: Blackwell.

Heller, A. (1994) 'The Elementary Ethics of Everyday Life', in G. Robinson and J. Rundell (eds), *Rethinking Imagination – Culture and Creativity*. London: Routledge.

Heller, A. and Feher, F. (1988) *The Postmodern Political Condition*. Cambridge: Polity Press.

Hennis, W. (1988) *Max Weber – Essays in Reconstruction*. London: Allen & Unwin.

Himmelfarb, G. (1995) *The De-Moralization of Society: From Victorian Virtues to Modern Values*. London: The Institute of Economic Affairs.

Hoggart, R. (1995) *The Way We Live Now*. London: Cape.

hooks, b. (1990) *Yearnings: Race, Gender and Cultural Politics*. Boston: South End Press.

Horowitz, I. (ed.) (1965) *The New Sociology: Essays in Social Science and Social Theory in Honor of C Wright Mills*. New York: Oxford University Press.

Hoy, D. (1988) 'Foucault: Modern or Postmodern?', in J. Arac (ed.), *After Foucault – Humanistic Knowledge, Postmodern Challenges*. London: Rutgers University Press.

Huyssen, A. (1984) 'Mapping the Postmodern', *New German Critique*, no. 33: 5–52.

Illich, I. (1973) *Deschooling Society*. Harmondsworth: Penguin.

Illich, I. (1978) *The Right to Useful Unemployment: and its Professional Enemies*. London: Marion Boyars.

Illich, I. (1985) *Tools for Conviviality*. London: Marion Boyars.

Irigaray, L. (1986) 'The Fecundity of the Caress: A Reading of Levinas, *Totality and Infinity*, section IV, B, "The Phenomenology of Eros"', in R.A. Cohen (ed.), *Face to Face with Levinas*. Albany: State University of New York Press.

Irigaray, L. (1993) *Je, Tu, Nous – Toward a Culture of Difference*. London: Routledge.

Jameson, F. (1984) 'Postmodernism or the Cultural Logic of Late Capitalism', *New Left Review*, no. 146: 53–92.

Jameson, F. (1988) 'Cognitive Mapping', in C. Nelson and L. Grossberg (eds), *Marxism and the Interpretation of Culture*. London: Macmillan.

Jameson, F. (1989) 'Marxism and Postmodernism', *New Left Review*, no. 176.

Jameson, F. (1991) *Postmodernism or the Cultural Logic of Late Capitalism*. London: Verso.

Jay, M. (1988) *Fin-de-Siecle Socialism*. London: Routledge.

Jenkins, S. (1996) 'Use and Abuse of Science', *The Times*, 27 March.

Jonas, H. (1984) *The Imperative of Responsibility: In Search of an Ethics for the Technological Age*. Chicago: University of Chicago Press.

Kamuf, P. (ed.) (1991) *A Derrida Reader – Between the Blinds*. London: Harvester Wheatsheaf.

Keith, M. and Pile, S. (eds) (1993) *Place and the Politics of Identity*. London: Routledge.

Kellner, D. (1988) 'Postmodernism as Social Theory: Some Challenges and Problems', *Theory, Culture & Society*, vol. 5, nos 2–3: 239–69.

Kellner, D. (1989) *Jean Baudrillard. From Marxism to Postmodernism and Beyond*. Cambridge: Polity Press.

Kroker, A. and Cook, D. (1988) *The Postmodern Scene: Excremental Culture and Hyper-Aesthetics*. London: Macmillan.

Kroker, A., Kroker, M. and Cook, D. (1989) *Panic Encyclopedia: The Definitive Guide to the Postmodern Scene*. London: Macmillan.

Kuhn, T. (1970) *The Structure of Scientific Revolutions*. London: University of Chicago Press.

Laclau, E. (1988) 'Politics and the Limits of Modernity', in A. Ross (ed.), *Universal Abandon? The Politics of Postmodernism*. Minneapolis: University of Minnesota Press.

Laclau, E. (1992) 'Beyond Emancipation', *Development and Change*, vol. 23, no. 3: 121–37.

Laclau, E. and Mouffe, C. (1985) *Hegemony and Socialist Strategy – Towards a Radical Democratic Politics*. London: Verso.

Lash, S. (1990) *Sociology of Postmodernism*. London: Routledge.

Lash, S. (1994) 'Reflexivity and its Doubles: Structure, Aesthetics, Community', in U. Beck, A. Giddens and S. Lash (eds), *Reflexive Modernization – Politics, Tradition and Aesthetics in the Modern Social Order*. Cambridge: Polity Press.

Lash, S. (1996) 'Introduction to the Ethics and Difference Debate', *Theory, Culture & Society*, vol. 13, no. 2.

Lash, S. and Urry, J. (1987) *The End of Organised Capitalism*. Cambridge: Polity Press.

Lash, S., Szerszynski, B. and Wynne, B. (eds) (1996) *Risk, Environment and Modernity – Towards a New Ecology*. London: Sage.

Lemert, C. (1990) 'The Uses of French Structuralism in Sociology', in G. Ritzer (ed.), *Frontiers of Social Theory: The New Synthesis*. New York: Columbia University Press.

Lee, R.L.M. (1992) 'Modernity, Anti-modernity and Post-modernity in Malaysia', *International Sociology*, vol. 7, no. 2.

Leonard, P. (1997) *Postmodern Welfare – Reconstructing an Emancipatory Project*. London: Sage.

Levinas, E. (1969) *Totality and Infinity – An Essay on Exteriority*. Pittsburgh: Duquesne University Press.

Levinas, E. (1981) *Otherwise than Being or Beyond Essence*. London: Martin Nijhoff.

Levinas, E. (1987a) *Time and the Other*. Pittsburgh: Dusquesne University Press.

Levinas, E. (1987b) *Collected Philosophical Papers*. Boston: Martin Nijhoff.

Levinas, E. (1988a) 'The Paradox of Morality: An Interview', in R. Bernasconi and D. Wood (eds), *The Provocation of Levinas: Rethinking the Other*. London: Routledge.

Levinas, E. (1988b) 'Useless Suffering', in R. Bernasconi and D. Wood (eds), *The Provocation of Levinas: Rethinking the Other*. London: Routledge.

Levinas, E. (1989) *The Levinas Reader*. Edited by Sean Hand. Oxford: Blackwell.

Levinas, E. (1992) *Ethics and Infinity*. Pittsburgh: Duquesne University Press.

Levinas, E. and Kearney, R. (1986) 'Dialogue with Emmanuel Levinas', in R.A. Cohen (ed.), *Face to Face with Levinas*. Albany: State University of New York Press.

Levine, D. (1985) *The Flight from Ambiguity – Essays in Social and Cultural Theory*. Chicago: University of Chicago Press.

Lukes, S. (1988) *Emile Durkheim: His Life and Work*. London: Penguin.

Lyotard, J-F. (1984a) *The Postmodern Condition*. Manchester: Manchester University Press.

Lyotard, J-F. (1984b) 'Interview', *Diacritics*, vol. 14, no. 3.

Lyotard, J-F. (1988a) *The Différend – Phrases in Dispute*. Manchester: Manchester University Press.

Lyotard, J-F. (1988b) 'Interview', *Theory, Culture & Society*, vol. 5, nos 2–3.

Lyotard, J-F. (1988c) *Peregrinations – Law, Form, Event*. New York: Columbia University Press.

Lyotard, J-F. (1989a) 'Universal History and Cultural Differences', in *The Lyotard Reader*. Edited by A. Benjamin. Oxford: Blackwell.

Lyotard, J-F. (1989b) 'Discussions, or Phrasing "after Auschwitz"', in *The Lyotard Reader*. Edited by A. Benjamin. Oxford: Blackwell.

Lyotard, J-F. (1989c) 'Complexity and the Sublime', in L. Appignanesi (ed.), *Postmodernism: ICA Documents*. London: Free Association Books.

Lyotard, J-F. (1991) *The Inhuman – Reflections on Time*. Cambridge: Polity Press.

Lyotard, J-F. (1992) *The Postmodern Explained to Children – Correspondence 1982–1985*. Sydney: Power Publications.

Lyotard, J-F. (1993) *Political Writings*. London: UCL Press.

Lyotard, J-F. and Thébaud J-L. (1985) *Just Gaming*. Manchester: Manchester University Press.

MacIntyre, A. (1987) *After Virtue – A Study in Moral Theory*. London: Duckworth.

MacIntyre, A. (1988) *Whose Justice? Which Rationality?* Notre Dame, IN: University of Notre Dame Press.

MacIntyre, A. (1993) 'Miller's Foucault, Foucault's Foucault', *Salmagundi*, no. 97, Winter.

McNay, L. (1992) *Foucault and Feminism*. Cambridge: Polity Press.

Maffesoli, M. (1990) 'Post-modern Sociality', *Telos*, 35: 89–92.

Maffesoli, M. (1996) *The Time of the Tribes – The Decline of Individualism in Mass Society*. London: Sage.

Malik, R. and Anderson, K. (1992) 'The Global News Agenda Survey', *Intermedia*, vol. 20, no. 1.

Marenbom, J. (1996) *Answering the Challenge of Communitarianism*. London: Politeia.

Marshall, T.H. (1963) *Sociology at the Crossroads and Other Essays*. London: Heinemann.

Marx, K. (1973) *Grundrisse – Foundations of the Critique of Political Economy*. Harmondsworth: Penguin.

Marx, K. and Engels, F. (1968) *The Communist Manifesto*. Harmondsworth: Penguin.

Midgley, M. (1996) 'Rights and Wrongs', *Guardian*, 16 January.

Miller, J. (1993) *The Passion of Michel Foucault*. London: Harper Collins.

Mulgan, G. (1997) 'On the Brink of a Real Society', *Guardian*, 1 February.

Nietzsche, F. ([1930]1968) *The Will to Power*. New York: Vintage Books.

Nietzsche, F. (1968) *Twilight of the Idols*. Harmondsworth: Penguin.

Norris, C. (1982) *Deconstruction: Theory and Practice*. London: Methuen.

O'Connor, N. (1988) 'The Personal is Political: Discursive Practice of the Face-to-Face', in R. Bernasconi and D. Wood (eds), *The Provocation of Levinas: Rethinking the Other*. London: Routledge.

O'Malley, J.B. (1971) *The Sociology of Meaning*. London: Human Context Books.

O'Neill, J. (1972) *Sociology as a Skin Trade – Essays Towards a Reflexive Sociology*. London: Heinemann.

O'Neill, J. (1985) *Five Bodies – The Human Shape of Modern Society*. London: Cornell University Press.

Parsons, T. (1977) *Social Systems and the Evolution of Action Theory*. New York: The Free Press.

Pavlich, G. (1996) *Justice Fragmented: Mediating Community Disputes Under Postmodern Conditions*. London: Routledge.

Pieterse, J.N. (1994) 'Globalisation as Hybridisation', *International Sociology*, vol. 9, no. 2: 161–84.

Polhemus, T. (1996) *The Customised Body*. London: Serpents Tail.

Poole, R. (1991) *Morality and Modernity*. London: Routledge.

Poster, M. (ed.) (1988) *Jean Baudrillard – Selected Writings*. Stanford: Stanford University Press.

Poster, M. (1990) *The Mode of Information – Poststructuralism and Social Context*. Cambridge: Polity Press.

Postman, N. (1996) 'School's Out, Forever', *Guardian*, 21 December.

Rabinow, P. (1986) 'Representations are Social Facts: Modernity and Post-Modernity in Anthropology', in J. Clifford and G.E. Marcus (eds), *Writing Culture – The Poetics and Politics of Ethnography*. London: University of California Press.

Rajchman, J. (1985) *Michel Foucault – The Freedom of Philosophy*. New York: Columbia University Press.

Rasch, W. (1994) 'In Search of the Lyotard Archipelago, or: How to Live with Paradox and Learn to Like It', *New German Critique*, no. 61.

Readings, B. (1991) *Introducing Lyotard – Art and Politics*. London: Routledge.

Readings, B. (1992) 'Pagans, Perverts, or Primitives? Experimental Justice in the Empire of Capital', in A. Benjamin (ed.), *Judging Lyotard*. London: Routledge.

Readings, B. (1993) 'Foreword: The End of the Political', in *Jean-Francois Lyotard Political Writings*. London: UCL Press.

Richters, A. (1988) 'Modernity–Postmodernity Controversies: Habermas and Foucault', *Theory, Culture & Society*, vol. 5, no. 4: 611–43.

Rieff, P. (1965) *Freud: The Mind of the Moralist*. London: Methuen.

Ritzer, G. and Smart, B. (eds) (1999) *Handbook of Social Theory*. London: Sage.

Robertson, R. and Lechner, F. (1985) 'Modernization, Globalization and the Problem of Culture in World-Systems Theory', *Theory, Culture and Society*, vol. 2, no. 3.

Rochlitz, R. (1992) 'The Aesthetics of Existence: Post-conventional morality and the theory of power in Michel Foucault', in T.J. Armstrong (ed.), *Michel Foucault Philosopher*. London: Harvester Wheatsheaf.

Rorty, R. (1983) 'Method and Morality', in N. Haan, R.N. Bellah, P. Rabinow and W.M. Sullivan (eds), *Social Science as Moral Inquiry*. New York; Cambridge University Press.

Rorty, R. (1989) *Contingency, Irony and Solidarity*. Cambridge: Cambridge University Press.

Rorty, R. (1991) *Objectivity, Relativism, and Truth – Philosophical Papers*, vol. 1. Cambridge: Cambridge University Press.

Roth, G. (1987) 'Rationalization in Max Weber's Developmental History', in S. Whimster and S. Lash (ed), *Max Weber, Rationality and Modernity*. London: Allen Lane.

Rouse, R. (1991) 'Mexican Migration and the Social Space of Postmodernism', *Diaspora*, vol. 1, no. 1.

Sacks, J. (1996) 'A School is a Moral Community', *The Times*, 16 January.

Sacks, J. (1997) 'Tradition and the Politics of Babel', *The Times*, 22 February.

Said, E. (1989) 'Representing the Colonized: Anthropology's Interlocutors', *Critical Inquiry*, vol. 15, no. 2.

Salemohamed, G. (1991) 'Of an Ethics that Cannot be Used', *Economy and Society*, vol. 20, no. 1.

Sayer, D. (1991) *Capitalism and Modernity – An Excursus on Marx and Weber*. London: Routledge.

Schirmacher, W. (1984) 'The End of Metaphysics – What Does This Mean?', *Social Science Information*, vol. 23, no. 3: 603–9.

Schutz, A. (1971) *Collected Papers*, vol. 1. The Hague: Martin Nijhoff.

Scruton, R. (1996a) *The Conservative Idea of Community*. London: Conservative 2000 Foundation.

Scruton, R. (1996b) 'The Party of Humbug', *The Times*, 6 November.

Segal, H. (1992) 'The Achievement of Ambivalence', *Common Knowledge*, vol. 1, no. 1.

Seidman, S. and Wagner, D. (eds) (1992) *Postmodernism and Social Theory: The Debate over General Theory*. New York: Blackwell.

Selznick, P. (1992) *The Moral Commonwealth – Social Theory and the Promise of Community*. Oxford: University of California Press.

Shilling, C. (1993) *The Body and Social Theory*. London: Sage.

Simmel, G. (1950) 'The Metropolis and Mental Life', in *The Sociology of Georg Simmel*. Edited by Kurt Wolff. New York: The Free Press.

Simmel, G. (1990) *The Philosophy of Money*. Edited by David Frisby. London: Routledge.

Smart, B. (1986) 'The Politics of Truth and the Problem of Hegemony', in D.C. Hoy (ed.), *Foucault: A Critical Reader*. Oxford: Blackwell.

Smart, B. (1990) 'Modernity, Postmodernity and the Present', in B.S. Turner (ed.), *Theories of Modernity and Postmodernity*. London: Sage.

Smart, B. (1991) 'On the Subjects of Sexuality, Ethics and Politics in the Work of Foucault', *Boundary 2*, vol. 18, no. 1.

Smart, B. (1992) *Modern Conditions, Postmodern Controversies*. London: Routledge.

Smart, B. (1993a) *Postmodernity*. London: Routledge.

Smart, B. (1993b) 'Europe/America – Baudrillard's Fatal Comparison', in B. Turner and C. Rojek (eds), *Forget Baudrillard?* London: Routledge.

Smart, B. (1994) 'Review of Ulrich Beck's *Risk Society: Towards a New Modernity*', *Thesis Eleven*, 37: 160–5.

Smith, A.D. (1990) 'Towards a Global Culture?', *Theory, Culture and Society*, vol. 7, nos 2–3.

Soja. E.W. (1989) *Postmodern Geographies – The Reassertion of Space in Critical Social Theory*. London: Verso.

Soja, E. and Hooper, B. (1993) 'The Spaces that Difference Makes: Some Notes on the Geographical Margins of the New Cultural Politics', in M. Keith and S. Pile (eds), *Place and the Politics of Identity*. London: Routledge.

Stauth, G. and Turner, B.S. (1988) *Nietzsche's Dance*. Oxford: Blackwell.

Stein, M. and Vidich, A. (eds) (1963) *Sociology on Trial*. Englewood Cliffs, NJ: Prentice-Hall Inc.

Steiner, G. (1996) *No Passion Spent*. London: Faber & Faber.

Stephanson, A. (1988) 'Regarding Postmodernism – A Conversation with Fredric Jameson', in A. Ross (ed.), *Universal Abandon? The Politics of Postmodernism*. Minneapolis; University of Minnesota Press.

Stout, J. (1990) *Ethics After Babel – The Languages of Morals and Their Discontents*. Cambridge: James Clarke & Co.

Straw, J. (1995) 'Putting the Heart Back into Communities', *The Times*, 8 November.

Tate, N. (1996) 'Deliver Us from These Fallacies', *The Times*, 31 October.

Taylor, C. (1989) *Sources of the Self – The Making of the Modern Identity*. Cambridge: Cambridge University Press.

Taylor, C. (1992) *Multiculturalism and 'The Politics of Recognition'*. Princeton: Princeton University Press.

Tester, K. (1993) *The Life and Times of Post-Modernity*. London: Routledge.

Tester, K. (1997) *Moral Culture*. London: Sage.

Titmuss, R. (1970) *The Gift Relationship*. London: Allen & Unwin.

Tololyan, K. (1991) 'The Nation-State and Its Other: In Lieu of a Preface', *Diaspora*, vol. 1, no. 1.

Touraine, A. (1984) 'The Waning Sociological Image of Social Life', *International Journal of Comparative Sociology*, vol. 25, nos 1–2.

Touraine, A. (1989) 'Is Sociology Still the Study of Society?', *Thesis Eleven*, no. 23.

Toynbee, A. (1954) *A Study of History*, vol. VIII. Oxford: Oxford University Press.

Turner, B. (1984) *The Body and Society – Explorations in Social Theory*. Oxford: Blackwell.

Turner, B. (1993) 'Outline of a Theory of Human Rights', *Sociology*, vol, 27, no. 3: 489–512.

Tyler, S.A. (1986) 'Post-Modern Ethnography: From Document of the Occult to Occult Document', in J. Clifford and G.E. Marcus (eds), *Writing Culture – The Poetics and Politics of Ethnography*. London: University of California Press.

Vattimo, G. (1988) *The End of Modernity: Nihilism and Hermeneutics in Post-modern Culture*. Cambridge: Polity Press.

Vattimo, G. (1992) *The Transparent Society*. Cambridge: Polity Press.

Vattimo, G. (1993) *The Adventure of Difference: Philosophy After Nietzsche and Heidegger*. Cambridge: Polity Press.

Wacquant, L.J.D. (1992) 'Towards a Social Praxeology: The Structure and Logic of Bourdieu's Sociology', in P. Bourdieu and L.J.D. Wacquant (eds), *An Invitation to Reflexive Sociology*. Chicago: University of Chicago Press.

Wacquant, L.J.D. (1993) 'Bourdieu in America: Notes on the Transatlantic Importation of Social Theory', in C. Calhoun, E. LiPuma and M. Postone (eds), *Bourdieu – Critical Perspectives*. Cambridge: Polity Press.

Wallerstein, I. (1995) 'The Language of Scholarship', *ISA Bulletin*, 67–68, Fall.

Wallerstein, I. (1997) 'Sociology at an Intellectual Crossroads', *ISA Presidential Letter*, no. 5.

Warnke, G. (1992) *Justice and Interpretation*. Cambridge: Polity Press.

Weber, M. (1970) *From Max Weber*. Edited by H.H. Gerth and C. Wright Mills. London: Routledge & Kegan Paul.

Weber, M. (1976) *The Protestant Ethic and the Spirit of Capitalism*. London: Allen & Unwin.

West, C. (1989) 'Black Culture and Postmodernism', in B. Kruger and P. Mariani (eds), *Remaking History*. Seattle: Bay Press.

White, S.K. (1987/88) 'Justice and the Postmodern Problematic', *Praxis International*, vol. 7, no. 3/4.

Wolff, K. (1989) 'From Nothing to Sociology', *Philosophy of the Social Sciences*, vol. 19, no. 3.

Woollacott, M. (1996) 'Risky Business, Safety', *Guardian*, 28 March.

Wright Mills, C. ([1959]1970) *The Sociological Imagination*. Harmondsworth: Penguin.

Wynne, B. (1996) 'May the Sheep Safely Graze? A Reflexive View of the Expert–Lay Knowledge Divide', in S. Lash, B. Szerszynski and B. Wynne (eds), *Risk, Environment and Modernity – Towards a New Ecology*. London: Sage.

Young, I. (1990) *Justice and the Politics of Difference*. Princeton: Princeton University Press.

Zweig, F. (1963) *The Student in the Age of Anxiety*. London: Heinemann.

Index